TRANS/gressive

How Transgender Activists Took on Gay Rights, Feminism, the Media & Congress... and Won!

RIKI WILCHINS

All photographs by
Mariette Pathy Allen

Cover photos. Clockwise from top-left:
Camp Trans at the Michigan Womyn's Music Festival (Hart MI);
Brandon Teena Memorial Vigil (Falls City KS);
First National Gender Lobby Day (Washington DC);
Christian Paige Memorial Vigil (Chicago IL).

For more information contact:
Riverdale Avenue Books
5676 Riverdale Avenue
Riverdale, NY 10471
www.riverdaleavebooks.com

Design by www.formatting4U.com
Cover by Scott Carpenter
Cover photo and interior images reprinted with permission from Mariette Pathy Allen
Digital ISBN 978-1-62601-367-4
Print ISBN 978-1-62601-368-1

First edition, June 2017

Table of Contents

Dedication

To Gina and Dylan Jade—you are my life. Thank you for patiently putting up with all my late-night scribbling. To Clare Howell, who is the inspiration and editor most writers can only dream of. And to all the "ghosts:" those transpeople, especially of color, who have been felled and continue to fall in unaddressed and unsolved hate crimes on society's margins. I swear someday you will have the recognition and justice you deserve. We will never forget.

Acknowledgments

To the people who reviewed and helped with sections of this book—Nancy Nangeroni, Tony Baretto-Neto, Barbara Warren, Cheryl Chase, Dana Beyer, Clare Howell, Susan Wright, and many others—thank you for correcting errors of fact and memory. To Camilla Saly Monzingo for taking this book to heart and giving it such a deep and close reading—your late night calls to argue punctuation and wording all produced a much stronger book than the rough manuscript you were given. And to Riverdale's Lori Perkins, for her passion for books and authors—your support makes all the difference.

Foreword
When I Was in Gender and You Were the Main Drag

In the early 1990s, no one talked about transgender people because nobody knew one. We were invisible; we did not appear on TV shows or in movies (except as deranged killers). Police harassed, arrested, and assaulted us. Courts and legislatures found new ways to strip away our rights.

Feminist theorists, psychiatrists, and right-wing bigots regularly prodded, dissected, and publicly denounced our bodies and identities: we were mentally unbalanced, "invading women's spaces," or "stealing women's body parts." Transmen were mostly ignored; transwomen of color especially suffered epidemic waves of violence that continue today.

There was no Gender Outlaw yet or Stone Butch Blues. There was no Internet or email. There was no LGBT movement, because Gay and Lesbian organizations still openly excluded transgender.

We were freaks. We were gendertrash. We were decidedly non-political, waging our isolated struggles for survival alone. What little community we had emerged one weekend at a time at conferences held in lonely hotels out on the interstate. But all that was about to change, because bringing a despised and marginalized people together is in itself a political act. We didn't know it yet, but we were about to reach critical mass.

When people start realizing that humiliation and degradation are not the result of personal failings, but of systemic oppressions, they stop begging for some social acceptance, and they start demanding their damn civil rights.

This is the inside story of how a handful of activists from an obscure community at the very margins of society launched a revolution that would challenge our most fundamental conception of

1

bodies, gender, and sex—a revolution whose ideas would one day circle the globe.

This is the story of the birth of the modern movement for gender rights.

Gender fluidity, transgender, genderqueerness—all of this in the age of "I Am Cait"—seems to have found wings. President Obama mentioned transgender people. The military is finally allowing us to serve openly. We've made the cover of *Time* and the front page of the *New York Times*. Even straight kids think being flexible about gender is cool.

I was recently interviewing a middle-aged mother in Chicago. Out of nowhere, she just mentioned offhand how her son told her he prefers to identify as "genderqueer" rather than male, because binary genders are *soooo* 20th century. He is 19, cisgender (someone whose gender identity matches the sex assigned at birth), and totally straight.

It wasn't always so.

Less than 20 years ago, I hadn't yet coined the term "genderqueer," and even after doing so, practically no one else used it. Transgender activists were busy fighting for air, for any kind of awareness or recognition from mainstream cisgender society—straight *and* gay.

We had been slowly pushed to the margins of every community. Mainstream feminists wanted nothing to do with crossdressers or transsexuals. Lesbians were uncomfortable with us. And many "radical lesbians" were implacably opposed to our very existence (still are—why does "radical" so often translate to kicking the crap out of some other minority even more dispossessed than you are?).

Lesbian and gay organizations saw no reason to embrace these weird transgender people who lurked in the same gay bars and attended the same Pride parades, but seemed to have totally separate issues and, even worse, made straight people (and many gays) extremely uncomfortable.

Gay men weren't effeminate; they didn't run around in pastels and dresses. Lesbians weren't butch and didn't want to wear men's clothes or ride motorcycles. Those were mainstream stereotypes that a newly emergent gay rights movement was eager to put behind it. Gay people were gender normative—just like straight people. Just like you and me—well, *you*, anyway.

But transpeople resurrected all these gender issues and put them front and center, and who needed *that* headache?

The *Queerer* Queers

As gay rights increasingly played to Main Street, trannies looked like a huge public relations nightmare—and a very avoidable one.

I use the word "trannie" deliberately. It was what we called ourselves then—many of us at least, and some still do. It may have fallen into politically correct disfavor (certainly when cisgenders use it). But I've never considered it pejorative, rather an affectionate shorthand.

All this rejection of trans was a bit weird in a gay community in which drag queens were still celebrated (on the down-low of course), gay men still teased other men with gender put-downs ("Get you, Mary!"), and Dykes on Bikes led Gay Pride Parades.

But we were the queerest of the queer—too out to be in.

Even among ourselves, there was self-consciousness, shame and the desire to pass as cisgender. We were mostly isolated. There was no email, no Internet to connect us. You found people by word of mouth or (more rarely) at the bars.

When I began transitioning in 1978, there were two other transwomen in Cleveland that anyone knew of—Joanne and Carmen. They were my whole support system and basically kept me alive through the whole awful affair. I assiduously tried to fit in and pass as cisgender for 15 years. Needless to say, with my frame, voice, and height, it worked a lot better in my mind than it ever did on the street.

Even when it did work, at a certain point, trying to fill all the cisgender standards for true femininity got really old, and really tiring. It's a good recipe for losing the last shreds of your self-respect, and losing any sense of self-worth independent of what others think.

I told myself over and over that I didn't really want to be active politically, but the truth was that I was afraid I'd be outed or evicted or both. Constantly being afraid of what the *cis-sies* will do to you feels awful, but that's the world they created for us.

After trying for years to look traditionally feminine—long hair, lipstick, high heels, etc.—I simply got tired of it. A cis woman doesn't have to do anything special and still looks like a cis woman. But without all the war paint and femmy clothes, I looked like a man with breasts. It's exhausting having to do all that prep just to walk out the door, get the right pronoun and not get all the stares.

At a certain point you just say, "fuck it" and decide to be you, whatever that is. So I developed this butch-y look with short hair, jeans and no makeup.

Interestingly enough, this tall butch dyke look had its advantages. Other transpeople gave me major points for being so "radical" and turning my back on cisgender femininity. Actually, I would have loved to have been more femme, but I just never thought it looked good on me. And anyway, for me, most of being femme is an "inside job," not about what other people think or how they perceive me.

So I became a visible part of the social fringe—a transsexual—a creature that many people had not even heard of, and few knew who or what we were. Even we were not sure what to call ourselves. The word "transgender" had barely been coined.

In fact "transgender" was introduced to refer to the excluded middle ground between transsexuals and crossdressers (and drag queens—there were no drag kings yet). *Genderqueer* and *genderfuck* were not really on the horizon. We were still mostly into very binary ideas of male/female gender.

But, over time, transgender would morph into this grab-bag term that included all of this, and all of us. And then, imperceptibly, inevitably, it would harden into another new identity—one with its own hierarchies and boundary issues, until one day it would become important to exclude people who weren't "really transgender."

It was a time when even our doctors encouraged and expected us to pass as cisgender. That was a large part of the "Real Life Test" or RLT: forcing us to live in the correct gender a year before being granted surgery. It wasn't just to make sure we really wanted it, but to make sure we could survive in the world as cisgender-ish persons.

My doctor even announced point blank that I was a "successful" transsexual woman to the degree to which no one could tell that I *was* transsexual, that I could "pass:" blend in and live life as a "normal woman." And I tried. I'd always wished I could pass, and was silently envious of those transwomen who could.

Partly as a result, there was little political activism. We didn't think of our troubles as a group struggle, or even as political. I often thought of my own poor genderqueer body as the reason and locus for my troubles, just as much as the intolerance of cisgender people. As a result, I wasted a lot of years hating it, and myself. And self-blame—blended liberally with shame—is an effective antidote for political awareness.

That doesn't mean, however, that there weren't some amazing and important early efforts. In 1970 STAR (Street Transvestite Action Revolutionaries) was formed in New York City in the wake of the Stonewall Riots by Sylvia Rivera and Marsha P. Johnson, and powered largely by drag queens of color.

In 1992 Texas attorney (now Judge) Phyllis Frye organized the first conference on transgender law: the International Conference on Transgender Law and Employment Policy (ICTLEP)—the first of its kind.

A few years later, in 1994, she and activist Karen Kerin would found It's Time America, an early lobbying group that sprouted chapters in several states.

Software developer Anne Ogborn in San Francisco would launch Transgender Nation, modeled on the street action group Queer Nation, which became an offshoot of that group. (Anne was a true original and a visionary. She left a profitable software job to go live with the Hijra—the sacred outcast transpeople of India—in the process almost dying from dysentery. And Anne could be really mind-blowing: when I first met her she was walking around wearing a T-shirt that read, **"Sex Change—Ask Me How."**)

But, for the most part, these courageous first efforts failed to scale up and catch on with the larger community. The rhythms and energy of the lives of most visible trans people were dominated by the affiliative need to find one another and connect, to share information and resources, and to win a small measure of tolerance from the cisgender world.

At the center of this effort for many of us lay the annual transgender conferences that organized the trans social calendar. In those pre-internet days, they were crucial and irreplaceable community watering holes.

The big tent-pole conferences—Southern Comfort every fall in Atlanta and the International Foundation for Gender Education (IFGE) months later—anchored each year.

IFGE outside Boston—was founded in 1987 by Merissa Sherrill Lynn. It was the national information conduit for the transgender community and its regular magazine, *Tapestry*, which was in many ways as close as we had to a national transgender newsletter.

Both were mostly focused on and for crossdressers, although the transsexual influence would grow. *Tapestry* had a robust personal ads section—the magazine reportedly had a huge "trans-fan" base of men attracted to crossdressers (one reason most early covers featured conventionally-feminine cross-dressers).

As Susan Stryker put it, describing *Transvestia*, the first trans publication, our magazines tended to focus on "social commentary, educational outreach, self-help advice, and autobiographical vignettes." Common topics for articles included how to find a supportive wife (or deal with an unsupportive one), interviews, transgender history, dealing with prejudice and accepting your transgender self.

These get-togethers proved so popular that new ones kept popping up. By the 1990s there was another medium or big regional conference almost every month, year-round, each with its own distinct regional flavor.

To these many of us flocked, if we could afford the travel, hotel, and admission costs. Inspired by the pioneering work of Tri-Ess and a support group founded by Virginia Prince to provide support to cross-dressers, they were very oriented towards mostly straight, white, middle-aged men who needed a safe space to dress up and express themselves in feminine attire.

In fact, it all started with cross-dressers—whom, I might add, still do not get on the cover of *Time* or land their own reality TV shows. It was a historical moment so hostile to trans issues that in 1961 federal agents were prosecuting Virginia on "obscenity" charges for corresponding about dressing-up fantasies with another cross-dresser.

Virginia did not lack for courage. She invited a group of individual cross-dressers to bring brown paper bags with their hose and heels and feminine attire to a hotel room, where they all put them on simultaneously, outing themselves to one another. It was an act of unbelievable bravery. It was also a deeply abhorrent activity—considered shameful and abnormal—which they knew was only barely legal and could easily get them all arrested, which would ruin both their families and careers forever.

Yet this small first gathering of transgender people—eventually named the "Hose & Heels" club—just three decades later would morph into the modern transgender rights movement. And it was all started by straight male crossdressers.

But, in the 70s and 80s, the movement of sex reassignment surgery (SRS) into the hospitals (it would eventually move back out again) was quietly creating a large, hidden wave of post-Christine Jorgenson transsexuals. By the 90s that wave began to break, with more and more of us showing up at crossdressing conferences, looking for comfort and looking to find people like ourselves.

At first, almost all of us were transwomen, so we fit right in with all the male crossdressers. But eventually transmen showed up as well, first only a couple, but then in numbers. More and more workshops addressed mostly transsexual topics like how to get "top surgery," finding a sympathetic surgeon, and going on estrogen and testosterone.

Politics By Any Other Name Would Still Smell as Sweet

These conferences were affiliative in nature, dedicated to the social side of being transgender: sharing information, support, and advice. They were determinedly non-sexual and avowedly non-political, and they were meant to be. But when you're dealing with despised identities that are isolated and hidden, organizing them in large groups for whatever reason is highly political.

Part of this has to do with the politics of gender and lifestyle. For many crossdressers it was sufficient to be able to dress up, and then go back home.

But for the transsexuals, being a gender outlaw was a full-time gig: there was no "home" to go back to. Anywhere we went, we were still outcasts and trannies, and on enemy turf. That made many of us angry and desperate—emotions that were new to these gatherings.

Second, it's much harder to keep feeling shame and self-hatred when you're no longer the only one in the room, when you start regularly seeing hundreds and hundreds of people who are just like you. Being you starts to seem more, well... *normal.*

Finally, you start slowly realizing that the oppression and humiliation you're dealing with every day isn't personal, it's political. Everyone is going through it. It's not about you or your body, but about a system of cisgender intolerance and hatred for your entire group. *Your group.* The conferences were the first time in my life I felt part of *any* group. Or had any group to feel a part of.

The first time I walked into a gay bar was the first time in my young life that I didn't feel like an outcast. But it took me 20 minutes, sitting outside in my car, to muster the nerve.

The bar was off the downtown Cleveland manufacturing area

simply called, The Flats and it was all straight out of a 1950's *film noir:* cobblestones shimmering wetly in the fitful street lamps, broken bottles in filthy gutters, the odd newspaper blowing down the street, with the constant sound of elevated traffic in the distance. If you put it in a movie today it would seem like a cliché.

The bar had no sign, just a plain, plank wooden door with number on it, illuminated by a single light. Small groups of men and women would go in, and I would watch them, thinking to myself, "THOSE are HOMOSEXUALS." I had never seen one before. Neither had anyone I knew. In 1968 they might as well have been unicorns—you could read about them, but these were never ever seen in the wild. But the moment I walked in—I don't know what it was—but I knew I belonged, and for once no one would ever tell me I shouldn't be there.

But they weren't me. It was almost all gay men, a few lesbians huddled in a corner, and the odd drag queen.

I didn't look like any of them. And they didn't really accept me either. But I'd been a queer for a long time without knowing it, and I was finally among other queers. I was home, baby, and it was powerful.

I suspect the conferences were like that for many people. Other than all the crossdressers going out at night in groups, dressed outrageously and clearly having the time of their lives ("Why do crossdressers wear three-inch heels? Because they can't find five-inch heels."), the conferences were actually pretty tame: group breakfasts, lunches, and dinners at circular tables in giant ballrooms, initiated with key speakers at a podium and terminated by us streaming out to workshops and panel presentations in small, over-air-conditioned conference rooms. We might have been the American Bankers Convention.

But, unlike the bars, at the conferences I found lots of people like me. It was radical feeling normal and accepted, if only for a brief, three-day weekend.

Hotels on the Beltway

Feeling normal, accepted, and un-hated are powerful experiences. Moreover, they are *political* experiences. And I wasn't alone in having them.

As Tony Barreto-Neto, who would become pivotal in many of the actions that followed, recalled: "It was like finding a family and like-minded people who were, if not doing, at least thinking about doing something. It was affirming, it was frightening, it was exhilarating, it was liberating."

There was a sense of suppressed potential at those conferences in the early 1990s. All those people, all that compressed energy, yet no real discussion of why we needed to keep gathering in these three-star hotels out on the beltway (*never* in city centers), served by smiling and conspicuously tolerant staff who'd been carefully briefed on our event, running into straight-laced and befuddled hotel guests in elevators and hallways (and women's rooms!) who probably made us the highlight of their trip stories when they got home to Topeka.

(I recall one occasion when the hotel failed to tell us we had been booked at the same time as a nationwide evangelical Christian gathering. The "Finding Jesus" workshops ran in break-out rooms right next to the "Finding SRS Surgeons." It made for some unique and animated conversations between the two groups as we rode elevators together.)

We were there, in short, because we were isolated and despised and it wasn't safe to be us and be out—particularly the crossdressers—anyplace else.

The conference was an island of safety, of gender sanity; but, like *Brigadoon,* it was a temporary sanctuary, an idyllic haven that quickly vanished again almost as soon as it appeared, leaving us once again stranded in our normal, everyday, transphobic lives. While we might be safe in groups of several hundred, especially at hotels where we were paying big bills, we weren't safe alone—or anywhere else.

Even the grown, male crossdressers who would hit the local bars at night (many of whom could only dress up the rest of the year in the privacy of their own bedrooms) made sure to go out and come back in large groups and only to visit hotspots that had been carefully screened in advance to make sure they'd be welcome. And even they went out only at night.

But we didn't talk about that much—and we certainly didn't hold workshops and plenaries to organize politically to change it.

In the politics of the moment, simply being *positive* about being transgender was a major step forward, which is another way of saying we were not only mocked and loathed, but too many of us had internalized that and scorned and loathed ourselves.

But this affiliative phase couldn't last for long. And it didn't.

Down to Its Roots

This book is about what happened when it ended, and the transition from a collection of individuals focused on affiliation and self-education, trying to feel better about ourselves and gaining cisgender acceptance to an upstart political movement bent on changing the world.

My intent is not to diminish the timeless contributions of people: Virginia Prince who started the first crossdressing publication and organizations; Lou Sullivan who started the first Transmen's support group in San Francisco; Ari Kane who launched one of the first transgender conferences; or people of color like Marsha P. Johnson and Sylvia Rivera, who stormed the Gay Liberation barricades and went on to found STAR.

These are leaders whose actions—often brave and alone—paved the way for all that was to come. They helped open our eyes to what we could be and do. Anything we accomplished was only possible because we were standing on the shoulders of giants.

All of them and more are covered in Susan Stryker's authoritative chronicle of transgender in the US, *Transgender History*, and in Patrick Califia's in-depth documentation of the politics of transsexuality in *Sex Changes.*

Rather, my intent is to share the story of my own experience at the birth of what has grown into modern transgender political activism.

At the time, it seemed like we were making no progress whatsoever. Looking back with 20 years of hindsight, it all now seems to have happened very quickly.

But it didn't. Really, back then, no one would listen to us, and no one paid attention to us. We were shock value, or comic relief, freaks on the Jerry Springer Show, and not much more. In fact, it was not until our first Lobby Day on Capitol Hill that any major city newspaper carried a "hard news" story about transgender. That was what we had to fight.

In fact, what made this movement unique was that we had to fight not only average Americans—who might deride or even despise us—but the progressive left which misunderstood us and wanted nothing to do with us, including feminist organizations, progressive groups and gay rights organizations.

It was a time when, just trying to buy food at the local grocery store, I would be openly mocked or laughed at. I'd go to my local gay community center, but they had nothing for transpeople. So that evening I would join a lesbian support group seeking help and a kind ear, and instead I'd get voted on and asked to leave. It was an interesting and lonely time.

It was also the time when a very small group of people was able to begin pushing very radical notions of gender non-conformity and fluidity—ones in the most direct possible conflict with deeply entrenched heterosexual ideals—and eventually move them right into mainstream culture.

In many ways, the emergence of transgender challenged mainstream ideals of boy/girl, masculine/feminine, and the Ozzie & Harriet nuclear family in more radical ways than homosexuality ever could and ever will.

We challenged heteronormativity right down to its roots. We couldn't say it was just about who we loved. This was about nearly everything important about bodies: how we looked, how we could desire, what genders we could inhabit, even how we could change embodiment itself.

I think it was Jacob Hale, now an accomplished academic, who first introduced me to the idea of "trans fags." There's a photo of him embedded forever in my mind: He—a transman—in feminine drag. That sat me down for a moment as gears stripped in my head. God only knows what identities like that (not to mention bois, andros, and boychix) are doing to the gourds of average Americans.

In other words, this is also the history of the power of identity. A small group of people, simply by being who and what they were and refusing the invisibility inevitably forced on genderqueers by cisgender society, challenged and eventually changed bedrock notions of sex and gender that have existed for millennia. They are changing them still.

One View, Many Movements

Since there was no organized national transgender political activism, almost anything we did became "the first…". Everything remained to be done—newsletters, political gatherings, street protests, political lobbying.

All of these happened through group efforts and collaboration.

There is no "lone wolf" method of political organizing. Leadership might be something exhibited by individuals, but leading is mostly about figuring out where people already want to go and then helping them get there.

Yet I was fortunate enough to be there at the inception of many of these efforts. This is that story.

Let me be clear: it is not *the* story, but rather *my story.* It is what *I* experienced, what it was like to be there and what it means now. Each chapter ends with an epilogue that covers what happened to the key players afterwards and where they are as of this writing.

At the moment of inception, trans political organizing required the skill-set of a good grassroots organizer: a sense of outrage, the ability to instigate (and occasionally inspire), nerve and a sense of humor... all leavened with a strong sense of the absurd, which was never far away.

It was not that I particularly wanted to do trans-activism. I'd never thought of myself as an activist, and when repeatedly invited in the early 1990s, I kept finding ways to beg off getting involved.

But Leslie Feinberg—who had enormous popularity—was passionately committed to socialism, and although that movement's gender politics were more than impeccable (and often prescient), the global class struggle was never going to be the foundational ideology for a transgender movement. And Kate Bornstein was busy performing her plays and bending people's minds, and well... being our own Auntie Kate (a full-time job if ever there was one).

In a weird way, I felt responsible. At least one of us should do the dirty work of trying to build a communal politics. I would much rather just write or speak. But, clearly, I was the last one standing when the music stopped.

Most of what is detailed in this book took place from 1994 to 1996. Yet, only five years later, many of the things done by people first set in motion during those two critical years would become organizations and regular events, and the structures that produced a trans political activism.

Check Your Privilege at the Door

This in turn would require a new and different skill-set: patience, coalition building and negotiation—not exactly my own strong suits.

In retrospect, we owed a huge debt to Black Civil Rights, which developed the tools for nearly every liberatory movement which has come after. But we also owed (and still owe) a huge debt to the crossdressing community. The foundation for almost everything that we did was the social network that crossdressers had more or less invented. When you read the history of transgender, most of the early *organizing* was done by crossdressers: the Hose & Heels Club, Fantasia Fair, the Outreach Institute, the Tiffany Club.

One of the strange things about what we and the public came to call "transgender politics" was that it was almost all focused on transsexuals. (Drag queens—and later kings—were more an outgrowth of both gayness and entertainment.) Crossdressers were—and still are—ignored and overlooked.

Some of them, perhaps even the majority (I don't know) are fine with this. They worry that more public attention to crossdressing will mean more danger to those doing it. And because it is, unlike transsexuality, something one can keep private for a lifetime, many of them are happy to do so. Sometimes political activists aren't the most radical people, but merely the ones who had fewer alternatives.

Being transsexual might have been despised, but it at least held out some small hope of limited legitimacy—if only through the medical diagnosis of Gender Identity Disorder and of a degree of tolerance (if not true acceptance) by mainstream America.

But a man wearing a bra and dress was then, and is still today, an object of nearly universal contempt and derision. Being outed can still easily cost you your wife, your kids and your job.

The nasty psychiatric diagnosis for a man who desires to experience his own (rather than his wife's) femininity is still "Fetishistic Crossdressing," which diminishes and trivializes him (like psychiatry still does with BDSM).

Declaring how much more difficult it was to be transsexual, some of us explained, "I don't get to just do this on the weekends or away at conferences—I have to live as a woman full-time."

I've since come to believe that being a crossdresser may actually be the more revolutionary identity. Even today, in the era of the public trans-celebrities like Laverne Cox, Jenny Boylan, Janet Mock and Caitlyn Jenner, I can think of no public crossdressers. It is the closet no one ever comes out of?

A man changing into a woman may finally be getting some respect, but a man wearing a dress is still considered frivolous and pathetic. We have accomplished so much, yet for them so little. It remains the impossible identity.

From the Bottom Up

It's an oft-cited truism that movements emerge from the bottom up. Being trans meant being at the bottom socially for many of us. Yet the key players who emerged were also mostly people with sufficient resources and luck to be functional in mainstream society. Thus they could focus on life beyond the issues of day-to-day survival that occupied so many of us, and devote time and energy to activism.

It also meant those of us who had steady incomes (a huge accomplishment by itself) could afford conference registration fees (not to mention hormones, electrolysis, and surgery if you were lucky), and travel to the new political events that emerged.

While there were important exceptions, nearly all of us were white, lower-to-middle-class, middle-aged, and transsexual women. For instance, in all the transgender conferences I attended over the years, I can only recall three or four people of color who were regularly in attendance.

And it's telling that the first three prominent trans books to emerge from this period of activism were by Kate Bornstein (*Gender Outlaw),* Leslie Feinberg (*Stone Butch Blues*) and your humble author (*Read My Lips*)—three white, middle-aged, middleclass-y, urban, Jewish, women-y people.

While, to her credit, Leslie was an early and visionary exception on addressing issues of both race and class, I still don't think, as a movement, we ever did—or still do—enough to address the core concerns of people of color, or transgender people struggling with economic injustice. And part of that is surely my responsibility as well.

Wait for the Cavalry

Taking on radical lesbians who attacked us as male intruders and rapists, combating psychiatry's relentless pathologizing of our identities and bodies, holding vigil after vigil to force attention to the epidemic of murders of trans women of color and picketing the gay rights establishment to demand they "just add the T!"—all of this is what I lived through.

Almost all of it was new. It was a national-level, trans activism taking its first steps towards policies, events and organizations now taken for granted. It may not have been politically correct or inclusive, but this is the way it happened.

It was also scary. Often you had no clear idea of what you were doing, or had no experience doing it. So you groped your way forward, often alone, or nearly so. Leadership seldom happens by committee. One or two, or at best, three people come together and decide to do something that needs doing.

You feel like you're all exposed, like raising a public flag on an empty field. You hope and pray that people will see. If you're lucky, they do and come running. Sometimes they don't. Those are the risks you take.

Being on unfamiliar ground with no landmarks, doing something new and untried—making a public issue of your cause—all this usually left me feeling sick and disoriented. All my instincts told me to retreat, to wait for someone else to take the lead, to wait for the cavalry to arrive. I've had that feeling in my stomach at a few key junctures. Every time I've followed my instincts and backed away, I've regretted it later.

I've finally learned a lesson, perhaps too late. That sick feeling of isolation and disorientation means you're doing something worthwhile and necessary. It's when you want most to retreat, when you wonder why no one else is doing it, when you feel most alone, that's when you most need to stand your ground. These are the moments you will look back on later and realize you were making the very best use of your life.

You Do Things at the National Level

Much of my own national activism stemmed from a brief conversation with New York City Rev. Lynn Walker. Lynn was short and solid and highly proper, with blond hair and a great pixie-ish grin. She carried herself with the equanimity one might expect from someone with a strong spiritual center and a degree in divinity.

She had also been a high-ranking officer in the military—one of the highest-ranking transgender officers ever—and we'd known each other for several years through one event after another.

Late one night we were discussing why none of the activism anyone was doing ever seemed to really "catch." We created local events and groups, as others were doing in other cities, but they never attracted large numbers, spread, and attracted sustained media attention.

Entirely frustrated, at one point I blurted out, "But how do you do national political activism?" She answered with one of the smartest statements I'd ever heard: "You do things at the national level." From then on, I never did another local event. Everything I participated in or helped organize—even if it was limited to a single city—was pitched as a *national* event.

For All the Ghosts

My partner once described what I do as being a "social entrepreneur." I never thought of it that way. I do know that what I've been good at is seeing what someone else is doing, and then figuring out if it would scale up, and how to make it catch with a wider audience.

I've even done this with communities with which I have no part, including S&M activism, transgender cops and intersex people. But my real focus has been gender equality and gender rights.

In looking back over everything, I'm a little crestfallen to notice almost nothing here originated with me. Lobbying Congress, Camp Trans, overturning Gender Identity Disorder, or doing ACT-UP style trans street activism—every one of those ideas was someone else's, and for that I take no credit.

As transpeople, we were used to being isolated, and I think, perhaps partly as a result, many of the amazing leaders who initiated these efforts were doing them alone or in small local groups. My contribution was recognizing how to take their efforts to a much wider audience, how to repackage them so they could scale up and have national impact.

In recent years, it's become fashionable to forget much of what's in this book. For instance, the *New York Times,* the nation's "newspaper of record," finally published a definitive history of transgender activism along with a timeline.

Nothing that follows appeared in it.

Banner of GenderPAC logos

In fact, that was the genesis for writing this book. The problem started with GenderPAC, the first national transgender political rights organization. I tried to stretch its mission beyond transgender people to gender rights broadly.

It surprised no one but me that this really pissed off a lot of the trans-leadership, and split the community down the middle.

Even before the major blow-up, there was a minor one which should have served as a warning. As a first step to ensuring GPAC would not neglect issues of racism, and would keep race and gender in focus, our board added "…and racial equality" to the mission statement. But if our directors supported the move, almost no one in the wider community leadership did.

It was around this time that the country's largest transgender conference invited me to keynote. My theme was how rigid gender regimes hurt *all* of us, and that the oppression of trans-people was its most visible expression.

Gender norms and expectations touch, engage, shape, reward, pressure and sometimes punish us across the entire plane of our contact with society and social institutions. In this way, rigid gender regimes are similar, in pervasiveness and impact, to structures of race and class, to which they are inextricably linked.

In fact, for me, the entire *point* of being transgender and suffering through all this shit is that it gives us what might be called "gender vision": a bone-deep comprehension of how gender regimes work, and the gift of a message on overturning them that has the revolutionary potential to (yes…) transform society.

I said all this in my keynote, ending with the rousing cry, "Gender rights are human rights, and they are for ALL of us!" This was followed by a standing ovation, and GenderPAC was awarded a grant to do the work.

Sort of. Next year, as we tried to implement this broader vision, GenderPAC was publicly disowned, and the grant was canceled. I asked one of the conference leaders, "What happened? I said all this last year, and you all loved it." Her reply: "We didn't think you meant it."

Well, I did. For the past five years, since sun-setting GenderPAC, my day job has been flying around the country teaching cisgender policy-makers and funders how rigid gender regimes hurt them too. The list of places is long, and includes the White House, the Office on Women's Health, the Office on Adolescent Health, the Centers for Disease Control, etc., etc., because, for several decades, studies have shown that when young people conform to rigid gender norms, they have markedly lower life outcomes.

For instance, boys who buy into masculine norms as defined by strength, aggression, sexual prowess and emotional toughness are more likely to get kicked out of school, engage in drug risk-taking, believe that pregnancy validates manhood and engage in partner violence and LGBTQ bullying.

For girls, those who internalize what I think of as the "three D's" of traditional femininity—being Deferential, Desirable, and Dependent—are more likely to drop out of school early, develop disordered eating, have unplanned pregnancies, defer to male sexual prerogatives and end up economically and psychologically dependent on older, stronger male partners.

Folks on the international front have already *drunk the Kool-Aid* on this: major institutions like CARE, PEPFAR, USAID, UNAIDS, UNFPA, the World Health Organization (WHO) and even the venerable World Bank have all moved gender norms to the center of their work.

Only the US lags behind. That's my part in the food chain. I believe once cisgender people understand how non-LGBTQ kids are hurt by conforming to rigid masculine and feminine ideals they will see how important it is to also address the hurt to those of us who are gender non-conforming. Not as another *me-too* subpopulation, and not only as another wedge of the identity pie, but as something that is an integral part of the challenges that every young person faces.

This was the argument I started to make that led to the break-up between GenderPAC and the trans leadership. I get why many in the current trans leadership from that time would be anxious to forget what is written here, and why all these early efforts from GPAC to the Menace that really launched national trans political rights go unmentioned in the *New York Times*, and remain conspicuous by their absence.

In the back of every room I face there are always one or two transpeople. I assume that they're going to hate me and hate my message—which always touches on transgender, but only within the bigger picture. Strangely enough, they never do. In fact, many of them are proud to see a transgender person up there. They actually like the message of inclusion, one that positions us as just the shock troops in a wider social narrative of how rigid gender regimes hurt everyone—gender conforming and non-conforming alike—and particularly the young. In fact, part of the reason I started insisting on adding the phrase "and non-conforming" every time "transgender" was used as an identity, was to remind people that the doors of identity must always remain open. My own painful experience at least taught me that.

So maybe I have at last transitioned from a transgender rights activist to a gender rights activist.

Today the fragmentation and enlargement of the movement that I pushed for back then is being driven by a host of novel new identities and non-binary genders which barely fit under the *transgender* umbrella and are stretching its boundaries like never before. But back then the community leadership wanted a transgender organization and nothing but a transgender organization. So be it.

There are now many of us "ghosts"— many other people who contributed greatly to the birth of trans political activism and then have been lost or forgotten.

So many ghosts, so many stories, so many silences. I only hope that, over time, they will tell their stories too. I've tried to mention many whom I was honored to know and work with in this book.

As for me, I confess that sometimes (like after two or three six-packs), I start feeling like some Kremlin apparatchik who has been judged *counter-revolutionary* and must then be airbrushed from pictures and purged from history books.

Well, good luck with that. The bitch is back. It's time someone told the story, the real story—someone who was there.

So this time, for *all* the ghosts. Here it is.

Riki Wilchins
January 2016

Chapter 1—Putting the Womyn Back in Michigyn

Where's Nancy?

It began, as all serious things do, with a fight. That was the easy part. But then there was the murder.

In the summer of 1991, Nancy Jean Burkholder, an electrical engineer from New Hampshire, was accosted by two security guards while attending the Michigan Womyn's Music Festival, the country's largest annual lesbian event, held each year in… Michigan.

Nancy had been minding her own business. And it's highly doubtful she was the first transwoman to attend (she had attended the festival without incident the previous year). However, that year she made the mistake of confiding in another attendee—who then dimed her out to the *po-po*. They (yes, they came in a group) told Nancy she was suspected of being… a man!

It helps to understand that Michigan prides itself, in fact *sells* itself, as entirely man-free. Male children aren't allowed, nor are male dogs (No, I am not making this up or exaggerating).

Even the porta-potties have been renamed from porta-*johns* to porta-*janes.* When the (male) sanitation crew has to come on "the Land" to empty them, women are detailed to yell out "Men on the land" to warn everyone within earshot.

Even the Y in "Womyn" is there so there's no "men" in it.

The Security women kept Nancy waiting while they collected her belongings, unceremoniously dumping them and Nancy outside the main gates at 2:00 a.m. She was not allowed to notify her friends of what had happened, or where she was.

Now MichFest is literally in the middle of nowhere. There are miles and miles of only miles and miles on either side. Across the road is simply a large, national park of tree-covered forest. There's nothing within easy walking distance, and this was not the age of cell phones. So, you do the math.

To justify the unjustifiable, sometime later, Festival owner Lisa Vogel retroactively declared a policy that "Womyn-Born-Womyn Only" were allowed to enter.

Trannie-Born Trannies

Now this—even ignoring the profusion of Y's sprouting from it—is really interesting. It's more than just a bit of nasty propaganda, posing as discriminatory rule making. In fact it was reflective of many similar efforts that had been made by lesbian and women's groups for at least the past decade and would unfortunately continue for at least another 15 years.

Their goal was to develop definitions of womanhood which excluded us linguistically and thus could be used to isolate us politically and expel us physically.

Other neologisms included "real women only," "biological women only," "genetic females only" and the ever-popular "no dogs allowed." But as queer theorist Judith Butler has noted, trans bodies have a tendency to fall off the grid of cultural intelligibility. What she means to say is we can be hard to talk about.

(This alone should have alerted the more reflective feminists that transbodies might not be just a threat to women's community, but also a way to overturn oppressive gender roles—something that would not be lost on their daughters.)

The existing language—created entirely by a deeply heterosexist cisgender culture and rooted firmly in rigid male-female binaries—tended to fall apart when applied to transbodies, even when it was employed in the service of justifying cisgender people's worst discriminatory impulses.

So Lisa couldn't just say "No Men Allowed," since that was already MWMF's *raison d'etre.* Announcing that would have no linguistic or political value. Everyone who heard it would just shrug and say, "Well… yeah, we already *knew* that."

She also couldn't simply hang a sign from the front gate announcing "No Trannies Allowed." Even in the rarified, High-Church, radicalesbian-feminism of the Festival, that would have smacked too nakedly of discrimination and intolerance. She couldn't even just come out and call Nancy a man. For one thing, the Festival had already taken her money and issued her tickets for the past two years. For another, Nancy didn't look particularly man-like and lived her normal everyday life as a female.

So, like many of her peers, Lisa punted. She invented a new super-class of women: those who not only *were real* women, but were *born that way.*

Gathering Firewood, Carrying Water

In doing so, she was trying to mine two concepts simultaneously that had been, and continue to be, used nearly universally to delegitimize transgender experience. First is the feminist ideal that there is a common experience of all women—most likely patriarchal oppression—and, whatever that might be, transwomen by definition didn't have it.

Leslie Feinberg, author of *Stone Butch Blues,* used to lampoon this by pointing out that "women's experience" for almost 90% of the world's three billion or so females was carrying water and gathering firewood—not exactly everyday experiences for Festival attendees living in the world's most industrialized culture.

The second thing Vogel was going for was that trans-women are not really women. We were some kind of second-class knock-off. Some of us might look sorta like women, we might live our lives as women, we might even *feel* like women (although god-only-knows what *that* means), but that didn't make us real ones. Only those who had started life as women counted… and of course they made the rules.

This is a point with which cisgender public discourse continues to struggle to this day. Are we men who become women—as the (now archaic) phrases "male-to-female transsexual" and "sex change surgery" implied? Or are we women only if we opt for some pretty radical genital adjustments (questions which only become important within cisgender gender regimes)?

For cisgender society, having a vagina and not a penis is the universal *sine qua non* of actually being a woman. This makes it very challenging to think of a woman who really is a woman, but who had (or has) a "woman's penis" (again, *pace* Butler, language breaks down).

On this score, I'm not sure that cisgender people of a certain age will ever really *get it*. For instance, I find it very sweet and considerate that my closest friends still go out of their way to treat me exactly the same as my lesbian partner. But then, I find it a bit depressing that they still always have to go out of their way.

23

Throughout the long political struggle that commenced in the mid-1990s, transgender activists would find themselves repeatedly struggling with these two discursive strategies employed by those who might be called (for lack of a better term) *cisgender supremacists* in the women's community: the production of The Real, with trans experience as derivative and inferior versions of it; and, the production of deliberately prejudicial notions of our bodies and experience in order to better delegitimize us.

The tools Vogel was refining had been used before at feminist events, but seldom ones so large and never in such a public way. And they would be the same tools that would be used against transgender people, once the movement broke out into the mainstream in earnest.

As the larger society began struggling with how to think about us, these tactics became so successful that, as Susan Stryker and Stephen Whittle have noted, there was no way to *be* transgender without being "automatically dismissed as damaged, deluded, second-rate, or somehow inherently compromised."

The Uses of 'The Real'

Oddly enough, MWMF made a point of embracing all the things usually considered mannish which women might have to suppress in the straight world. For instance, letting mustache, leg or armpit hair grow naturally is almost a rite of passage for first-timers. Bearded women with obvious chin-hair are valued. In addition, many attendees are simply so butch they made us look like Mary Poppins. This genderqueer masculinity is honored, and rightly so. Ours, not so much.

It might be tempting to say that the very fact of being transsexual, of having the "wrong body" is such an extreme dislocation of accepted gender norms that mainstream confusion about how to think about us was inevitable.

Perhaps. But it was certainly cisgender supremacists and trans-hating theorists within lesbian feminism who provided the intellectual firepower for transgender rejection and legitimated it as not just politically acceptable but politically correct.

Yet, issues of "realness," which transgender politics surfaced within lesbian feminism and then the wider public, were part of a half century of politicizing and/or rejecting female bodies, genders, and desires that were inconvenient.

For instance, in the decades immediately before and after WWII, any woman who publicly questioned or pushed against the "normal" female roles in childbearing, homemaking and beautifying herself was considered to be in rebellion against her God-given natural role and risked being pathologized as a "deviant."

In the 1950s, lesbians were called "inverts" because they had the "unnatural" desires and gender expressions of males. Even some lesbians considered themselves a Third Sex (a formulation later pressed into use for intersex individuals).

In 1969, the National Organization for Women (NOW)—relentlessly dyke-baited by feminist-hating Republicans—evicted all members suspected of being lesbian or bisexual. Lesbians were accused (as we would later be *by* lesbians) of having male psyches, being male identified and bringing "male energy" into women's space.

This was especially true for butches, who created discomfort with their short hair, mannish clothes and disconcerting habit of occasionally cruising the straight girls (for shame!).

Do That to Me One More Time

Even within the lesbian community, gender had been rigidly policed. By the 1980s, anything that smacked of hetero power-relations was dismissed as internalized oppression. Butch/fem couples—even the *idea* of roles in women-on-women relationships—were openly mocked and condemned.

Real Lesbians didn't want to look like straight girls, screw women who looked like men or ask them for penetration. Lesbian butches were frequently shut out of meetings (as we would be) for being "male-identified" and lacking "women's experience."

It would take a lot of work by historians like Joan Nestle and others to resuscitate butch/fem as specifically *lesbian* genders that did not (and were not meant to) mimic heterosexual roles.

A decade or so later, it was S/M lesbians who weren't Real Lesbians, because they recycled oppressive male roles and privileges, using pain to re-enact men's rape and degradation of women. (At MWMF leather and S/M women had to camp out in an empty area of the distant woods named The Twilight Zone to escape protests, hostility, and threats of violence.)

So, the rhetorical and political tools that Lisa reached for to create a basis for evicting transsexuals had a long history of use against nontransgender women too—in particular lesbians, who were considered somehow genderqueer.

These tools were pressed into use by each generation as it struggled to define and defend some new gender line by pushing out some other non-dominant group, with the same dismal conflicts over hierarchy and power.

My favorite example occurred in 1995 in New York City. The Lesbian Sex Mafia—a support group for self-proclaimed BDSM practitioners who paraded around in leather and studs and chains and other things I haven't worn for months now, announced a policy of "post-ops only."

Now stay with me a moment here: cisgender lesbian sex perverts were now telling pre-ops that they weren't *woman enough* to get tied up and whipped... I mean, really?

(Today, it is impossible to appreciate just how much the social legitimacy and legal recognition of one's gender identity was dependent upon one's genital and/or surgical status. If the very idea of pre-op *vs.* post-op seems vaguely archaic now, even politically incorrect, back then it was a widely-recognized dividing line in a hierarchy forced on us by cisgender society, and constantly policed and enforced by them. The *cis-sies* were transfixed on our genitals as gender, and sometimes we internalized this as well. For instance, the small annual "New Woman" festival was open to post-ops only, and I was widely denounced when I proposed to challenge this rule for not recognizing the post-ops' need to have their own spaces.)

The Transexual Menace immediately began crashing LSM events, announcing that we were all pre-op and refusing to leave until the policy was changed. Alas, the international lesbian SM conference in Seattle, PowerSurge, moved to adopt the same policy.

It was like there was this perpetual feminist circular firing squad that mustered into formation as each new generation and group confronted the "problem" of gender non-conformity, but, with no awareness of prior similar situations, it was doomed to repeat past actions.

With the surfacing of women's, gay, and then transgender rights, gender was becoming permanently blurred, and each new project to "correct" this was doomed from its inception. Defined gender norms were about to be gone for good.

YOUR Biology IS Destiny

What made all this particularly ironic among the kind of High-Church lesbian feminism over-represented at Michigan and elsewhere was that feminists had also been busily declaring for decades that "biology was NOT destiny"—that, as Simone de Beauvoir put it, "One is not born a woman, but becomes one."

Such arguments refuted longstanding prejudices that Woman's confinement to a narrow range of roles and privileges was natural, the inevitable result of her function in pregnancy, child-rearing and supporting Man's role as family leader and provider.

"Biology is not destiny" declared that women's role and status was a cultural—not a biological—fact, a product of a repressive patriarchy. Women could be and become whatever they wanted. But bodies are inherently unstable as a foundation for identity and politics. Once you unmoor them from biology, the whole enterprise becomes unstable.

It became obvious that perhaps it wasn't just the *social position* of Woman that was culturally determined; it was the entire gendered *category* of Woman. The logical extension of this argument made room for all sorts of unpleasant bodies: trannies, boychix, faggot-identified dykes, transmen and so on.

In an effort to stem the incoming tide of gendertrash, lesbian-feminists ended up availing themselves of the very same biological-determinism many had spent decades refuting. And all to keep a handful of transwomen from quietly attending women's events. It was crazy.

As Gayle Rubin succinctly put it in her landmark essay, *Of Catamites and Kings*, "After decades of feminist insistence that women are 'made, not born,' after fighting to establish that 'anatomy is not destiny,' it is astounding that ostensibly progressive events can get away with discriminatory policies based so blatantly on recycled biological determinism."

Whenever categories of bodies are marginalized, excluded, and (as Butler puts it) abjected, they inevitably find each other, organize, and return with pitchforks demanding political legitimacy—exactly what was about to happen at Michigan.

Resistance Is Futile

Isolating and evicting transsexual women like Nancy had a long and shameful precedent in women's politics. As early as 1972, a

27

transsexual woman seeking to join the Daughters of Bilitis, the prototypical lesbian organization, was evicted.

In 1983, sound engineer Sandy Stone was forced from early feminist music collective Olivia Records in a hate campaign by enraged radical lesbian cisgender supremacists and egged on by arch-transphobe Janice Raymond.

Heavy drums on record arrangements were introduced as evidence of "throbbing male energy" (I am not making this up). And Olivia was threatened with a nationwide boycott—and Sandy was threatened with death.

One Seattle group calling themselves the Gorgons (catchy, no?) announced they were coming armed to an Olivia concert to kill Sandy—resulting in the first and only women's tour to feature love, children, Mother Gaia and heavy-muscle male security.

Camp Trans activists across from Michigan Womyn's Music Festival

A dozen or so women signed a public statement denouncing Sandy, and sought to force Olivia to evict Sandy. One of those signers was... Lisa Vogel. Say what you will, her animous towards transwomen has been remarkably consistent and unyeilding.

In 1991, even the National Lesbian Conference was still banning "non-genetic women" from its gathering (another interesting discursive creation that leveraged chromosomal difference).

I was familiar with being drummed out of women's events and lesbian gatherings, and with being the target of long and hate-filled debates over bodies like mine and whether cisgender women thought we should be admitted to "women's space" going back to my own 1978 transition in Cleveland, Ohio.

Alice Walker says, *Never be the only one in the room,* but I was always there alone.

Moreover, even if I'd wanted to fight back, there was always little or no support among my intended audience, so that it would have been pointless.

As The Borg says, *Resistance is Futile.* With feminists, that had always been the case, at least in my experience.

So it's possible to wonder why MWMF grew into such an emotional cause for so many. For me it had to do with what an older transwoman once said about the life she'd never lived: the groups she never attended, parties she didn't go to, events she never tried to enter—because she feared being rejected and evicted.

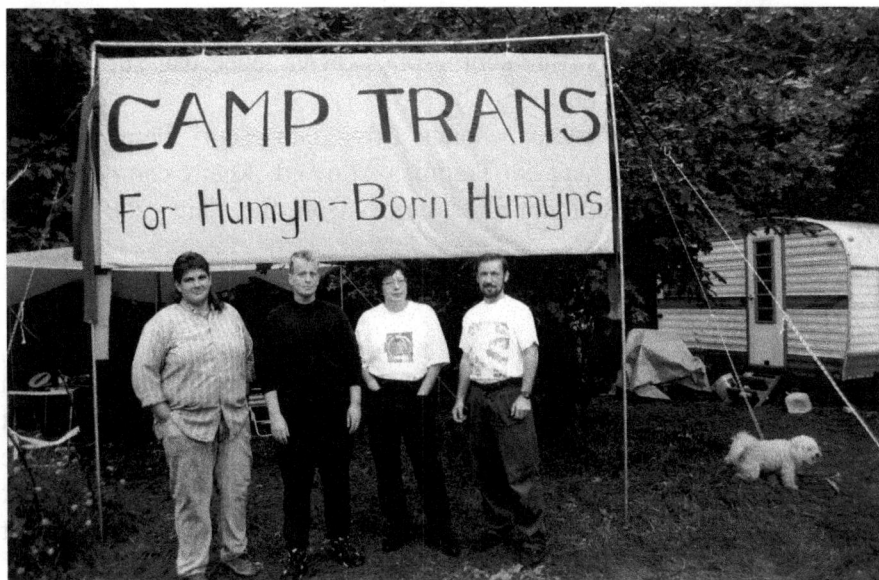

Leslie Feinberg (second from left), Jamison Green (far right) and other Camp Trans activists in front of camp sign.

I had missed out on a whole life like that, too, but it had never moved me to action until now. But Nancy being shoved out of the front gates alone in the dead of night represented my own personal nightmare of what would happen if I'd ever tried to live that life and participate in the women's community.

It was such an unfeeling act of naked hostility—this one lone woman among 7,000 attendees minding her own business—that I think it sparked outrage among a broad cross-section of feminists who might have started out only mildly sympathetic to our cause, but ended up feeling totally opposed to the shabby and nasty treatment accorded her.

Where's Nancy?

The next year, Nancy, Janice and two friends showed up and camped across from the main gate, handing out buttons ("Where's Nancy?") and fliers and holding four scheduled workshops and many impromptu discussions with whoever wandered out. And a lot of women did.

I was invited to join them the next year, 1993, after Nancy and three trans friends had again attempted to attend. At first, Security told them they had to leave because they couldn't "guarantee their safety" from radical separatists (threatening physical violence was supposed to be evidence of our "male energy").

When S/M and leather lesbians offered to escort them, Security then retreated to the usual: No Trannies Allowed. Again, camped in the empty woods of the national forest across from the main gate, we held more workshops.

A Scalable Love-in

Hundreds of women walked the mile or so out from the main Festival grounds to stop by and dialogue, camp out with us for a night or two, and offer support. The energy was amazing. This moveable four-day feast in the woods outside Michigan was a freakin' love-in. It was something I'd never experienced. It was more than gratifying; it was...*scalable*.

If we could do this with an ad-hoc effort and a half-dozen women, what could we do with a year of planning, dozens of women and real speakers? And we still needed a name. The only one I could think of was "Camp Trans," and then it quickly caught on. We had a rallying cry and a banner, and folks came running.

A Gathering of the Tribe

I called for a fund-raising event at NYC's Lesbian and Gay Community Center, and reached out to anyone and everyone with name recognition who I thought might be supportive. I didn't have high expectations. But everyone invited said *yes*.

For the first time, a transsexual event drew mainstream gay support from groups like the Lesbian Avengers and the Gay and Lesbian Alliance Against Defamation (GLAAD) and recognized activists like Ann Northrop, Amber Hollibaugh, Cheryl Clarke, Holly Hughes as well as our own author/playwright/actor Kate Bornstein and Leslie Feinberg and her partner, poet Minnie Bruce Pratt.

The event was like a gathering of the tribe. Amber Hollibaugh stole the show with a quiet but powerful speech comparing the constructedness of her fem identity with the constructedness of transbodies, calling for all our constructions of gender and desire to be honored instead of holding up some for ridicule because they failed to meet arbitrary standards of "naturalness"—an argument that is still ahead of its time today.

The next year over 30 trans-activists and friends announced plans to attend a new, expanded and very structured Camp Trans featuring two dozen workshops. I recruited Leslie Feinberg to be our keynote speaker, and community leaders like transman Jamison Green said they would attend and hold workshops.

A Queer *Weltanschauung*

Camp Trans was a huge success. For one wonderful week, 30+ trans women, men and friends created a totally gender-free community in the woods across from the Festival gate.

One couple provided music as the Transexual Celtic Modal Band from Hell. An ordained minister held a marriage ceremony for a couple who wanted to wed. Photojournalist Mariette Pathy Allen documented everything. I regularly cleaned the outhouse-style toilets Janice had rigged in a failed attempt at Buddhist-style self-abnegation that might keep my ego in check (it didn't).

We ate meals over campfires and talked endlessly about trans and gender politics, endlessly engaging the thousands of women who wandered out of the Festival main gate in singles, couples and great waves at all hours of the day and night to talk.

The year before, attendees who stopped by to visit us were afraid to wear their "Where's Nancy" buttons back inside the Festival, for fear of being harassed. This year, I'd taken four dozen brand new Transexual Menace T-shirts with me to sell. They were all gone within hours—including the one I'd worn in. Support was so strong that you would see them worn openly all over the Festival.

For the first time, a very public statement was being made at the heart of lesbian feminism about transgender. We were no longer *the only ones in the room.* And it felt amazing. It was a tide slowly starting to turn. If there is such a thing as a queer *Weltanschauung*, it was definitely moving in our direction.

Triggered by our presence, small gender confrontations began suddenly occurring all over of the Festival. For instance, one tall, gorgeously genderqueer guard who wore her Menace T-shirt during her Security shift found herself taunted by co-workers for "being a man." Later she was fired.

In a sign of things to come, the popular young rock group, Tribe-8, announced themselves transgender, promoted our issue during their set on the festival main stage and called a town meeting out at Camp Trans.

Janice had done amazing logistical work and everything ran smoothly—things like food, toilet paper, cooking utensils and tents for workshops in the rain somehow appeared just when we needed them. She was good.

For some reason, one of my favorite memories was when we tried to hand out invitation fliers and workshop schedules to women in all the cars lined up outside the front gate. Festival Security had shown up and kept blockading us, staying between us and the cars, encouraging them from slowing down and discouraging women from listening to us and taking our fliers.

They were discouragingly successful. In part that was by design. Janice, anticipating this move by Lisa, had sent a number of Camp Trans women a mile up the road out of sight at sunrise that morning. Armed with boxes of fliers, they made sure all those cars passing us by at the main gate already had our schedules. As I said, she was that good.

Men-ace on the Land

Leslie Feinberg addresses Michigan Womyn's Music Festival attendees on trans-exclusion.

On the last day of the Festival, we were invited to speak by a contingent of leather-wearing Lesbian Avengers from Chicago.

We approached the main gate, entered, and went right to the ticket table. There, after affirming that we considered ourselves "womyn-born womyn," each of us was allowed to pay the one-day rate and enter.

As we entered the Festival, an angry middle-aged woman ran up and screamed out at us, "You're not wanted here!" Later I was told that it was Festival-owner Lisa Vogel.

Two women marched alongside us yelling "Men on the land!" at the top of their lungs every few minutes to warn others. It was nerve-wracking. A gray-haired, grandmother driving by smiled at me, leaned out of her truck window, and declared, "If you'd stand still, I'd love to run you over."

But our presence was an overwhelming success. I heard a lot of comments like "Thanks for coming," "Glad you're finally here" and "About time." The Festival runs on volunteer work and Camp Trans folks did food prep duty in the meal area, hauled garbage and washed dishes.

The Lesbian Avengers had called a public town meeting in their area of the Festival. *Stone Butch Blues* had been out a couple years, and Leslie was immensely popular. Hundreds of attendees came and sat quietly in a circle to hear Leslie speak, just as hundreds more had just a day earlier at Camp Trans.

A Transgender Baton

The Festival is held on an immense empty wooded land that runs on for acres and acres with scattered campgrounds, dotted by areas for meeting or showering, with a huge sprawling eating and meeting area.

As long as I stayed in the Avengers' area, I was okay, but when I went off after Leslie's speech, I needed protection. One moment I'd be walking along and enjoying the sun, and the next some hostile attendee (invariably my age or older) would try to confront me. It was strange, dislocating and anxiety-producing.

So, some woman—often genderqueer and usually about half my age—would act as my escort. And when she had to go, she'd find someone else who would take me in hand. In this way I was passed hand-to-hand from one young woman to the next, like a transgender baton. They were all very sweet and very protective.

When darkness fell, the only place I felt really safe was inside the Twilight Zone—the darkened S/M woods where, with the other outcasts sitting around campfires, I belonged and fit in.

Jamison Green at Camp Trans

34

Bearded, Hairy-Chested Women?

During all this, the real elephant in the room, the dog that never barked (putting all my animal metaphors to use) was transmen. Jamison Green, a leading transman activist, was part of Camp Trans and hosted workshops on transmen, but did not try to enter.

In fact, he did explain to Festival personnel that since their policy was *once a man always a man,* the reverse must also be true: *once a woman always a woman,* adding, "I don't think you want me in your festival." What happened next is informative: "They were shocked. They looked like I had just slapped them in the face." He was right. Clearly Lisa had never envisioned the possibility of female-to-male transsexuals when declaring that biology was the litmus test for womanhood.

Had there been the desire within the trans community, it would have been *extremely* interesting to see the effect of a cohort of strong, bearded, hairy-chested transmen showing up at the Festival, demanding entry as women. Queer bodies almost always refute the cisgender conventions created to contain them.

Forearms on the Land!

As Tony explained his reasoning to me at the time, "First of all, I don't always identify as fully FTM; sometimes I still think of myself as a woman, and sometimes people still call me 'she'. Second, according to Festival policy, if it's 'once a man, always a man' for you, then it should be 'once a woman, always a woman' for me: they can't have it both ways. All that aside, the bottom line is—I've fought for this movement as a lesbian, organized and marched as a lesbian, I grew up as a lesbian and spent almost my entire adult life as a lesbian. The surgery changed my body—it didn't change my mind or my experience." (InYourFace Interviews Tony Barreto-Neto)

Perhaps even more weirdly, at a later date, a transman did enter the Festival (with me). Being part Native American, Hillsborough County (FL) Deputy Sheriff Tony Barreto-Neto did not have a beard or hairy chest.

What he did have was a newly constructed phallus made from skin from his arm. Hot and sweaty once inside, he asked a woman nearby and a Festival staffer if they would mind if he washed off. They both (probably seeing a very butch woman, which he sometimes still identified as) said "yes."

By noon the same day, Holy Hell had broken loose. Word ran like wildfire through attendees that Camp Trans had snuck a man in and radical separatists complained that there were now "Penises on the Land." They also spread rumors that a man had waved his "erect penis" at women in the shower stalls, terrorizing them.

Remember, this is a sworn peace officer, not Jack-the-Ripper. And to be entirely accurate, they should spread rumors that there were "Forearms on the Land." But I could see that lacked the original formulation's rhetorical punch.

There had been a young Lesbian Avenger from Chicago who was transsexual and pre-op and had entered with her crew. She didn't get naked or anything, but we learned that several hundred women surrounded her at one point and got very angry and confrontational.

We were working furiously with five Festival coordinators, wracking our brains about how to find her—when she comes out of the main gates alone, completely oblivious, walks up to the Coordinators and asks, "Does anyone have a razor? I need to shave, and I left mine back in Chicago." They just turned and looked at us like, "What on earth are we supposed to say to this?"—and we just burst out laughing.

I've hardly mentioned Kodi, who lived as a butch lesbian (and had been repeatedly assaulted for it) but who identified as intersex and who entered with us. Cody was a big part of Camp Trans. Queer identities strike again.

Lisa eventually responded to the new and unanticipated Transmen Menace in the person of Jamison's handsome, bearded presence by expanding the policy so that, henceforth, all attendees would have to also have government issued female ID.

So radical lesbian separatists were depending on accreditation by patriarchal government agencies to establish attendees' womanhood. I felt like I'd missed an email somewhere.

Man-Made Womyn Only

Even Camp Trans was not entirely immune to the charms of gender regulation. Our plan to enter the Festival immediately split the Camp over whether the post-ops thought the pre-ops should be allowed to enter.

The fact that post-ops even felt authorized to question anyone else's surgical status and pass judgment on it speaks volumes. But this is how gender hierarchies work: as soon someone gets a little status, they tend to use it against someone farther down the totem pole.

Alas, this circular firing squad was going to be all transgender. We had apparently learned nothing from the festival's own prejudices. A core of feminist-identified post-ops held that only they should be allowed to enter because they were real women, while those nasty, penis-bearing pre-ops should be excluded because they were still men. To this day, I find the semantics of that position so bizarre I still don't know what to say (especially now that gender status has finally been decoupled from genitals).

Luckily, activists Nicole Storm and Liby Pease do. Noting that issues of race and class were also at stake, they declared it was completely, totally "objectionable to suggest that surgical procedures beyond the means of many are the proper price for inclusion in women's culture." They added that female-ness which could be bought was oppressive in its own right.

Since no one definitively knew my surgical status, I immediately declared myself pre-op, adding that a shift in policy from "womyn-born womyn only" to "man-made womyn only" didn't seem like much of an improvement. For reasons that weren't entire clear, none of the feminist post-ops involved found this the slightest bit amusing.

A Capitalist Enterprise

It was clear that our presence had dramatically upped the stakes. While it might have been possible for Lisa to throw out one lone woman like Nancy, it was logistically and politically impossible to have all of us evicted.

Unable to throw us out and unwilling to throw in the towel, Lisa consulted with the US military, adopting its policy of Don't Ask, Don't Tell, which had worked so well for lesbians. Henceforth, the Festival wouldn't ask us if we were transgender, and transwomen could attend as long as we didn't publicly assert our identities. That has been her policy ever since, and now appears to be the policy the Festival will end with.

I took a lot of heat inside the lesbian community and the trans-feminist community for making Camp Trans so confrontational. More than a few chalked it up to my "male energy" (why is this *never* a compliment?).

They thought that the true feminist approach would be to dialogue and reason, which would eventually change hearts and minds. It's true, I was confrontational. I thought if we just sat quietly outside educating, nothing would change.

It was already clear that a majority of the attendees were on the side of admitting us if it were ever put to an open vote. But it never would be. The Festival was not a democracy. As Leslie repeatedly pointed out, it may have looked like a giant feminist collective, but in reality it was a for-profit capitalist enterprise, controlled by a single owner.

So we could patiently dialog our way to winning over all the hearts and minds we wanted. But Lisa and her private leadership group at the top were not going to give an inch they didn't have to. Sad to say, time has proven this true.

No, We Can't All Just Get Along

We had numerous interactions with Festival Coordinators. They clearly didn't like us and didn't want to be talking with us and they did so only when there were logistical details that couldn't be avoided.

For instance, I was invited in to do a workshop inside one day. Coordinators showed up that morning to dissuade me, right before I was to depart for the Main Gate. They claimed they hadn't had enough time to prepare for my coming in. I said others had scheduled the workshop well in advance, and my invitation to participate required no special preparation on their part.

Then they claimed Security couldn't guarantee my safety if I entered. I said I wasn't really worried about my physical safety, and even if I was, the Avengers would be glad to watch my back. Then they claimed that the dog ate their homework, and the sun was in their eyes. Anything and everything to get me to change, delay or cancel my plans.

And this happened over and over in every interaction with them. It wasn't in good faith and it wasn't meant to be. They didn't care how many of their attendees actually wanted us in, much less about singing *kumbaya* around the campfire and holding a heartfelt feminist dialogue.

The Festival might be a public event and accommodation, but they made clear it was on private property. They didn't want us on that land any longer than they could possibly help. That was their goal. It was obvious to me that they would only react when we acted.

The only reason Lisa switched to Don't Ask, Don't Tell was

because Camp Trans aided by the entirely awesome Lesbian Avengers forced her to. Afterwards she has repeatedly claimed that the policy never really changed, and was in place to allow us to enter if we chose all along. Go tell that to Nancy.

Years later (see Epilogue), a coalition of local and national groups joined together and signed a petition demanding the policy be changed. Lisa cried foul, and pled for them to back off and engage in... yet more heartfelt dialogue. They did, announcing in the best feminist tradition, and with the best of intentions, that they were going to honor all sides in the debate and instead engage in conversation and negotiation.

Lisa responded by closing the Festival for good. So much for the power of dialogue. It is worth recalling that this was a woman who signed the first public letter condemning Sandy Stone for being a transwoman in an effort to force Olivia Records (who knew and welcomed her) to expel her—an effort that ultimately succeeded.

She had remained implacably opposed to transwomen in lesbian spaces for more than three decades. Why anyone would believe that she was suddenly and voluntarily going to enter into good-faith negotiations after 30 years remains a mystery to me. Lisa was never going to negotiate anything or give an inch she didn't absolutely have to. Say what you will, she was at least entirely consistent in her prejudices. Sometimes even good feminists have to be confrontational. I thought we had learned that.

A Turning Point

Although it seemed like a small private action in a small corner of the feminist community, Camp Trans proved to be a political watershed.

First, it marked the first time transgender activists had coordinated and pulled-off a complex political event on the national level.

Second, although trans-exclusive policies would sputter on for another 10-15 years, it was the beginning of the end for them in women's' spaces.

It was the high-water mark for the cisgender supremacist arguments that had defined and poisoned our presence in (and absence from) women's' spaces for more than a decade. Henceforth, it would no longer be possible for cisgender women to impose their prejudices on an isolated transgender woman. None of us would have to be *the only one in the room* again.

And, third, all of this was because trans issues were moving beyond transgender people, attracting broad-based support from within the women's community itself—particularly among the young genderqueer lesbians who would turn out to be shock-troops within feminist and LGB-but-not-yet-T circles in the struggles to come.

It quickly became clear that these young lesbians weren't just allies, they understood gender non-conformity as their issue too. Following one particularly nasty shouting match inside the Festival, I thanked a young, genderqueer dyke for her energetic support. She quickly corrected me: "I wasn't supporting you. If you're not welcome, I'm not safe here either. This is my issue, too." All over the Festival young feminists were arguing passionately in favor of trans-inclusion with the bewildered mothers who had brought them.

These edgy young lesbians kept fracturing the category of Woman that old-school feminists were trying so hard to keep intact. As a result, the post-binary feminism they were calling for shared few of the familiar boundaries and landmarks by which their feminist elders navigated and were still determined to defend.

This was a clash of generations moving quickly in opposite directions. It was a huge change from being summarily and unanimously voted out of women's' spaces in Cleveland just 15 years earlier.

Transgender was moving from being seen as something affecting a very small minority, to being perceived as the bleeding edge of something that affected every woman's right to resist rigid gender regimes.

The idea of a common and unitary and universal "women's experience" shared by stone butches, intersex activists, transmen, boychix and genderqueer women made little sense, as did equating *genitals with gender*, or a feminism that saw as one of its primary tasks enforcing gender conformity and keeping trannies from muddying the category.

Underscoring this profound shift, in 2000 at Camp Trans Y2K, eight young attendees with names like Casey, Gunner and Jack stood in the main dining area before thousands of women and held up signs which read: "Boy," "Intersex," "Drag Queen," etc. and "End Binary Gender!"

They were part of a larger group of 60 genderqueer activists attending the Festival. That larger number alone spoke volumes about the tectonic shifts that were silently reshaping feminist topography. After engaging Festival Security, they declared that none of them could or would affirm that they were "womyn-born womyn." And—just like us—Security then forcibly evicted them.

Realizing the protest could spread (!), the Festival called the Sheriff's office so that armed officers were on hand at the front gate the following morning to support further evictions. (Apparently males were okay in this capacity.)

Think of that—the Festival now saw *itself* as the party under siege. But this was purely a defensive reaction. If you had to call the cops to suppress other women in a community of 6,000 feminists camping out, you'd already lost the war. The struggle had escalated and metastasized. New battle lines had been drawn. The Gender Genie was out of the bottle for good.

The End of the Gender Wars

Explained one of the Y2K evictees, "We aren't silent. We don't identify as womyn-born-womyn. We don't even know what it even means or why it should be used against us or our trannie friends." Amen, sister.

In the coming years we would find an army of radical young lesbians ready to fight on the front lines of a new gender struggle. They couldn't know it then, but in the political hothouse that was Michigan, their actions presaged much of what was to follow.

Their generation would one day help to finally put an end to that circular firing squad. It would mark the beginning of the end to more than a half-century of feminist Gender Wars over the limits of non-conformity. As for trans-activism, it was the end of the beginning.

The affiliative phase of the transgender community as manifest in the conference culture was about to be eclipsed. It would take a few more actions and protests, but without fully realizing it, the community's attention and energy would begin quietly turning towards the coming political struggle.

Transgender was on its way to becoming not just an identity, but a cause, a movement. Yet just as young lesbians were showing feminism a way out of identity struggles, the pre-op/post-op conflict at Camp Trans foreshadowed splits in the trans community, which—as it began accumulating some small degree of its own power—would end up having similar issues with boundaries, identities and hierarchy. Just seven years after the first Camp Trans and only a year

41

after Camp Trans Y2K in 2000, these issues split the transgender community down the middle.

Ironically, that conflict would come in the form of a young, genderqueer lesbian—very much like the ones who took up our cause at Camp Trans—who was taunted and then fired for being "too butch."

The moment that GenderPAC, the new national trans organization, took on Dawn Dawson's cause, our board and then the trans community split in a bitter feud because she wasn't "really transgender." It was ironic, and in its own way heartbreaking.

I said at the beginning that it all started with a fight, which was the easy part. The hard part was building a movement. That was to come next. But first there would be a few more good fights, too many deaths and one terrible murder.

An Epilogue

After the first Camp Trans that action languished, until five years later, in 1997,when Tony Baretto-Neto and I returned to stage "Son of Camp Trans." The idea was to reignite the spirit and the debate of the original.

It mostly worked. Unfortunately, a young MTF who entered the Festival with a Lesbian Avengers contingent was verbally assaulted during a large and angry assembly of lesbian-feminists who took turns at a microphone attacking her identity, body and presence. According to her report, one speaker even announced herself in possession of a knife and unsure if she could continue to keep herself from using it on the young MTF woman. No action was taken.

(It was one of the more outrageous inconsistencies of those who hated transwomen's presence that if we did anything that might remotely be considered aggressive it was inevitably introduced as proof of our "male energy," and several of them would announce that they felt "unsafe" and were "deeply traumatized" by us. Yet when cisgender women threatened actual physical violence on us, or S/M lesbians, or whomever was pissing them off at the moment, that was totally accepted as *womyn's righteous anger.*)

By Camp Trans Y2K in 2000, the whole event was taken over by a younger generation who shifted from our focus of entering MWMF to staging a genderqueer counter-festival outside of it, complete with its own sound stage and musical acts. It was simply amazing.

Early on, Lisa's intransigence (pun intended?) and intolerance were widely seen as acceptable, if problematic. But as the larger gay discourse continued to swing towards trans-inclusion, big name acts have begun refusing to perform at Michigan. In 2013, the Indigo Girls declared they would not perform again until the policy was changed.

In 2014, *Orange is the New Black* star and long-time lesbian comic Lea DeLaria declared that she would not perform at MWMF because her transgender co-star Laverne Cox could not attend. Equality Michigan, the National Center for Lesbian Rights and the Task Force signed a petition calling for change (although NCLR and the Task Force later rescinded theirs).

Attendance at the Festival has dwindled from 7,000 to 2,000 or less. The conflict over trans-inclusion has contributed to this. The tide was clearly going out and perhaps recognizing this, in 2015, Lisa Vogel announced there would be no more Festivals after the current one, the 40th.

The National Women's Music Festival, which has always welcomed transwomen (and still does), continues to this day.

Jamison Green continues to be considered a manly man by practically everyone (perhaps excepting biological essentialists). He wrote an autobiographical book, *Becoming a Visible Man,* which went on to win the Lambda Literary Award.

Sandy Stone went on to write and publish *The Empire Strikes Back: A Post-Transsexual Manifesto* in 1987. Calling on transpeople to come out, it marked the official launch of the transgender counter-discourse, boldly refuting the radical feminist narrative of transwomen as inauthentic perpetrators, which had been used against her and dominated women's spaces for two decades.

Finally, those who launched the original attacks to isolate, demonize, and expel transgender women have increasingly found themselves the ones under attack as a younger, more gender fluid and tolerant generation of feminists take over.

There's even a name for them, TERF for Trans-Exclusive Radical Feminist. It is not a compliment. Tired of TERFs endless bigotry and rhetorical violence towards transwomen, women's groups and events have begun dis-inviting and/or ejecting angry TERFs.

Perhaps ironically but certainly predictably, this has led to TERFs complaining loudly of discrimination, and of the unfairness of being excluded from women's spaces (I am not making this up). As Dr. Martin Luther King once said (almost), the moral arc of the universe is long, but it bends towards men in dresses.

Chapter 2—Boys DO Cry: The Killing of Brandon Teena

Non-Humans

And then the murder. Nothing in recent memory transfixed the transgender community like the violence killing Brandon Teena.

Nothing in recent memory transfixed the transgender community like the murder of Brandon Teena. It was not the most recent transgender murder; it wasn't even the first that year. But it was different.

It was simply so egregious, in so many ways, that I felt like I had to do something, even if that was only to show up and—by the sheer presence of my (transgender) body—bear silent moral witness in reply.

For me, the response by the community was not entirely expected. Because Brandon's murder was highly atypical. Our victims have been overwhelmingly young Black transwomen from low-income communities in major urban centers.

All that Brandon had in common with them was that he was also young and low-income (both contributing to social vulnerability), and attacked violently by more than one guy. Otherwise he was a white man living on a farm out way in the country.

In other words, this is a crime that probably never would have happened, except that the actions of the local Sheriff made it almost inevitable. If the rest of this chapter runs the risks of dwelling too long on facts, it is because it was these actions by law enforcement—omitted from a romanticized movie version and overlooked by a sensationalized media coverage—that led to his beating and rape and entirely avoidable murder.

Brandon's death was different in that it proved beyond a doubt that transpeople could be considered so worthless, such non-humans, that we could be violently attacked, sexually assaulted, threatened with death, and even then, the police would not only fail to protect us but would actually help our assailants.

That's what got everyone's attention. That, and the media coverage.

In the midst of this bloody and senseless murder, media writers straight and gay had a field day blaming Brandon for his own murder (*What could you expect? 'She' tried to pass himself off as the wrong sex*), playing up the most salacious aspects of his surgical status (*Was 'she' packing? Did 'she' have sex with him?*) while making sure to use the wrong name and pronouns.

Even in violent death, we had no respect and were granted no dignity. Looking at that, none of us were safe. But a lot of us were angry.

A Trailer Park in Lincoln

He was born Teena Renae Brandon in a trailer park in Lincoln, Nebraska to JoAnn Brandon. He was reportedly sexually abused repeatedly by his uncle. (Sexual abuse of transgender youth is common, as many of us are confused, socially isolated, used to keeping secrets and afraid of publicly discussing sexuality.)

Brandon began self-identifying as male in adolescence, frequently dressing in masculine clothes and even trying to enlist in the Army as a man.

In 1993, when he was 20 years old, he moved to Humboldt, 80 miles from Lincoln, where no one knew him and—fulfilling what he'd been trying to do in Falls City for years—living completely as a man.

He stayed at the remote, rented farmhouse of a young woman, Lisa Lambert, and her infant son. Soon he was dating the local it-girl, 19-year-old Lana Tisdel. Unfortunately, he also started hanging out with two of her friends, former beaux, John Lotter, and his pal, ex-convict, Marvin "Tom" Nissen.

Brandon was always out of money, and frequently kited checks. He did the same in Humboldt. When he was arrested, Lana got him out. But he'd been held in the women's section, and the arrest report published in the local paper used his birth name. That let the cat out of the bag.

Soon after, on Christmas, Nissen and Lotter—who now suspected he'd been born female—got drunk and decided to "prove" his sex to Lana by attacking and then stripping him in front of her.

After Lana left, they beat him, drove him to a secluded spot and took turns raping him vaginally and anally.

Warning him that if he reported them to the Sheriff they would kill him, they drove him back and demanded he take a shower to remove all the evidence. It was through the bathroom window that Brandon finally escaped them and made his way back to Lana, hurt, coatless and shoeless in the freezing night. It was Lana who convinced him to go file a report.

"I Don't See Why I Have To"

Naively believing law enforcement might be interested in several violent crimes, that it might want to protect someone who had been raped and threatened with death, Brandon went to Sheriff Charles Laux.

He was wrong on both counts. Remember, Brandon is just a kid, violently beaten, raped, without money or a home. Here are some outtakes of that very long interview:

Sheriff's Office*: And what did you have in your underpants?... You didn't have a sock? Do you run around once in a while with a sock in your pants to make you look like a boy?*

Brandon Teena*: Yeah.*

SO*: How come you forgot to tell us about this?*

BT*: Well, I didn't see it as important.*

SO*: It's all important when we are doing an investigation. We ask you to start at the beginning and you skipped half of it...*

...

SO*: Okay. So then after he could stick it in your vagina he stuck it in your box or in your buttocks, is that right?*

BT*: Yes, sir.*

...

SO*: All right, did it feel like he stuck it in very far? Or not?*

BT*: I don't know how far. It hurt.*

SO*: Did you holler all the time he was putting it in?...*

...

SO*:... Did he have a hard-on when he got back there or what?*

BT*: I don't know. I didn't look.*

SO: You didn't look. Did he take a little time working it up, or what? Did you work it up for him?

BT: No, I didn't.

SO: You didn't work it up for him?

BT: No.

...

SO: ...Why do you run around with girls instead of guys being you are a girl yourself?

BT: Why do I what?

SO: Why do you run around with girls instead of guys being you are a girl yourself. Why do you make girls think you are a guy?

BT: I haven't the slightest idea.

SO: You haven't the slightest idea? You go around kissing every girl?...

...

SO: The ones, the girls that don't know about you, think you are a guy. Do you kiss them?

BT: [Inaudible] what [inaudible] that happened last night?

SO: Because I'm trying to get some answers so I know exactly what is going on. Now, do you want to answer that question for me or not?

BT: I don't see why I have to.

Every time Brandon balks, Laux pulls the old "just the facts" routine, like he's an extra on the old TV show *Dragnet*. But he obviously has no interest in facts about an actual *crime* that's been committed, just in dragging out every detail about Brandon's gender by trivializing and sexualizing the assault on him as much as possible.

You can just feel him trying to humiliate this uppity, mannish-looking female to force him to acknowledge his femininity. But this is one tough kid: even alone, wounded and traumatized, it never happens.

Brandon hangs in there, gamely answering every demeaning and maddeningly irrelevant question, until that final "I don't see why I have to," when it seems to strike him that this endless verbal assault has no end in sight and Laux is only interested in degrading him. For the rest of the transcript, which goes on quite a bit longer, he clearly gives up and is non-responsive to further questioning by Laux.

Two Facts

The Sheriff's deputies bring in Nissen and Lotter to question them based on Brandon's report. But according to published reports, Laux refuses to let deputies arrest them, although several wanted to.

So now Nissen and Lotter—who have demonstrated a capacity for profound violence and threatened Brandon with death if he goes to the cops—know that he has in fact gone to the cops.

Laux's response to the danger he's now placed Brandon in by bringing Nissen and Lotter in but not placing them under arrest, is to advise Brandon to hang around for more "questioning."

These two facts doom Brandon.

He calls his mother, and JoAnne begs him to come home immediately. Brandon promises to do so in a few days. He never makes it. Fulfilling their threat made just five days earlier, on Christmas Day 1993, Nissen and Lotter get drunk again, find a knife and gun and go looking for Brandon.

They check out a few places before finally driving out to Lisa Lambert's farmhouse, where a black male friend, Philip DeVine, happens to be visiting after breaking up with his girlfriend.

They put the gun under Brandon's jaw and pull the trigger, shooting him twice in the head. And then, while he lies there twitching, they stab him in the stomach to make sure he's dead.

They then shoot and kill Lambert, and then Phillip DeVine. Only Lisa's toddler in its crib is spared. After their arrest, Nissen accuses Lotter of the murders, and turns state's evidence in exchange for being spared the death sentence. Based largely on his testimony, Lotter is sentenced to death.

Commented Hillsborough County (Florida) Deputy-Sheriff Tony Barreto-Neto, who had founded the first support group for transgender cops, TOPS (for Transgender Officers Protect & Serve): "In my opinion, Charles Laux is guilty of criminally culpable negligence in the triple murders. I have examined Brandon's original signed complaint, and there is no question that [Laux] had probable cause to make an investigation and take the perpetrators into custody before they carried out their threat to kill Brandon. He didn't act because Brandon, like me, was a transsexual."

The Media Strikes

The story had sex, gender transgression and violent death, but unlike dozens of such murders that had been totally ignored, for once it wasn't some inner city black girl but a photogenic white butch. The media was all over it.

Playboy was among the first in the Blame the Victim parade, with a horrendously-titled article "Death of Deceiver" by Eric Konigsberg in January, 1995. Adding insult to injury, the article, like almost all coverage—straight and gay—relentlessly identified to Brandon as "Teena" and "her" throughout.

Dwelling at length on Brandon's gender crossing, Konigsberg concluded that Brandon brought on his own murder: "Posing as a man got Teena Brandon what she couldn't get as a woman—adoring girlfriends and a fiancée. It also got her killed." Note the absence of the actual killers—and the Sheriff—from that formulation.

Being *Playboy*, if they could have done a naked fold-out photo to make it more salacious for their cisgender straight-boy readers, they would have. No one expected *Playboy* to have any interest in male-identified individuals, much less understanding transmen. Sexualizing and objectifying women's bodies was their business model. And the trans-community wasn't exactly *Playboy*'s target demographic.

And a *New Yorker* piece by true-crime writer John Gregory Dunne managed to be authoritative on every detail—while still getting names, pronouns and identity wrong and referring dismissively to Brandon's "gender disorientation."

But it was an April, 1994 article in the *Village Voice* by bad-boy lesbian author Donna Minkowitz that really ignited rage in the trans-community. Interestingly, Minkowitz had also publicly noted that among her very fertile and fluid identifications is, "a sort of sexy, holy kid on a motorcycle. The kid may be male. He's an effeminate boy with long hair." She's even gone undercover as a boy to report.

In her piece, "Love Hurts: Brandon Teena Was a Woman Who Lived and Loved As a Man" Donna used her trademark style of throwing her consciousness hook, line and sinker at a story to experience it from the inside.

For many writers, it can be a rich way to engage complex topics. In this case, the approach led her to mine her own sexual feelings for

Brandon as "the handsomest butch item in history—not just good looking, but arrogant, audacious, cocky—everything [the local girls] and I look for in lovers."

Perhaps mining her own wish fulfillment, she portrayed Brandon as a confused, cross-dressing butch who suffered from profound internalized homophobia, which—had "she" only been able to overcome it—would have let "her" live happily ever after as a lesbian dreamboat.

What really pissed many of us off was the rampant sexualization. The article made 11 references to Brandon's sexual practices, seven references to his genitals and five to a dildo he allegedly owned. Through all this, it never managed to get the pronouns or names right once, or to even explain how this young man, who had been raped and beaten, threatened with death and reported all this to the cops, happened to still be in the same small town just waiting around to be murdered.

An interview with Dyke TV by Leslie Feinberg summed it up: "The article is sleazy, salacious psycho-sexual babble. But worst of all, this article lets the cops off the hook for their culpability in instigating the violence... in the first place. We demand an investigation into the criminal role of the police."

It's true that Brandon's identity has never been totally clear. This is often true of people who have not had the resources to physically transition and who are not around to answer questions.

What is clear is that he was vehement that he was not a lesbian, that he had repeatedly told those important to him that he identified as a male for years, that he moved to another city so he could live freely as a man, that he took a male name and that he told girls he was going to have surgery.

This is not the profile of a closeted butch dreamboat.

I don't think the article meant to be hurtful—to a large extent, it was just Minkowitz being Minkowitz. I doubt she or anyone else writing about us knew much about transgender. Most people didn't back then.

And minus the gratuitous sexualization, her take on Brandon wasn't that far off from how many of the gay media outlets covered him. Boston gay and lesbian newspaper, *Bay Windows*, didn't even want to run the story because, if he was trans, he wasn't gay or lesbian.

But the *Voice* article was ill-considered and ill-timed. It wasn't love that hurt Brandon, it was two psychopathic murderers. And looking a little further outside a writer's own personal frame of reference (or even interviewing a live transman) might have been more appropriate when dealing with someone who had been so recently and violently murdered.

For a community still reeling from his death and the egregious abuse of police power that had led to it, the article, the noxious title, the gratuitous sexualization of a dead transman—all came like a slap in the face.

Moreover, Minkowitz was from the community, writing for a left-wing publication, located right in NYC. It was a bridge too far. Everyone felt that a line had to be drawn. But how? Within days, we put out a call to picket the East Village offices of the *Village Voice*. And on a cool, sunny Monday morning on April 18, 1994, we did.

This was a time when the trans community was still defined by going to conferences, getting medical care and being accepted. Most of us didn't out ourselves unless we absolutely had to. We didn't picket or demonstrate or pick public fights. In fact, except for Anne Ogborn and Transgender Nation, and Denise Norris and her activists friends inviting me to picket Gay Pride earlier that year, I don't think any of us knew the first thing about picketing and demonstrations.

As a result, no one had any idea what to expect. But dozens of us showed up anyway, many wearing black Menace t-shirts to make our presence more high-profile. It may have been our first street demonstration, but it would prove to be the first of many. We arrayed ourselves around the East Village front entrance, holding up hand-lettered signs and pictures of Brandon.

We made sure to give out handbills denouncing Minkowitz and the *Village Voice* with specific details from the piece to everyone entering or coming near the building. A trio of police cars quickly drove up, braking hard, and disgorged a host of uniformed patrolmen. No doubt summoned by a panicked *Voice* management, they were probably expecting rabid protesters, ready for a confrontation.

What they found were a bunch of transsexuals mourning one of their own and pleading their case with *Voice* employees (more than a few of whom were quite sympathetic), along with scores of bemused businessmen and women who worked in the same building and got our fliers.

After a few minutes of conversation with us, and a sit-rep on the terrain and tactical situation in which they found themselves, the cops withdrew. After an hour or so of picketing and leafleting, we did the same.

The action eventually won me a hearing from the *Voice*'s Editor-in-Chief, for whom I ended up writing a couple of pieces. One of them was a respectful memorial on the death of Marsha P. Johnson—so maybe they'd learned something.

Donna Minkowitz was still in full-on denial, though. She was scheduled to speak at Beit Simchat Torah, the gay synagogue in the West Village. I reached out to the rabbi, explained our situation and pushed hard for the opportunity to be there when Donna spoke. The rabbi consented.

When several dozen Jewish women gathered soon after at the temple, Donna and I faced off again with the rabbi—looking both concerned and a little baffled—watching. Being a rabbi can be very routine; in retrospect, I suspect we were the high point of her week.

There was also a lesbian speak-out scheduled soon after where Donna was one of the speakers. I contacted Joan Nestle of the Lesbian Herstory Archives and again asked to be allowed to challenge her. I ended up being the one challenged. I'd exaggerated in some of the things I'd said about her and the moment she spotted me, she made a beeline and screamed at me, "Get your facts straight!"

She was totally right. If you attack someone publicly for something they've done, you never go beyond the facts. It was a lesson I never forgot. Something else interesting happened at that speak-out. I had made a list of "our stories" and when it was finally my turn to speak, I started going through them.

When I got to MWMF, about half the 300 or so lesbians in attendance started hissing loudly. I knew it was intended to intimidate me but I thought "screw this," and just glared back at them and said loudly, "These ARE our stories." It wasn't until later that Joan told me they'd been hissing not me, but the Festival. They were expressing support. The thought had simply never occurred to me.

Rounding Up the Troops

One productive thing that all of the awful mainstream media coverage *had* done was to focus our attention on Nissen's and Lotter's trial and sentencing, which was coming up the very next month in Falls City, Nebraska. We'd done one demonstration successfully; could we do another? The logistics were daunting, since no one knew where Falls City was, or if anyone would show up there if we announced a demo.

Friend and fellow activist Nancy Nangeroni from Boston had been pushing for some sort of action. I reached out to Tony, the transgender cop, to see if he'd provide security for whatever event emerged.

In all our street actions, Tony was always a lynchpin. He had silver hair, a pronounced Southern drawl and a gunslinger's loping, loose-hipped walk. Always passionate and ready to help out, Tony was our emotional ballast if things might get tough and—in the best cop tradition—totally unflappable when they did.

His presence would be critical, because we would be in hostile territory where we already knew local law enforcement couldn't be counted on. And there would be no calling call a cab or hopping a nearby subway to head home if things went south on us.

Tony quickly agreed to come as always, and I started reaching out to others from the Camp Trans crew—Nancy, Mariette Pathy Allen our photojournalist, Leslie Feinberg and her partner poet Minnie Bruce Pratt, playwright/author Kate Bornstein and two women named Davina Anne Gabrielle and Hannah Blackwell.

Nancy, Tony and I would work together often in the coming years. Nancy and I catalyzed one another in productive ways, often providing sparks of conflict, while Tony would bring a certain sober and unflappable masculinity that kept all our efforts grounded.

Nancy had been a high-powered, highly-paid engineer and tech expert, with her gender issues deeply closeted. While redlining her motorcycle one day on a long stretch of road, she ditched it, splitting herself up the middle, more or less like you might a wishbone.

She always suspected the real cause of her accident was an unconscious effort to both escape and deal with the pain of being transgender. Nancy's recovery was long and slow, but she emerged from it a more self-reflective, confident and determined person, a natural leader, and one finally prepared to dive headfirst into trans-activism.

Davina had been one of Janice's original Michigan activists before Camp Trans was launched. More importantly, she lived in Kansas City, which was the nearest major airport to Falls City and our logistical jumping off point. Hannah had also been an important part of Camp

54

Trans, and lived not far from Davina. Davina's house became our staging point on the way in, and our debriefing place on the way out. Their knowledge of the area and presence in the community was crucial.

A Memorial Vigil

A demonstration or picketing was inappropriate for a murder trial. We wanted to honor Brandon, not make a scene or—even worse—influence the courtroom in any way. We decided to call for a quiet "memorial vigil" and the concept stuck. We blasted announcements in every way possible—word of mouth, email, phone trees.

I didn't care if a lot of people showed up, but I knew there would be safety in numbers and I just didn't want four or five of us standing outside the courthouse alone. The night before the vigils, activists in Kansas City hosted a memorial gathering, and Leslie, Kate and Minnie Bruce addressed a crowd of 150.

The room was rocking with feelings and emotion ran high as they got up to speak. Brandon's death wasn't some distant event for them, an article in a periodical. It was something that had happened not far from their homes.

We gathered back at Davina's and spent the night of May 14th getting ready. Local folks provided cars and we rented a couple extra. Not knowing what to expect, I had a fitful night's sleep. The next morning we got into half a dozen cars, lined up end-to-end near the highway, and our little caravan started off for the 200-mile round trip to the Richardson County Courthouse in Falls City.

Sitting on the back seat of our car was a small, dark, tightly wound young woman with sculpted muscles and conspicuously short hair. She was a boyishly handsome graduate student at Columbia Film School, where she'd been working on a script about Pauline Cushman, a black woman who crossdressed as a man and passed as white during the Civil War to avoid being incarcerated.

She explained that she'd read Donna's piece in the *Village Voice* and had become mesmerized by Brandon and his story. She had come with us because she'd even been working to develop it into a movie script, which seemed kind of a long-shot at the time. Her name was Kimberly Pierce.

Just as with Michigan, I had that anxious sensation of vulnerability from being in hostile territory. We stopped to at a self-serve gas station on the outskirts of Falls City. Without thinking, I jumped out of the driver's seat and starting pumping gas. Just then, a car of good ole boys drove up. They looked at me and then at the rest of us really hard.

It suddenly occurred to me that I was only miles from where Brandon had been murdered and I was wearing a black Transexual Menace T-shirt out in the open. I'd been beaten up by locals while hitchhiking when I was young. I knew if these guys decided to assault us there was nothing we could do, and not much the cops would do, either.

I just thought, *well if this goes down, it will be part of the process—whatever is supposed to happen.* I looked back and they looked at me and us for a long few seconds that seemed like minutes and then they went on their way. But it was a warning, an indication of things to come. This wasn't fun and games in the East Village.

Like Brandon, But with a Badge and Gun

At mid-morning we pulled into Falls City. Tony, Nancy and I went off to see the new Sheriff. He wasn't around (or didn't want to talk with us) but we got his deputy. This was an interesting interaction. These guys had just let a transsexual man get murdered under their noses because their boss considered him some kind of non-human. So a year later, in walks another transsexual man, but this time carrying a gun—a Deputy Sheriff, just like them, who tosses his badge onto their desk and asks, 'Would you let this [murder], happen to me?"

You could see this was a bit of a mind-fuck. They looked at Tony the transsexual cop and saw a brother officer. It was an exceptional moment—when something in the universe just seemed to click. I can only wonder what Brandon would have thought.

The two Deputy Sheriffs—one from Nebraska and one from Florida—talked at length about where we planned to be, where we *could* be, what to expect and so forth. We all wanted this not to become an incident.

Then, ignoring Nancy and I, they started conversing about prominent cases, the challenges of policing, and a dozen other topics of routine cop-talk. It was interesting for a little while, but I eventually detached myself and wandered out to help set things up and communicate everything with the rest of the group.

What I didn't know was that the Deputy was one of those who wanted to arrest Lotter and Nissen—there was plenty of Probable Cause—but Sheriff Laux wouldn't allow it. And Tony somehow wrangled from him a copy of Brandon's police interview, which is excerpted in this chapter.

He was a very useful guy. His willingness to put himself on the line personally and professionally, wherever he was needed to ensure our safety and cooperation from local police, made many of our political actions possible. Plus I learned another valuable life lesson: always make sure someone has your back, and if possible try to make it a transman with a handgun.

Between Us and Them

In the end, 40 of us came together in Falls City. We were from Arkansas, Boston, California, Florida, Kansas, Minnesota, Missouri, Nebraska, New Jersey and New York.

Almost everyone wore Menace T-shirts—to make sure we did stand out and people knew who and what we were. Also to communicate something about transpeople to the townies who had re-elected John Laux the Sheriff, and then County Commissioner.

Almost everyone who attended tried—and failed—to explain their presence in Falls City in the same words: *I don't know why I need to be here, but I do.*

I understood. I felt the same. Why else fly hours to the middle of nowhere where you weren't even wanted to stand outside a small nondescript courthouse with townspeople glaring at you, except that something in you said, "It could have been me"?

Just before noon we saw Lotter and Nissen brought in by the cops and hustled in around back. We'd been asked to stay away, so as not to cause any kind of scene that could contaminate the proceedings, and we complied.

Kimberly, Kate, Tony and Mariette took off to find the farmhouse where the three had been murdered. That took a lot more guts than I had. Kimberly later returned saying they had seen and touched his blood on the floor and also retraced Brandon's steps.

In early afternoon, a woman came by who identified herself as Lana Tisdale's aunt. She drove an old, immense Cadillac and was big and strong and very, very butch. We also briefly saw Lana. Considering her, and the slight and almost effeminate Nissen, you couldn't help but wonder if there wasn't a whole other gender story just under the surface that everyone had missed.

We leafleted the entire square, and anyone going into or out of the courthouse. Some were interested, some were hostile, and some even expressed sympathy for the two murderers. Few had anything good to say about Brandon or expressed regret at his violent demise. And more than a few shared with us that what really angered them was all the bad publicity the murder had brought on the town.

Others were upset because all the additional legal fees for the trial had caused taxes to go up, and some people were at risk of losing their farms. It was an interesting sense of priorities.

The *Dead Fish* Stare

By mid-afternoon, word of our presence had spread, and the local neo-Nazis and hard guys started showing up. While we held our signs across the road from the courthouse square, they would circle the block in their trucks, taunting, threatening, holding up their hands palm-down in "Sieg Heil"—style salutes.

We didn't budge, and eventually it escalated. They started spitting at us as they drove by, and then riding up close to sideswipe us with their pickups. I'm sure they had no love for us, but the Sheriff's office had to maintain order with a sentencing trial going on. So they formed up and came out to protect us, along with a couple of State Highway Patrol officers.

So, here are some of the same officers involved in Brandon's murder out in the square a year later protecting three or four dozen transsexuals in black Menace T-shirts from the local tough guys. It was priceless. And the Deputy who led them was the same one who'd been prevented from arresting Lotter and Nissen.

I give them credit—they did a great job. Tony and I walked over to stand with them as they confronted the neo-Nazis, who by now were out of their trucks and lined up on the courthouse side as if for battle, with the line of law enforcement men between us ready for trouble.

It was plain these peace officers were very serious about keeping things under control and not being embarrassed again on their own turf.

It was also plain that the neo-Nazis meant to do us as much bodily harm as possible, and only the presence of the law was stopping them from starting a bloodbath then and there.

I've never been a physically brave person. But I thought it important to walk up and stand in front of them, look them in the face, to let them see us and know that transpeople would stand their ground. The Deputy Sheriff was talking to them forcefully, reasoning with them, explaining that no one here wanted an incident on the steps of the courthouse with a legal proceeding going on.

If they were on Lotter's and Nissen's side, it would hurt rather than help their case with a sentencing going on. But several of the neo-Nazis were looking right past the Deputy at us, giving us that dead, unblinking, totally expressionless fish-eyed state, full of hatred, that said, *"If we ever find you without these men with guns between us you'll be dead."*

I can still see that face—I've never forgotten it. Eventually they were persuaded to go, and our vigil continued. By late afternoon, tired and out of fliers, we packed up for the drive back to Kansas City.

Sitting Ducks

On the way back, I must have picked the wrong car. About halfway home, we got separated from the others. Then, it turned out that whosever car I was in, hadn't topped off their tank, and the needle now read just barely above "Empty." We were on a deserted two-lane state highway with no farm, no intersection, no structure of any kind in sight—not even plowed land. And no cell phone signal or place to grab a payphone.

In fact, we couldn't even go looking for a gas station since we don't really know where we were and we didn't have enough in the tank to make a mistake. Plus we had a pretty good idea that the neo-Nazis hadn't just given up and gone home to play checkers, but were likely still cruising around out here somewhere hoping to catch us alone and unprotected—which was precisely what we were.

And it's not like we were hard to find. Falls City is just a dot on the map with two main roads—only one of which leading to KC and back to civilization, so they'd have a pretty good idea which one we'd be on.

Keeping the car in the high gear to conserve gas and avoiding breaking as much possible, we drove on, checking the rearview mirror constantly. If we ran out of gas and got stranded, we were sitting ducks. If we took a wrong turn and got lost, we'd also run out of gas, and again we'd be sitting ducks. If a couple of truck-loads of them found us out here stranded with night coming on, there'd be no wall of cops to stop them.

I may have led a sheltered life, but this was the only time I'd ever been in a place where I knew for certain there were men nearby who wanted me dead.

Just as the sun set and, we finally saw the outskirts of KC and then found a small gas station. But only after the needle had struck "Empty," and we were deep into the last of the reserve tank. Thank god for that reserve tank.

Whack-a-Mole

It was the second time in less than a year that transgender people had pulled off a complex political action at the national level. And this one was different. Michigan was about access to women's events. This had been about violence and murder. The ante had gone up, and the issue involved had escalated.

With Nancy's ejection, the *Village Voice* article, or Lotter and Nissen's sentencing, I don't think any of us set out to be political. We just felt our backs were against the wall, and that the community had no choice but to respond. In that sense, we were all accidental activists. But for the first time we were starting to believe that, with timing and organizing, we could now mount serious actions at the national level and the community would support them.

Back at Davina's, we shared a small sense of empowerment, a sense that the community had finally begun pushing back a bit, if only a little. Maybe things could change. We were wrong. We thought we were drawing a line when it came to the epidemic of murders of transgender people. We didn't know yet that we were in a nation-sized game of whack-a-mole with bigotry and violence.

As we were packing up to leave the vigil for Brandon's murder in Falls city, Nebraska, back in Haverhill, MA, not too far from the offices of IFGE (the international Foundation for Gender Education), a young transwoman named Deborah Forte was being violently murdered. Falls City had been only the beginning. A decade of murder vigils and the Menace had begun.

Epilogue

Donna Minkowitz eventually apologized for her article on Brandon Teena, telling *The Bay Area Reporter* in October of 2014 that, "I did not understand a lot about transgender people when I wrote that story, so I wrote a lot of things that were insensitive. I did a lot of misgendering. I wasn't sure whether to think of him as a transman or a lesbian. I'd like to apologize to the transgender community."

In 1998, Donna won the Lambda Literary Award for *Ferocious Romance*, about her going undercover with anti-gay Christian Right groups, disguised as an evangelical boy.

The day after our demonstration, Marvin "Tom" Nissen—who had already been convicted of murder—agreed to testify against Lotter in return for life without parole. Most of what we think we know about the actual events of Brandon's murder come from his testimony. He is currently serving three life sentences at the Lincoln Correctional Center. However, he eventually recanted his testimony, and admitted that it was he who shot and stabbed Brandon, Lisa Lambert, and Phillip DeVine. However, because of a three-year statute of limitations on new evidence in Nebraska, his confession is inadmissible.

John Lotter has unsuccessfully appealed his death sentence all the way to the US Supreme Court, based on Nissen's recantation. He remains on death row, and has largely exhausted his appeals. As of this writing in 2016, Nebraska still uses lethal injection.

On *Saturday Night Live*'s popular Weekend Update faux-news segment, bad-boy wannabe and SNL regular Norm MacDonald noted the recent death sentence to Lotter for the murder of a transsexual man and two friends, joking to a hushed audience, "I believe everyone involved in this story should die." Despite complaints, neither NBC nor MacDonald apologized. Not to compare horrors, but it was impossible to imagine similar treatment for the shocking death of Mathew Shepherd.

JoAnn Brandon successfully sued Richardson County and Sheriff Laux and was awarded $80,000. However, a local judge reduced the amount by 85% on appeal, tacking on an additional one percent reduction for Brandon's own "fault" in the matter, leaving about $17,000. The Nebraska State Supreme Court reinstated the full $80,000, eventually increasing the total award to $110,000.

***GenderPAC speak-out for Boys Don't Cry with director Kimberly
Peirce (second from right), star Hilary Swank (second from left), Riki
(far right) and cast at the NYC Lesbian and Gay Community Services
Center***

Kimberly Pierce's screenplay became the huge 2000 indie hit,
Boys Don't Cry. The film was a remarkable achievement capping five
years of script development and fund-raising. The final screenplay
greatly simplified the facts, leaving out Sheriff Laux, Lisa Lambert and
Philip DeVine entirely, instead recasting Brandon's life and death as a
small town tale of star-crossed lovers, complete with him finding final
happiness in a last sex scene with Lana just before he's killed.

Despite her professed feelings of deep connection with Brandon,
Kimberly was still prone to making unfortunate public statements like,
"I fell in love with her," and (referring to casting for Brandon) "We still
hadn't found the girl."

She went on to direct two major movies—a remake of *Carrie*, and
Stop Loss (which she also wrote). Both were unsuccessful at the box
office.

Hilary Swank, a virtual unknown (she had been in the ill-stared
The Next Karate Kid), won an Academy Award for Best Actress for her
portrayal of Brandon, besting Meryl Streep (*Music of the Heart*) and

Annette Bening (*American Beauty*). The film launched Swank's career, as it did that of actor Peter Sarsgaard, who played a creepy but affecting John Lotter. According to published reports, Hilary refused to disrobe for the final sex scene at the last minute—feeling it was untrue to Brandon's character, and only relented when Kimberly threatened to sue her for breach of contract.

Chloë Sevigny as Lana Tisdel was also nominated for an Oscar, but lost to Angelina Jolie (*Girl, Interrupted*).

Star Hilary Swank (second from left), director Kimberly Peirce (third from left), Gina Reiss (far left), Riki (middle) and cast of Boys Don't Cry pose in front of movie poster after GenderPAC event

Lana Tisdel sued the movie's producers for misrepresentation and use of her name, settling for an undisclosed sum. Kimberly reports that she eventually met and spoke with Lana about Brandon and the film.

Somehow—after weeks of phone calls, agents dodging her and the director bailing at the last minute—on January 20, 2000 GenderPAC's Managing Director Gina Reiss reunited Pierce with cast members, including Hilary Swank, at an anti-hate event held at NYC's Lesbian and Gay Community Center. Swank, now an Oscar-nominated actress, was amazingly gracious, entering by a dingy back stairwell before offering her hand to GPAC staffers immediately and explaining (unnecessarily), "Hi, I'm Hilary Swank." Even then, with every question the whole cast still deferred to Kimberly as their leader. Hilary was wearing a very low-cut, unstructured and braless dress and was about to fall out of it during the media photo shoot. She was rescued from embarrassment at the last moment when Gina bounded across the stage, grabbing her bodice just before cameras could go off, and pulled it closed.

JoAnn Brandon continues to insist that Brandon was female.

Brandon himself is buried in Lincoln, in his favorite black rugby shirt, matching cowboy hat and cowboy boots. The family headstone bears his birth name, Teena, and reads "Daughter, Sister & Friend."

The PFLAG Omaha chapter conducted LGBT diversity training for the Falls City Sheriff's office years later when it was under new management. Sheriff Charles Laux was eventually voted out as Richardson County Sheriff. However, in an indication of how deeply the locals mourned Brandon's murder, he was subsequently elected Richardson County Commissioner. The vote was a tie; it was decided by a coin-toss.

Chapter 3—The Murders and the Menace

Getting on a Treadmill

As we relaxed back at Davina's on May 15, back east, Deborah Forte was being strangled, beaten and stabbed in the chest six times with a steak knife by Michael Thompson. She was found naked lying on her back with the knife still in her.

The new murder, coming so quickly on the heels of the Brandon mobilization, hit everyone emotionally, especially Nancy, since it was so near her in Boston. Any small sense of accomplishment still lingering from the Falls City vigil quickly evaporated. Practically no one outside of the community knew these crimes were even happening, or that we had people dying every month. And it was impossible to get anyone to address an epidemic they never had to acknowledge.

Part of the problem was that, at that time, we were often totally dependent on the print media for facts. And usually the straight—and often even the gay—media under-covered, mis-covered or outright ignored these assaults. Had the ultra-violent murders that usually occurred to transpeople happened to middle class white girls, it would have led any front page in the nation, above the fold.

But the vast majority of our victims were young, black, transgender women from low-income communities. No one in power paid them the slightest attention. We would end up carefully sifting news items, trying to divine transgender deaths. These were often identifiable only from headlines like "Man Accused of Killing Transvestite" (in the case of Chanelle Pickett) or describing young male victims "who wore makeup and dressed in women's clothing" (in the case of Gwen Araujo).

Articles unerringly used the victims' male names, referred to them by the wrong pronouns and dismissed their terrible deaths with a few terse paragraphs relegated to the obscure back pages of the local news section. Follow-up stories—like arrests and convictions—were rare.

As Gordene MacKenzie and Mary Marcel documented in *Media Coverage of the Murder of US Transwomen of Color*, even this small coverage tended to play up victims as being sexual deceivers, and assailants as likely falling prey to "transgender panic" at discovering their victims' pre-op status. Moreover, they tended to present transwomen as hyper-sexualized outcasts who—lacking family connections of friends—lived deviant lives well beyond the boundaries of social norms.

(In fact, some *were* outcasts from their families, because they'd been pushed out to survive on the streets when they came out as teenagers. And more than a few victims' bodies went unclaimed because families were too hostile, or humiliated, to claim them, and were interred in unmarked graves.)

In Your Face!

The coverage was so horrendous it was a problem in itself. It was impossible to know who had been attacked, where and when, and thus impossible to form any kind of informed, coherent picture of trans-violence across the country as a whole. There wasn't even any central clearinghouse for information, even when community activists did respond to these and other outrages.

Logo for InYourFace trans-activism newsletter.

So I started a newsletter called *InYourFace!* with Nancy Nangeroni, Lynn Walker and JoAnne Roberts.

I would end up writing most of the body copy, and Nancy and her Ninja Designs would do the entire layout. We borrowed the lit time-bomb from the Lesbian Avengers, and subtitled it "political activism against gender oppression." (Even back then I was thinking of trans as a window on wider issues of gender oppression.)

The Internet was still very new, and email was a novelty that few people had. (When I tried to convince her to get it, Mariette had asked me why she would want email—exactly the same question I'd asked my computer consultant just a half year earlier. It was testimony to the power of network effects. These marginal new technology were becoming something you couldn't live without.)

Every few months, I would phone everyone I knew around the country, one city at a time: Jamison Green in California, Phyllis Frye in Texas, Terry McCorcal in New Jersey, Holly Boswell in North Carolina and so on. I would try to find out the political news in their part of the jungle, writing up stories, collating news items and building larger story lines.

Rather than build a distribution network, we decided to jumpstart our distribution by offering free copies to all the transgender publications—*Tapestry, Transsexual News Telegraph* and *Chrysalis*—if they'd stuff it in their issues. In its own small way, it was a big step for us and for them.

Many apolitical publications devoted to conferences, social connection and self-acceptance were suddenly carrying highly political news about assaults, legal injustice, legislative setbacks and unfair media coverage. Over time, the information had the effect of radicalizing the communal discourse, shifting it to a more political vein.

People finally could see what was happening. And the more they knew, the more pissed off they became. And the writing was funny—at least to me. Ours was still a very staid community. While it certainly knew how to party and joke at its own gender foibles, it still tended to be very self-conscious and serious.

I wanted to upend that. I wanted IYF's voice to be subversive, irreverent, impudent, at times even juvenile. I wanted to energize and empower folks to spark a revolution, not put people to sleep. This was a voice that had little history in the community. I think it was Judith Butler who said that humor is a necessary attribute when confronting serious categories. I took that to heart.

On a deeper level, I wanted to totally shift the discourse on trans. Our bodies and genders were inevitably the object of the cisgender gaze. It's hard to mount a revolutionary movement when people feel themselves to be the object of constant discussion and surveillance, and as a result feel the need to always be on their best behavior.

Instead, I wanted us to puncture our self-consciousness and go on the offensive. I wanted to reverse that gaze, and hold up for ridicule cisgender people's endless fascination with and paranoia towards our queer bodies.

For all these causes, low humor and high parody were often admirable weapons. And so the following (with apologies) from our inaugural spring, 1995 issue of InYourFace!:

MISSION: Cover all actions related to overthrowing gender oppression, transphobia, genderphobia, binary genders or any political structure which oppresses us or just really pisses us off. Articles on what's happening, how to, how not to, and how to do it again even deeper.

PUBLISHING PERVERTS: Riki Wilchins, along with various disgusting, unprintable, and anatomically improbable suggestions from Lynn Walker, JoAnn Roberts, and Nancy "Ninja" Nangeroni (in fact, layout & production by Ninja Design).

DISCLAIMER: IYF refuses to disclose our sources; we will not disclose our sources, no matter what you do to us, not even if you tie us up and do unspeakable things to our unmentionable parts, not even if we're tightly handcuffed and obviously enjoying it, except where they're clearly printed below. In addition, we want you to know that our sources are all completely honorable, reliable and 100% accurate, while IYF is responsible for all misrepresentations, distortions and garbling of their stories contained herein (even though most of them were drunk, engaged in having sex with small barking animals, or both, when we spoke with them). Finally, all stories you agree with were written up by Riki Wilchins; those you hate were written up by Lynn, Nancy or JoAnn (probably all three).

IYF was not only openly political, it encouraged activism, assertiveness, and (when necessary, which given the politics of the day, was almost always) open confrontation. As the first issue's closing paragraphs declared with a strange mixture of prescience and presumptuousness:

The fight against gender oppression has been joined for centuries, perhaps millennia. What's new is that today it's moving into open political activism. And this is not just one more struggle for a single, narrowly-defined minority. It's about all of us who are genderqueer. We're not invisible anymore. We're not well-behaved. And we're not going away. Political activism is here to stay. So get out. Get active. Picket someone's transphobic ass. Get in someone's genderphobic face.

And while you're at it, pass the word: The gendeRevolution has just begun, and we're going to win.

In Your FACE!

political activism against gender oppression

The complete listing of all subversive actions against gender oppression around the US, along with occasional instructions on how to roll your own.

MISSION: Cover all actions related to overthrowing gender oppression, transphobia, genderphobia, the monocracy or any political structure which oppresses us or just really pisses us off. Articles on what's happening, how to, how not to, and how to do it again even deeper.

PUBLISHING PERVERTS: Riki Wilchins, along with various disgusting, unprintable, and anatomically improbable suggestions from Lynn Walker, JoAnn Roberts, and Nancy "Ninja" Nangeroni (in fact, layout & production by Ninja Design). You can reach us at:

- IYF, c/o Riki Anne Wilchins (RAW), 274 W11 St, NYC 10014
- E-Male to Riki@PipeLine.Com -- or -- nm@world.std.com (that's Nancy)

COST: Free. Made available to you courtesy of your favorite gender magazine as a free insert. Don't forget to tell 'em you love 'em (and us).

PUBLISHED: 2-3 times a year or whenever we damn well feel like it so just don't give us any crap, okay?

DISCLAIMER: IYF refuses to disclose our sources; we will not disclose our sources, no matter what you do to us, not even if you tie us up and do unspeakable things to our unmentionable parts, not even if we're tightly handcuffed and obviously enjoying it, except where they're clearly printed below. In addition, we want you to know that our sources are all completely honorable, reliable and 100% accurate, while IYF is responsible for all misrepresentations, distortions and garbling of their stories contained herein (even though most of them were drunk, engaged in having sex with small barking animals, or both, at the time we spoke with them). Finally, all stories you agree with were written up by Riki Anne Wilchins; those you hate were written up by Lynn, Nancy or JoAnn (probably all three).

IMPORTANT NOTICE: As part of our continuing effort to raise our political consciousness to the highest possible levels here at IYF, we will be picketing outside our own office next week where I will personally protest the squalid, degrading and humiliating conditions under which I force myself to work. Persons interested in taking part in this action should contact me directly or simply seek professional help.

◆ LATE BREAKING NEWS ◆

A recent lobbying trip to Washington by four transpeople and friends was outrageously successful. Lobbyists met with legislative assistants, Congresspeople and Senators including the offices of Paul Wellstone, Gerry Studds, Barney Frank, Louis Slaughter, Henry Gonzales, Ted Kennedy, Carol Mosley-Braun, Jay Rockefeller, Mark Foley, Daniel Patrick Moynihan, and Jerry Nadler to name a few. In addition, they met with lesbigay organizations National Gay & Lesbian Task Force and the Human Rights Campaign Funds. In all cases, we underlined the same message: the importance of transinclusion in health care and employment non- discrimination. The folks we met on the Hill were extremely interested and friendly; they had just never even considered transpeople or their needs. I guess visibility is everything. The effort was so successful, a broad coalition of activists is calling for a National Transgender Lobbying Day, Oct. 2-3 (see ad on back cover).

The Sexual Behaviors Consultation Unit at Johns Hopkins University continues to mistreat, demean, and extort our brothers and sisters, while denying effective treatment and working to eliminate surgical and hormonal options. It's time to picket their transphobic asses. **Please contact Dallas Denny, Jessica Zavier, or this rag if you're interested in participating.**

◆ ATLANTA / AEGIS

Source: Dallas Denny

Most people know AEGIS as an organization deeply into the issues of trans healthcare and medicine. They have recently made the jump to a membership organization, and have announced plans to move AEGIS more towards political activism, awareness and advocacy. And... (are you listening James?) AEGIS is beginning work towards a non-discrimination ordinance in local Atlanta.

◆ BAY AREA

Source: James Green

The City and County of San Francisco has finally passed Article 33, officially amending the city's non-discrimination policy to specifically include transgendered and transexual people. Hallelujah! James and dozens number of San Franciscan transpeople and friends have been working on this since just after the Ark docked at low tide, and it's finally a reality.

By the time you read this, it will have been signed into law. James says this is "just the tip of the iceberg," with additional legislation being introduced to define and extend the general concepts in Article 33. Yes!

◆ BRANDON TEENA TRIAL DEMO

Sources: Nancy Nangeroni & Hannah Blackwell c/o IYF

Last year M2M Brandon Teena (AKA Teena Brandon) was brutally beaten and raped in Lincoln, Nebraska. When he went to the police, the sheriff ("You can call it 'it', as far as I'm concerned.") said there was insufficient evidence. Just for good measure, they publicly outed Brandon. Not long afterwards, he was beaten, raped, and this time, murdered, execution-style. Nancy Nangeroni has repeatedly stressed the need for transpeople to stand up, show up, be there. Hannah Blackwell

Issue #1 (cover, page 1) of InYourFace trans political activism newsletter -- Spring, 1995

Riki Wilchins

In Your FACE!

political activism against gender oppression

The complete listing of all subversive actions against gender oppression around the US, along with occasional instructions on how to roll your own.

Issue 2, Fall 1995

MISSION: To cover all actions related to overthrowing gender oppression, transphobia, genderphobia, homophobia or any other political structure which oppresses us or just really pisses us off. Articles on what's happening, how to, how not to, and how to do it again even deeper.

PUBLISHING PERVERTS: Riki Wilchins, along with various disgusting, unprintable, and anatomically improbable suggestions by Lynn Walker, JoAnn Roberts, and Nancy "Ninja" Naugeron. You can reach us at: IYF, c/o Riki Anne Wilchins, 274 W.11 St., NYC 10014, or E-Mail: Riki@pipeline.com . Editing, Layout, Production & Attitude by Ninja Design.

COST: Freebie: We're included courtesy of your favorite magazine as a free insert. Don't forget to tell 'em you love 'em (and us). Also published on the Web by JoAnn "CyberBitch" Roberts at http://www.cdspub.com . **Or Not**: Or you dirtwads could get off your butts and donate a few beans to the cause (since this is all coming out of our back pockets) and send $10 payable to Riki for a year of IYF, delivered hot to your doorstep.

PUBLISHED: 2-3 times a year or whenever we damn well feel like it so just don't give us any crap, okay?

DISCLAIMER: IYF refuses to disclose our sources; we will not disclose our sources, no matter what you do to us, not even if you tie us up and do unspeakable things to our unmentionable parts, not even if we're tightly handcuffed and obviously enjoying it, except where they're clearly printed below. In addition, we want you to know that our sources are all completely honorable, reliable and 100% accurate, while IYF is responsible for all misrepresentations, distortions and garbling of their stories contained herein (even though most of them were drunk, engaged in having sex with small barking animals, or both, at the time we spoke with them). Finally, all stories you agree with were written up by Riki Anne Wilchins; those you hate were written up by Lynn, Nancy or JoAnn (probably all three).

NO, WE DON'T CARRY ADVERTISING....but thanks to our distributors, here's where you can get IYF for free (alphabetically): Anything That Moves, Chrysalis Quarterly, Dare To Be Different, FTM International, ITA Newsletter, ITCLEP News, Renaissance News, SCHEMail, Transgender Tapestry, Transsexual News Telegraph.

WITH A LITTLE HELP FROM OUR FRIENDS

IYF is distributed free! We *know* this is stupid, but we here at IYF can't help it. So why would you ever want to subscribe? Well, some of you have asked about getting your own copy directly, delivered hot off the IYF presses. But mainly you'll want to subscribe because this little intra-community rag has now grown all over the US to a distribution of ~15,000 pieces, and frankly we're running out of cash. We just can't grow without your help.

To support IYF's important and depraved contribution to gender political activism, plus receive your VERY OWN subscription delivered right to your doorstep it's only going to cost you 10 beans a year. That's right, just 10 shekels: a cheap activism high if ever there was one!

Now, we here at ITF Central realize this is a ridiculous amount to spend for only 2-3 issues a year. But then, we ask ourselves: how bright can you be if you're sitting here reading this? Lynn promises to give the first dozen subscribers 15 minutes of free oral sex. Of course, the second dozen subscribers get 30 minutes of free oral sex. And then it gets really ugly. So subscribe today!

IYF GOES ONLINE

You can now get your IYF monthly, just like... well, never mind. Anyway, IYF press releases up-to-the-minute is available through IYF_online@zoom.com. You'll see news as it happens, well before the great unwashed sees it in the regular twice-a-year snailmail version. Just call up and say "I want my IYF," but say it nicer than that. And don't forget, you can also view each issue online as it's published at JoAnn's Web site: http://www.cdspub.com

1995: A BREAKOUT YEAR IN REVIEW

This was a breakout year for political activism against gender-based oppression. As it draws to a close, some highlights:

☛ **Brandon Teena Murder Trial Vigil, the Tyra Hunter Demo** - In an unprecedented display of outrage and unity, 40 gender activists and friends show up in Falls City NB for the opening day of the murder trial of Brandon Teena. During

National Gender Lobbying Day, 35 activists from across the US picket outside Mayor Marion Barry's office to express their anger over the cover-up in the death of Tyra Hunter.

☛ **TOPS** - Following a particularly vicious media outing of Lt. Janet Aiello of Hoboken NJ, police and fire fighters around the country join together to form TOPS, "Transgender Officers Protect & Serve," a national organization dedicated to fighting discrimination.

☛ **National Gender Lobbying Day** - 100 gender activists and friends descend on our nation's capital for the first National Gender Lobbying Day, lobbying on critical issues such as employment discrimination, medical care and hate crimes.

☛ **Conferences** - In NYC, the first National Transexual & Transgender Health Conference. In California, the first Male-to-Male convention is held, and is nearly overwhelmed by enthusiastic attendees.

☛ **Media** - ABC's 20/20 schedules a ground-breaking segment on the emergence of transgender political activism.

☛ **Demos, ENDA, & HRCF** - Edged out of the Employment Non-Discrimination bill again, outraged TG activists respond with unprecedented series of demos in over 18 cities. After 6 months of leafleting and picketing by transactivists, HRCF agrees to inclusion and cooperation.

NATIONAL GENDER LOBBYING DAY TAKES OFF

Contacts: Riki, or Phyllis Frye

WASHINGTON DC (Oct 4) - Over 100 TG/TS activists and friends took to the nation's capital in the first National Gender Lobbying Day, far exceeding organizer's most optimistic predictions. For many this unprecedented and historic event marked the coming-of-age of the transgender movement, the first time activists from across the US have worked openly in unison for national political change. It also signaled a definitive step past the "conference culture" [*no diss intended -ed.*] which has long been the primary feature of the gender community.

Phyllis Frye (Transgender Law Conference) and Karen Kerin

IN YOUR FACE   i   Fall 1995

Issue #2 (cover. page 1) of InYourFace trans political activism newsletter - Fall, 1995

70

In Your FACE!

political activism against gender oppression

The complete listing of all subversive actions against gender oppression around the US, along with occasional instructions on how to roll your own.

Issue 3. Summer 1996

MISSION: Cover all actions related to overthrowing gender oppression, transphobia, genderphobia, homophobia and related oppressive political structures.
PUBLISHERS: Riki Anne Wilchins, with help from JoAnn Roberts, Lynn Walker, and Nancy Nangeroni. You can reach us at: IYF, c/o Riki Anne Wilchins, 274 W.11 St., NYC 10014, or E-Male: Riki@pipeline.com, Editing and Layout by Ninja Design.
Please do NOT add the IYF address to your mailing list. We're DELUGED with local newsletters and stuff. Please use our address only for press releases (or subscriptions).
COST: Included courtesy of your favorite magazine as a free insert. Also published on the Web at http://www.cdspub.com . **Subscriptions:** $10/year .
PUBLISHED: Twice annually, under the auspices of GenderPAC, "dedicated to gender, affectional and racial equality."
NO, WE DON'T CARRY ADVERTISING...but we welcome subscriptions and contributions towards the cost of printing and distribution.

♦ 2ND NAT'L GENDER LOBBY DAY SET FOR MAY '97

New York City, May 15, 1996: GenderPAC, the national activism organization dedicated to "gender, affectional and racial equality" has announced the 2nd National Gender Lobbying Day for Monday and Tuesday, May 5-6, in Washington, DC.

Last year's Lobbying Day on October 2-3 drew over 100 activists to Capitol Hill to lobby around issues like the Employment Non-Discrimination Bill (ENDA) and the Hate Crimes Statistic Act (HCSA), as well as trans health care and the treatment of transpeople in the military. In over 2 days of intense lobbying, activists called on the offices of nearly every one of the 503 Senators and Representatives.

Phyllis Frye and ICTLEP have announced their own separate lobby effort for the preceding February.

Dana Priesing, Washington DC lobbyist for GenderPAC, declared "...it's clear that we made an real impression in 1995. Telling our stories humanized us: it made them see us as real people instead of tabloid television subjects. This time we'll be returning with a focused, polished and more professional approach."

Said Alison Laing, acting co-Chair of GenderPAC: "This is a chance for anyone concerned to show up in Washington and have their voices heard. We welcome all people to participate, to let the incoming Congress know that we are not going away, that no American is free until *all* of us have our rights."

♦ 1ST NAT'L GENDER ACTIVISM CONFERENCE TO BE HELD

New York City, May 15, 1996: Seizing the announcement of the 2nd National Gender Lobbying Day as a chance to rally the rising tide of transactivism sweeping the country, GenderPAC has announced that on May 4, the Sunday preceding Lobbying Day, the first National Conference for Gender Activists will be held, also in Washington DC. The all-day event will be strictly devoted to gender activism. Topping the agenda are strategy discussions on national issues like transviolence, hate crimes, employment discrimination, child custody rights, and so on. There will also be "how to" sessions on topics such as how to lobby, getting press coverage, and more.

While recent years have seen the rise of out-front gender activism, until now there has been no conference where activists could join together and work on skills, consensus, coordination of effort, and the transfer of knowledge.

The event will be held at the Quality Inn in College Park, Maryland, where rooms are already being reserved for lobbyists attending Lobby Day. GenderPAC's Activists Conference will be a no-or-low cost, non-profit event.

Declared a GenderPAC spokesteam, "As activists, we need a place to plot a national effort and strategy for the coming years' activism. We are very excited about this chance to coordinate on the issues that affect us all."

♦ REGISTER NOW FOR NATIONAL GENDER LOBBY DAY '97 & ACTIVIST CONFERENCE ♦

Name: _____

Address: _____

City, State, Zip: _____

Phone: _____ E-mail: _____

☐ Yes, I'll attend the First Activist Conference Sunday May 4th
My senators (2) _____ and _____

My representative (1) _____

Military/Veteran's experience _____

Advice to Riki re: her attitude problem: _____

I can donate $_____to help someone else attend Lobby Day.

I can help out by putting (#) _____ people up in my room.

Activist Conference
➤➤➤ *May 4, 1997* ◄◄◄
Lobby Day
➤➤➤ *May 5-6, 1997* ◄◄◄
Both in **Washington, DC**
Conference at same Inn where lobbyists stay.
**CATCH THIS EVENT
GAIN EMPOWERMENT -- DO GOOD**

please mail this form to:
GenderPAC, c/o Wilchins, 274 W. 11th #4R, New York, NY 10014

Issue #3 (cover. page 1) of InYourFace trans political activism newsletter -- Summer, 1996

A Word Document

One consequence of IYF was a new awareness of just how many murders were occurring. Once you put them all in one place it was shocking. There were suddenly so many victims, I couldn't remember them all. So I started keeping a personal list in a Word document titled "Remembering Our Dead."

My hope was that it would not only help us ensure that no victim was ever forgotten, but the constantly lengthening list would focus community attention and spark real outrage.

Whenever folks would inquire about trans-murders, I'd email back the list. Two years later, in 1997, it morphed into a more formal online webpage on the GenderPAC site called "In Memoriam." Around that time, SF trans-activist Gwendolyn Ann Smith launched an elaborate online site titled, "Remembering Our Dead." It was clearly a much better effort, and we began simply linking directly to it, and it became the place of record.

Lines in the Sand

Deborah Forte's death, coming right on the heels of the Brandon Teena vigil, had created a real sense of despair, which morphed into urgency and anger. Nancy had been pushing me since Camp Trans to begin focusing on something more serious that trans-exclusion from women's festivals.

In talking with Nancy and Tony after Deborah's death, we made a decision that this was a line in the sand. From then on, whenever a transgender person fell, someone would show up. No assault was too obscure, no one would be forgotten. *We* would acknowledge them even if media, law enforcement and policy-makers wouldn't.

Over time, we hoped our efforts would eventually force these powers-that-be to recognize and respond to these murders. In retrospect, we were drawing other lines the dimensions of which we weren't fully aware.

For one thing, we wouldn't be playing inside the relatively friendly (if somewhat transphobic or at least trans-indifferent) gay ghetto anymore. We were now trying to influence the real world. For a second, this wasn't some one-off event where we could all go home at the end. This was a commitment to an ongoing campaign.

Without realizing it, we'd stepped onto a treadmill. Because no one really knew the true scale of transgender murders. In fact, we still don't—but it's enormous, and we now know it's bigger than anyone suspects.

So Far Off

In 2006, GenderPAC—with a lot of dedicated time from a Director named Taneika Taylor—did an exhaustive study of every known trans youth murdered over the preceding ten years from 1996 to 2006.

It found that victims were overwhelmingly (about 80%) young, poor, black and female, police almost never identified their deaths as hate crimes, and the killers were seldom caught. If you murdered a black transwoman, chances were excellent—as high as two out of three—that you could walk away free. I can't help but think this fact wasn't lost on potential assailants.

Titled *"50 Under 30: Masculinity & the War on America's Youth,"* and developed with guidance from Global Rights, the report put the rate of murder at about one victim every two to three months. It was a statistic that was widely used in the media and elsewhere at the time. But we were off, way off.

As of this writing, in the fall of 2015, according to the National Coalition of Anti-Violence Projects (NCAVP), there have already been 26 recorded homicides... just *this year*. A report from the Trans People of Color Coalition and the Human Rights Campaign (HRC) puts the number at 21.

This makes 2015 the worst year on record, surpassing even 2014, which at the time *was itself* the worst year on record. How could we have been so far off?

Definitely *Not* a Hate Crime

To begin with, it's hard to believe that transgender murders have suddenly doubled or tripled. What is more likely is that we're simply paying more attention, and more victims are being reported. It may also be that, in the perception of a more informed and tolerant atmosphere, more transpeople are being out, or more of our assailants recognize and seek us out.

Certainly the former is at work in the identification of Keyshia

Blige of Aurora, Illinois in March of 2015. Ms. Blige was originally identified by the media by her male name. It wasn't until nearly six months later that her best friend stepped forward to report her real gender identity, feminine name, and the fact that she was (quite happily) finally in the process of transitioning.

On 7 March 2015, 33-year-old Keyisha was driving a car with a friend when shots were fired into the car, killing her. "It's definitely not a hate crime," declared spokesperson Dan Ferrilli of the Aurora PD. It never is.

Somehow police spokespeople *always* just *know* this fact… even before the crime is investigated, even before all the facts are in, even before an accused is apprehended. Call it a sixth sense. Because a hate crime designation means they have to report it to the Department of Justice, which means increased media attention, along with highly inconvenient calls from community leaders for action—all things Police Departments reflexively hate to their very bones.

This why PDs never, ever *just know* that murder is a hate crime. Not in all of recorded transgender history. Not even if the killer was heard to shout, "I hate transgender people!" before the attack and, after also killing himself in a double-homicide, leaves a hand-written suicide note on his body reading, "I did it, and it was a hate crime." The most you'd get from some police media flack was that they "have some theories" but are still "collecting all the facts."

The second thing, as the attack on Keyisha shows, is that as a culture we've accepted that trans hate crimes are common, and thus have widened our lens to identify them.

When we compiled *50 Under 30* we were trying to establish the breadth of the problem. We anticipated attacks from the right, and a certain degree of incredulity ("These figures are obviously inflated"). So we were very defensive about who was included, and even left out a few where we thought the cases might be vulnerable to outside review, so as not to undercut the main thrust of the report.

Taneika, who complied and analyzed the data, made sure we only included attacks where there was a colorable argument that hate was a main motivation. Today we understand that if someone starts transitioning, and is violently murdered shortly thereafter, gender intolerance is probably a main cause. You could read it as a sign of our success, having spent all those years trying to get mainstream society's attention.

In Your FACE!

political activism against gender oppression

The complete listing of all subversive actions against gender oppression around the US, along with occasional instructions on how to roll your own.

Issue 4, Spring 1997

MISSION: Cover all actions related to overthrowing gender oppression, transphobia, genderphobia, homophobia and related oppressive political structures.
PUBLISHERS: EDITORS: Riki Anne Wilchins, Nancy Nangeroni, and Claire Howell. You can reach us at: IYF, c/o, 274 W.11 St. #4R., NYC 10014, or E-Male: Riki@pipeline.com   Layout by Nancy.
Please do NOT add the IYF address to your mailing list. We're DELUGED with local newsletters and stuff. Please use our address only for press releases (or subscriptions).
COST: Included courtesy of your favorite magazine as a free insert. Also published on the Web at http://www.cdspub.com .   **Subscriptions:** $10/year .
PUBLISHED: Twice annually, through funding by GenderPAC, "gender, affectional and racial equality."

FORTE KILLER PLEADS GUILTY, GETS LIFE

[Lawrence, MA: Sep 16, 1996] Michael Thompson was sentenced to life in prison after pleading guilty to the murder of Debbie Forte. Thompson confessed that he had taken Ms. Forte home on May 15, 1995, began "Messing around" with her and, upon discovering she had a penis, killed her. A dozen members of Transexual Menace, GenderPAC, and IFGE gathered in a quiet memorial vigil outside the courthouse. Members of Debbie's family emerged from the sentencing appearing shaken but resolute, declaring themselves satisfied with the conviction and sentence. Many of them stopped by the demonstrators, thanking them for their support.

NATIONAL PUSH FOR GID REFORM HEATS UP

ACTIVISTS PICKET APA HEADQUARTERS IN WASHINGTON
[Washington, DC: Nov 8, 1996] A broad coalition of national queer groups banded together for their first protest on genderqueer issues. Forty activists held a demonstration outside the national offices of the American Psychiatric Association in Washington this morning.

The effort was jointly sponsored by the Transexual Menace, the National Gay & Lesbian Task Force (NGLTF), Bi-Net USA, and the International Gay & Lesbian Human Rights Commission (IGLHRC). Demonstrators protested the APA's continued use of Gender Identity Disorder (GID) as a mental illness, claiming it unfairly pathologizes gender-variant youth and transpeople.

Protesters were met by a representative of the APA's Public Relations Department, as well as 5 members of the DC Police. The demonstration was largely a friendly affair on all sides. The action drew a broad cross-section from the queer community, including bi, trans, gay, lesbian, and hetero activists of several races and all age groups.

GID has historically been used as a diagnosis for transexuals seeking hormones for sex-change surgery. However of late, fewer and fewer insurance carriers or HMO's have been covering trans-related medical care, and many now explicitly exclude it. Simultaneously, an increasingly militant combination of gender and queers activists is demanding that the APA reform GID, claiming it diagnoses them as mentally ill simply because they are gender-different.

TRANSACTIVISTS PICKET APA IN CHICAGO
[Chicago: Oct 19, 1996] Forty-eight demonstrators held an hour-long meeting with representatives of the American Psychiatric Association (APA) today during their national conference for hospital administrators and managers to protest the APA's use of Gender Identity Disorder (GID) as a diagnostic practice. A remarkably diverse group of demonstrators, including members of Transexual Menace (NYC, Chicago, LA, Tampa), It's Time America (IL, WI), Queer Nation, the Lesbian Avengers, TOPS, various leatherboys, and at least one intersexed person spent the morning outside this conference vigorously protesting the APA's use of GID.

Demonstrators carried signs and handed out a thousand fliers. In a bit of guerrilla theater, some protesters managed to insert the fliers in hundreds of the APA program guides so they were the first thing attendees saw when registering. Said one Menace spokestrans, "If I want my nose done, it's a 'nose job,' if I want my breasts done, it's a 'boob job,' but if I want my groin done, suddenly I have a 'mental disease.' GID is NOT about psychiatry, it's about punishing difference under the guise of practicing medicine."

MILLION IN TAX $ FOR 'TREATING' GENDER-VARIANT KIDS
According to Phyllis Burke's new book, GENDER SHOCK, for almost 3 decades, the US government has been funding millions in taxpayer dollars to locate, diagnose, and "treat" scores of children for

---

REGISTER NOW FOR NATIONAL GENDER LOBBY DAY & ACTIVISTS CONFERENCE

Name: _____

Address: _____

City, State, Zip: _____

Phone: _____ E-mail: _____

☐ Yes, I'll attend the First Activist Conference Sunday May 4th
My senator(2) _____ and _____

My representative _____

I can donate $_____ to help someone else attend Lobby Day.
I can help out by putting (#) _____ people up in my room.

Questions??? (212)645-1753 or Riki@Pipeline.Com

1st Activists Conference
▷▷▷ *May 4, 1997* ◁◁◁
Lobby Day
▷▷▷ *May 5-6, 1997* ◁◁◁
Both in **Washington, DC**
Conference at same Inn where lobbyists stay.
MAKE A LITTLE HISTORY
please mail this form to: GenderPAC, 274 W. 11th St. #4R NYC 10014 or GPac@GPac.Org

Issue #4 (cover. page 1) of InYourFace trans political activism newsletter -- Spring, 1997

In Your FACE!

political activism against gender oppression

The complete listing of all subversive actions against gender oppression around the US, along with occasional instructions on how to roll your own.

Issue 5, Early 1998

MISSION: Cover all actions related to overthrowing gender oppression, transphobia, genderphobia, homophobia and related oppressive political structures.
PUBLISHERS: EDITORS: Riki Anne Wilchins, Nancy Nangeroni, and Clare Howell. You can reach us at: IYF, c/o, 274 W.11 St. #4R., NYC 10014, or E-Male: Riki@pipeline.com   Layout by Nancy.
Please do NOT add the IYF address to your mailing list. We're DELUGED with local newsletters and stuff. Please use our address only for press releases (or subscriptions).
COST: Included courtesy of your favorite magazine as a free insert. Also published on the Web at http://www.cdspub.com . **Subscriptions:** $10/year .
PUBLISHED: Twice annually, through funding by GenderPAC, "gender, affectional and racial equality."

◆ NOW PASSES TRANSINCLUSION RESOLUTION

(Memphis, TN: 6 Jul 97) After years of debate and dialog, the National Organization for Women (NOW) has finally passed a resolution on transinclusion. The successful vote followed personal support by NOW President Patricia Ireland, and concentrated efforts by NOW-NJ President Bear Atwood and NOW Lesbian Rights Coordinator Kim Ward.

The measure was originally introduced and unanimously passed at NOW-NJ's State Conference in 1994, and then introduced at the 1995 National Conference in Columbus, OH.

A dozen gender activists in Menace T-shirts showed up to get signatures on petitions supporting the measure. But, in spite of signatures by over half the attendees and apparently overwhelming support, the measure was tabled to the National Board, where it languished for the next 2 conventions.

The breakthrough was prompted by an invitation Ms. Atwood extended to activists from GenderPAC and other groups to address the State Coordinators' Conference in San Francisco several months ago. As more State Presidents got behind the measure, Ms. Ireland asked activists to address the NOW National Board at the current conference.

◆ CONSERVATIVE CONFERENCE LABELS HOMOSEXUALITY A "TRAGIC AFFLICTION"

(San Francisco: 20 Jun 97) Gays and lesbians suffer from "gender disturbances" and an "infantile refusal to accept reality" maintains the American Public Philosophy Institute, a group of conservative 'intellectuals' who held a 3-day conference at Georgetown University. The San Francisco Chronicle reports that 350 people from around the country attended, including William Kristol, editor of the Weekly Standard, who addressed the conference.

Organizers said their purpose is to understand homosexuality "as a tragic affliction, with harmful consequences for both individuals and society...." George Rekers, a professor at South Carolina Medical School, opened the conference with a discussion of gender roles in children.

He said that lesbians tend to be tomboys in childhood, preferring "masculine" toys and demonstrating, "a distinct dislike for doll play and other female activities." Male homosexuals show the opposite pattern, "preferring the company of girls and wanting to wear lipstick and dresses." He maintains that "gender disturbance" can be corrected by therapy during childhood.

Funded by Taxpayers

Rekers' work, which is heavily funded by the federal government through research grants from the National Institute of Mental Health, features "aversion therapy," a technique that punishes nonconforming behavior (limp wrists in boys or swaggering in girls) and rewards conforming behavior (girls playing dolls, boys playing baseball).

Said another panelist, Joseph Nicolosi, "There is no such thing as a gay person," because homosexuality is "a fictitious identity that is seized on to resolve painful emotional challenges." Homosexuals engage in "a narcissistic refusal to accept a gendered world and the human biological reality on which that world is based."

◆ REGISTER NOW FOR NATIONAL GENDER LOBBY DAY & ACTIVISTS CONFERENCE ◆

Name: _____

Address: _____

City, State, Zip: _____

Phone: _____ E-mail: _____

☐ Yes, I'll attend the First Activist Conference Sunday April 19th

My senator(2) _____ and _____

My representative _____

I can donate $_____ to help someone else attend Lobby Day.

I can help out by putting (#) _____ people up in my room.

Questions??? (212)645-1753 or Riki@Pipeline.Com

2nd Activists Conference
➤➤➤ *April 19, 1998* ◄◄◄

Lobby Day
➤➤➤ *April 20-21, 1998* ◄◄◄

Both in **Washington, DC**

Conference at same Inn where lobbyists stay.

MAKE A LITTLE HISTORY

please mail this form to: GenderPAC, 274 W. 11th St. #4R NYC 10014 or GPac@GPac.Org

Issue #5 (cover. page 1) of InYourFace trans political activism newsletter -- Spring, 1997

A Heart Issue

There was a third hidden line being crossed. Trans-exclusion from Michigan had been an issue that appealed mainly to lesbian-identified transwomen, and even then, only that fraction actually interested in attending.

Brandon Teena's death, while it angered many, was also something that had happened in Nebraska—not exactly the center of the trans universe. In any case, it had taken place years before, and the judicial process was grinding to its inevitable conclusion. There was little left to do. But violence was different. Fear of violence was ubiquitous, it was personal and it stalked us all.

I remember one woman who transitioned in a quiet Midwestern town and had bricks thrown through her window at night. When I transitioned in Rocky River, a quiet, tree-lined, middle-class Cleveland suburb, no one had to tell me that I wasn't safe in daylight and could only go out dressed at night.

Even when I moved to Manhattan years later, I knew there were streets and neighborhoods where a transgender woman just didn't go. I'd been followed by groups of young men, (and once—pretty stupidly—even dashed into an Army-Navy store, bought a nightstick, and stalked one back, myself).

Clare Howell, a fellow Menace, transitioned on the job as a librarian at the Brooklyn Public Library and was first stationed in a small branch in East New York, not a hotbed of liberality.

She regularly endured casual verbal abuse of young men lounging near bodegas (come-ons with sucking noises, and name calling, laughter at her) as she walked the mile from her library to the Pennsylvania Ave subway station where there was at least the hope of safety in the presence—if not kindness—of strangers.

Being among strangers has the ever-present threat of shaming, less visibly destructive than physical violence, but perhaps more insidious, in that it's meant to wound the heart and mind. And it does hurt, though we try to be strong in the face of it.

Sometimes its wounds persist long after those from a physical attack would have healed. An especially difficult situation is finding yourself in a confined space where you are a captive target for your tormentors.

Carrie Davis, NYC trans activist, writes movingly about being humiliated on the subway (the A train), "The subway car is crowded, but I manage to get a seat. Across from me sit a woman and her male friend... The woman points her finger at me... 'That's not a woman, that's a man'... Her friend looks away, as if embarrassed... She will not be deterred. She turns to her left. 'Who's he trying to fool? Those breasts aren't real. He's a man. That's a man...

"A festive atmosphere of loud jokes and rude comments at my expense fills the car... all acting as if I can't hear them... Soon the entire group is laughing and joining in... The invective is relentless, the sound deafening... Now I try not to cry. I want to die."

So, violence—both physical and psychological—is an issue that touches all of us, and is always present. This violence is a "heart issue," one that is deeply felt throughout the community—which means it is also something you can build on and organize around.

Witnessing, reading, and hearing about this kind of violence cuts to the quick of every trans person and has become an animating force that defined and propelled emerging transgender political activism, engaging a much wider circle of folks who might never before have considered themselves activists.

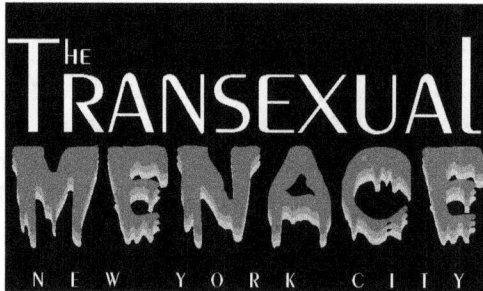

T-shirt art for NYC chapter of The Transexual Menace

The Menace

But perhaps the biggest line we unwittingly crossed with that decision to go forth as *a visible* political presence was the growth of what came to be known simply as "The Menace."

The year before, there had been anger about leaving the "T" out of LGB Pride marches. The June 1994 march was to be the 25th anniversary of the Stonewall Riots.

A number of activists vowed to fight for recognition and inclusion. Activists Phyllis Frye and Sharon Stuart threatened to lie down and obstruct NYC's half-million-person-strong Gay Pride Parade cum Stonewall Anniversary Celebration if transpeople weren't included. (This threat, strangely enough, succeeded at making the rest of us look like moderates.)

Stonewall organizers were concerned enough to assign a team to encircle the two of them if they lay in the street, so marchers could go around them.

NYC activist Denise Norris and a friend reached out to me about doing a local action to put additional pressure on organizers. I wasn't enthusiastic. I'd never attended the March and I'd never seen myself as an activist—in fact my life and career were finally settling down into something approximating normal.

But they were persuasive. We decided we needed something that would make us and the other troops we sincerely hoped would show up visible, and at the same time mock organizers for their fears of being inclusive of transgender people.

In 1968 lesbian and bisexual women were purged from NOW. According to reports, NOW co-founder Betty Friedan personally accused writer Rita Mae Brown (*Rubyfruit Jungle*) of being the "Lavender Menace." The following year Rita and her friends stormed the podium wearing T-shirts that read… "The Lavender Menace."

We thought that was a dandy example. We cheekily called our group "The Transexual Menace" (I'd always preferred the British spelling—with one 's'—which seemed to at least make a single word out of "trans-sexual"). Luckily my partner at the time, Montine Jordan, was a gifted graphic designer. I told her we wanted to channel *The Rocky Horror Picture Show* (a huge underground hit at the time) with its blood-dripping red letters.

She came up with a killer logo, one of those inspired designs that just "clicks" visually the first time you see it. We had three dozen printed up and started giving them out to anyone who promised to attend and protest the March.

It was wild putting one on. It's hard to explain now, but this was a time when *passing* as cisgender was everything. My surgeons had even told me that I would be successful *as* a transsexual to the degree to which no one suspected me of being one. Acceptance by passing and blending in were important goals for many transgender women.

There really wasn't such a thing as "genderqueer" even within the community. Certainly Leslie had been doing something that tripped the boundaries between butch lesbian and transmen. And Kate was always exploring gender beyond the binary.

But, in the main, most of us thought in terms of binary men and women and wanted very much to fit into one or the other. For me this meant being accepted as a "real woman," by looking like one. It was all very cisgender-oriented. And of course you wanted to be safe. That was a big unspoken part of passing. If you passed, you were safe.

But pulling on the T-shirt screwed all of that forever.

Pissed-Off Trannies with Knives

Right around then, *Esquire* Magazine had reached out to do a story on the new transgender activism. "Good ink" from an edgy national publication was a huge break for us. I decided to give their largely male cisgender readers something different than the I-hope-I'm-passing feminine dress-up they no doubt expected, posing in short hair and a black Menace T-shirt.

Towards the end of the shoot, my eye fell on a large cleaver I'd just purchased (I was learning Japanese kitchen techniques). I looked at the photographer, he looked at me. I said, "You know your male readers will all be fixated on surgery and penises. Why not give them a worst nightmare: a pissed off trannie with a cleaver."

As soon as it was in the camera we both knew they'd run with it, which they did. (One day my daughter will discover that image and I'll have a lot of explaining to do.) But here's the weird thing. Bear in mind that this was a *friendly* story, written by a writer who considered himself a *friend* of the community and a magazine that was trying to make nice.

Yet his story was titled: *"The Third Sex—Now the men who have decided they're actually women are on the march. Welcome to the transgender revolution."*

With friends like this, you don't need many enemies.

We were so angry, the NYC Menace immediately picketed the

office building that housed *Esquire*'s midtown headquarters the day the issue hit the streets. And we made damn sure *every single person* going into or out of that office building had a copy of our flier in their hands.

It was our longest and most literate flier, because I wanted to respond to them on their level and let them know we were just as intelligent as they were and that we got all the nuanced ways we were being dissected for fun and talked down to by a sophisticated national men's magazine.

I also made sure to mock the writer personally (just as he'd done to us), so as to embarrass him in front of his peers (just as he'd done to us). After an hour or so, he actually came down to talk. He was very, very hurt. Can't imagine why—probably thought we were harmless men in dresses who wouldn't bite back.

Try to imagine this kind of coverage today, and you'll get a good sense of the general climate in which we were trying to operate for everything that follows. And bear in mind—these were not hostiles; this was all incoming "friendly fire."

Riki Wilchins

ESQUIRE TO TRANSEXUALS:
THIRD SEX FREAKS!

"What makes the transgendered fascinating is the almost mythological proportions of their strangeness... their very freakishness conveys their magical, quasi-divine status."
Hey John, we thought it was Esquire's bizarre obsession with us was that was freakish. But we'll still respect your quasi-mystical, semi-divine status as a hack writer for a trendy, up-market, intellectually-challenged rag.

"The Third Sex: Now the men who have decided they're actually women are on the march."
Tell us: what happened to transsexual men? And are they the 4th sex, the 5th, the 6th? Hey can you guys even count beyond 13 <u>without</u> taking off your jockstraps?

"She pulled it over her ample estrogen-induced breasts."
Gosh, John, don't you think maybe your readers would like to hear how her eyes were riveted on you pulling your jean's zipper over your adorable, ample, testosterone-induced dick?

"She was tall and ungainly, radiating self-conscious awkwardness...hunching her shoulders to look less conspicuous. Pale, downy hairs grew on her chin."
Let's reverse the gaze: "John was a gaunt, bookish man, radiating self-importance over his Geraldo-style trans-hype hack-job. Dark, wiry hairs grew down the backs of his hands, knuckles, and even (yecch) his back. It was all we could do to avoid blowing chunks on the spot."

"Pre-op transsexuals perform a ritualistic farewell masturbation before surgery: 'wringing the turkey's neck.'"
Actually John, we all performed a ritualistic farewell masturbation after you left. Hey...I'm "wringing my turkey's neck" right now!

Flier for Esquire magazine protest

Shortly after the *Esquire* incident, we learned that the Pride Parade half-capitulated. They refused to add "T" to the name of the March, but promised more inclusive language at the event and a name change the following year. In a gesture of good will they gave Leslie time on the main podium, and she was electric, as always.

We also took on the Gay Games (more about this in my book *Read My Lips)*, which had allowed one rather voluble lesbian transphobe who was obsessed with the idea of "men competing as women" to push through some terribly onerous restrictions on transgender participation without any oversight (or, of course, consulting with us).

Unlike any other participants, transwomen had to jump through a long series of demeaning hoops, a full gender verification regime: producing doctor papers, demonstrating hormone levels, etc. etc. All disputes were decided by a group of cisgender-only March personnel.

Or else we could compete as males (it was aimed mostly at transwomen, although the elevated testosterone levels of transmen on "Vitamin T" was also mentioned).

All this was done in the name of ensuring a "level playing field"— meaning level for the *cisgender* athletes. What might constitute a level playing field for the trannies was never a consideration. Certainly trans-people were never consulted or part of the process.

A dozen Menace/NYC members crashed the March's board meeting, demanding to be heard. And heard we were. The leadership, including the ever-wonderful Ann Northrop of ACT-UP listened to our protest and actually changed the regs.

Alas, the same transphobic lesbian returned ("She's baaaack!) four years later in the next city with a fresh steering committee, and got the regs re-instituted. Sigh....

Southern Dis-Comfort

After the Parade, *Esquire*, and the Games, eight of us from MenaceNYC announced we were going to go down to Southern Comfort to shake up the conference.

I don't know exactly what we expected to do, other than be generally impressed with our own fabulousness. But it sounded radical and cool, and the community seemed a little overdue for a bit of controversy. Apparently long overdue. I was promptly denounced by one prominent DC activist as coming to "destroy" the conference. Oh my, that *did* sound ominous. Now I really *had* to go.

Unfortunately, every one of the other eight destroyers bailed. After all the publicity and controversy, I had way too much pride to back down. After all, I couldn't very well go from destroying a conference of almost a thousand transgender people to simply not showing up.

The show must go on. I got a couple dozen T-shirts hot from the printers, hopped into a rental car from Avis, and made the 12-hour drive to Atlanta alone, stopping only long enough to get food in fast food drive-through windows at interstate Rest Areas. It was not fun.

Just outside of Spartanburg, South Carolina, I could no longer wait and had to use a restroom. Looking the way I looked, it was not safe to use the Men's Room by myself. Then again, wearing that T-shirt, the Women's Room presented its own problems. Luckily it was deserted.

I ran in, did my business as quickly as possible, and just as I was washing my hands, to my horror I saw two young, pretty girls walking in. I'm six feet tall and while I don't exactly look like The Rock, my body wasn't really in orbit around the same gender galaxy as those tiny, blond Southern Belles. I dashed for the door before they could say anything, counting my blessings. Except that outside were their two, big Southern boyfriends, glaring right at me.

Just when it seemed something ugly was inevitable (*"Whatchoo doin' in there with our womenfolk, faggot?"*), they both noticed the T-shirt. Okay, so they moved their lips when they read it, but still. You could practically see the thought-balloons form over their heads: *"Well, yeah, we knew that, but, umm..."*

Something clicked. They went back off their DefCon 5 alert postures, and I walked right through them, quickly got in my car and got the hell out of Dodge.

I had assumed that wearing that T-shirt was asking for trouble. *That* marked the first time it occurred to me that wearing it might actually *inoculate* me from trouble—that by outing myself it would proactively puncture the deranged myth that we're all out to deceive cisgender people. Interesting.

No such inoculation was present or necessary as I entered the Southern Comfort reception area in Atlanta's Buckhead Hilton neighborhood, where there was plenty of stares as I plopped down with two dozen black T-shirts and waited to see what would happen.

You have to understand, it was still primarily a dress-up conference, where folks came to be *en femme* in ways they couldn't at home. Pearls, expensive dresses, heels and full make-up at breakfast, lunch and dinner were the rule, rather than the exception.

I thought, *this is going to be interesting.* And it was, just not the way I expected. By the next morning, every single T-shirt was gone. The last one—the one I'd worn down—went to a female psychologist who was a featured presenter.

I'll never forget one couple. They were on the far side of middle age. He was tall, quite heavy set, in a wig and an elaborate, formal, long-sleeve dress although it was just mid-morning. Probably this was his one big, public dress-up of the year. His wife, smiling tightly, was trying her best to be supportive of her husband's strange pastime.

He was a crossdresser not even one of us bleeding-heart liberal transsexuals. For reasons no one entirely understands, most crossdressers tend to be straight, white, males and rather conservative— most of the ones I know are Republicans. (Say hey, J. Edgar Hoover!) Although the contradictions of a man who likes to wear a bra and panties voting Republican has always been a bit of a mystery to me. *Old joke: What's the difference between a crossdresser and a transsexual? Answer: About three drinks.*

But he took my last extra-large, pulled it on *over* his expensive dress with the long-sleeves still sticking out, and wore it proudly throughout the rest of the conference. He wasn't the only one. People wore them everywhere. Passing, looking good for the cisgender world—all that went out the window. People were ready to be out. They were ready to be proud. More importantly they were ready to be a little rebellious.

Go Picket Someone

This was a sea change. Like Michigan, this could *scale.* And over the next year it did, like crazy. As the idea caught, more and more people called or emailed to order T-shirts with their city's name on them. I'd been filling orders myself at the printers at cost, but eventually, I just couldn't keep up with the orders and reorders. I started handing new cities off directly to the printers.

In the end they told me they'd printed over a thousand Menace shirts for chapters in 40 plus cities. And not just SF and NYC either—

most were in the "fly-over states" of heartland USA. There was no structure. The Menace was always more of a dis-organization than an organization. People who asked me if they could start a new chapter were informed that simply by inquiring, they had *already* started one.

I'd learned the mistake of protesting or attacking someone, and getting overly self-righteous. It was an occupational hazard of activism. So the only bit of structure was our motto: "Confront With Love."

It was mean to encourage people to confront injustice wherever they could—but from a place of changing hearts and minds, not trampling on the bones of their enemies and hearing the lamentations of their enemies.

It was hokey, I know. But we were a community with an abundance of resentment and hair-trigger personalities. In those days having a chip on your shoulder and a quick trigger were practically requirements for transgender survival. I hoped the general tone it set might prevent my reading one day in the gay news about some Menace chapter that had gone frothing-at-the-mouth at some deserving transphobe, and mostly it did.

The T-shirts provided an attitude and something even more important—solidarity and instant visibility. NYC Menace stalwart, Clare, recalled a photo shoot we did for the cover of Leslie's book *Transgender Warriors* (a photo that was never used): "Forty or 50 of us met at NYC's legendary West 4th Street basketball courts. You and I were shooting baskets with several of the young black men there before it started, when one looked up and saw a contingent of half a dozen or more Menace T-shirts coming. 'Oh my God,' he said. 'There's more of them.'"

People would phone or email me for advice over some local conflict, and my advice was always to go picket someone. A little public demonstration never hurt anyone. Except, perhaps me, when Clare and I, in Menace T's, leafleted the IFGE Board—in session—at that Southern Comfort conference in Atlanta.

A Perpetual Defensive Crouch

But moreover, as a community, it felt like we were locked perpetually in a defensive crouch, ashamed of our bodies, highly self-conscious, desperate for cisgender approval and constantly navigating the need for real acceptance which never, ever came.

The idea of demonstrating, of a protest group, was both foreign and invigorating. It required us to stand up for ourselves, to own our own power, to throw off the perpetual and crippling worry about what cisgender folks thought of us. You didn't hide or negotiate or try to work around your poor, genderqueer, transgender body. You owned it, you outed it proudly, and you used it as a foundation for political resistance.

This was new. And for many of us it was a huge psychological sea change. The notion that transpeople were "menacing" society was a way to mock and ridicule cisgender fear, loathing, and hysteria around gender non-conformity.

Genderqueer might be considered cool today, but back then being trans really made you an outlaw and an outcast. For instance, when I came out, I instantly lost my job and my life partner of seven years, and half my family stopped speaking to me.

One day I finally decoded what had been bugging me all my life, that is, my gender identity conflict, and starting telling people. In quick succession pretty much everyone around me (except for a few gay male friends) lost their minds.

My mother cried every time she heard my voice. My sister stopped talking to me or letting me visit my nieces. One cousin even stopped letting me visit her sons ("A mother has a right to protect her children!"). Shortly thereafter my partner stopped speaking to me permanently. (Thirty years later, she still won't acknowledge my friend requests on Facebook.)

I ended up in a dead-end tutoring job at an urban community college where one of my young charges, mistaking me for a gay man dying of terminal effeminacy, instead of our reading lesson for the day offered me his penis instead. School workers refused to meet my gaze, students taunted me in the halls. And I took massive doses of Valium every day just to attend work.

So, no, it was not "cool" to be trans back then.

But, for me, the Menace was particularly liberating. Some part of me was still very ashamed, and blamed myself for being "wrong" somehow. On some level I wouldn't admit, I was still trying—even after all these years—to pass. And I was getting harassed enough just walking down the street that passing seemed the only solution.

But my experience in that Spartanburg rest stop convinced me that I might be able to address both problems at once. I made a vow to wear that stupid black T-shirt every day, everywhere, except for work. In winter, I wore one of our heavy black Menace hoodies (which were really popular).

As Phyllis Frye would explain, "I wear 'Transgender Menace' T-shirts in my neighborhood quite often. When I go to the bank, or I go to the grocery store, or I go to the pharmacy or anywhere else I need to go in my neighborhood, I'm wearing my "Transgender Menace" T-shirt. And it's not necessarily just being in their faces because I can easily pass. I blend in very well. I don't wear a sign that says I'm transsexual, but sometimes I think it's important for people to be reminded. I discover otherwise that people forget about me, and then they think, 'Well, I don't know any transgender people. Who are they?'"

The first thing I noticed was that street harassment stopped… just like that, like a door suddenly closing. It was weird. I realized that what apparently enrages the straight cisgender male is the possibility that a transsexual woman might think she is "fooling" him into thinking she's "real." And the only way to prove that one is not "taken in" (i.e., possibly attracted to another "male" by mistake) is to out us publicly (if not physically assault us).

But with the shirt, what would be the point? It made clear that I was beyond both their outing and my own embarrassment. When I finally took that stupid shirt off, it was fully three years later. And I was finally over a lot of my own shit.

In *InYourFace* #2, published in the fall of 1995, we toted up all the new Menace chapters, which eventually grew to over 40 cities (last names have been removed to protect the innocent, or people who have become respectable citizens and might sue me for defamation).

Menace Chapters around the country

Alabama: Catherine S.
Atlanta: Caitlin F.
Baltimore: Bobbi L.
Boston: Nancy Nangeroni
Cincinnati: Diane M. T.
Cleveland-Akron: Emilio L.
Denver: Robin Diane B.
Fort Wayne: Michael D.
Houston: Phyllis F.

Los Angeles: Shirley B.
Louisville: Julia R.
Michigan: Gloria S.
Milwaukee-Chicago J. Debbie
New Jersey: Kate M.
New Orleans: Nancy S.
New York: Riki Wilchins
Oklahoma: Kendra Marie F.
Philadelphia: Angela G.
Pittsburgh: Diana S.
Phoenix: Janet P.
San Antonio: Tere F.
San Francisco: Katherine C.
San Jose: Marie T.
South Carolina T. Ming
St. Louis: Jordynne L.
Tampa-St. Pete: Tony Barreto-Neto

Two Years of Murders

As with Falls City, we decided to use the T-shirts for the murder vigils. They were a bit irreverent, but the black certainly suited the occasion. And they would at least make our group visible, so we stood out and didn't blend in. They would also identify us, so people knew we were there in solidarity with the victim. Like all uniforms, they provided us with a sense of solidarity and unit cohesion.

Deborah Forte

Michael Thompson had confessed to a coworker that he had taken her home, begun "messing around," and, upon discovering she was transgender, killed her.

As with so many deaths, there was violence well beyond that simply required to kill. The autopsy found that Thompson had strangled Debbie, beaten her head very badly, and then stabbed her deeply many times in the chest. Her death, also like so many, was largely ignored by mainstream and gay media.

A few dozen of us showed up at a vigil organized by Nancy Nangeroni and Rob Johnson outside the red-stone courthouse in

Lawrence, MA where Thompson was to stand trial. Members of IFGE from nearby Waltham, MA joined us.

We stood around on a cool, breezy and very bleak Monday, September 16, 1995, distributing hundreds of fliers headed "*Transpeople Are NOT Disposable People*" and carrying signs reading "*In Memoriam: Debbie Forte*" and "*Difference is NOT a Crime Punishable by Death.*"

A law enforcement officer guarding the courthouse tried to bully us into moving off, but we cited our rights and stood our ground and eventually he gave up.

Jury selection was scheduled to begin Tuesday and then the trial Wednesday. But at 10:00 a.m. that morning as we stood outside, Thompson entered a guilty plea to Second Degree Murder under a negotiated plea bargain. He was immediately sentenced to Life Imprisonment, with the possibility of parole in 15 years. The plea to just Second instead of First Degree Murder was probably due to lack of evidence of premeditation. First Degree would have denied Thompson the possibility of parole.

Members of Debbie's surviving family, including her older sister, emerged from the courthouse and appeared shaken but resolute. They were interviewed by the press, declaring themselves satisfied with the conviction and sentence. Many stopped by to thank us repeatedly for showing up and honoring her memory.

The trial and sentencing, at least, were well covered by local media. In a fortuitous turn, a journalist from the *Boston Globe* happened to be inside the courthouse, encountered our vigil on his way out and called the story in to his editor. It was an accident, but for once we went mainstream.

It was the vigil, if not the murder itself, that was considered newsworthy. This was a revelation for me. Apparently just the fact that you're staying around publicly making a statement is enough to generate news by itself. It reinforced our conviction to use the vigils to push our way into the news cycle.

Tyra Hunter

Just a few months later, Tyra Hunter was struck by a hit-and-run driver in DC. EMS technicians at the scene treated her for severe injuries. In the course of treatment, an EMS technician cut open her pants and discovered that Tyra was transgender.

He began laughing, referred to the prostrate, bleeding woman as a "bitch" and refused to render further medical assistance. He remained unmoved even when bystanders began pleading with him to continue treatment, saying "It don't make any difference, he's [sic] a person, he's a human being" for the next three to five minutes. Finally an EMS supervisor came over and began treating Tyra, who died at a local hospital shortly thereafter.

Two thousand people attended her funeral on August 12. The DC Fire Department Chief, Otis J. Latin, punted on the entire incident following an exhaustive "internal inquiry" which somehow managed to overlook interviewing at least eight known eye-witnesses to the incident.

On October 4, three dozen Menace activists from across the US (many in town for an upcoming first National Gender Lobby Day on Capitol Hill) picketed DC Mayor Marion Barry's office, handing out a thousand fliers and calling for a formal investigation.

Tony Barreto-Neto (now head of TOPS) was somehow able to arrange for a meeting with the Mayor, at which he pressed Barry to call for a full inquiry into EMS mistreatment of Tyra Hunter. He even wrangled a sit-down meeting between TOPS members (including Sgt. Stephen Thorn, Fire Captain Michelle Kamerer, and Officer Marla Anselona) and DC Fire Chief Latin. To this day, I don't know how Tony does these things, but clearly Chief Latin had no idea who he was up against.

Tony and the TOPS representatives pushed hard for a full investigation, more trans sensitivity training and a formal apology to Tyra's mother (which had been promised two months earlier but never materialized).

Chief Latin was having none of it, and the meeting became quite heated. There's nothing like the reality shock of being confronted with "one of us"—especially Los Angeles Fire Captain Kamerer—who actually turns out to be "one of them."

Chanelle Pickett

On November 20, 1995 Chanelle Pickett, a 33-year-old black transgender woman was found badly beaten and strangled to death, after her killer's lawyer informed police that they would find a dead body in William Palmer's Boston bedroom. He was a well-known patron at trannie bars.

Chanelle and her twin sister Gabrielle—also transgender—had been working steadily at NYNEX until a transphobic supervisor repeatedly harassed them and they ended up being fired.

Stunned, exhausted and unable to find work, both women fell quickly into desperate poverty. Chanelle was a prime target for a man with a predatory attitude toward transgender women, turning up dead in William Palmer's apartment, her body battered.

Despite strong physical evidence against Palmer, he was convicted only of assault and battery and received just two years of jail time—and even that was a longer sentence than the prosecutor had asked for.

Boston's gay community responded vigorously, primarily because of Nancy Nangeroni. She featured the story on her GenderTalk radio show, calling for action, and led the organizing effort. The National Gay Task Force's Sue Hyde and Robb Johnson of the Fenway Victim Recovery Program responded with suggestions like holding a vigil and contacting the press.

Nancy went on to lead a 'Remember Chanelle' committee that held the vigil and made subsequent efforts with the media.

In all the hate crimes I was exposed to, by far the saddest memory I have was of Chanelle's surviving identical twin Gabrielle looking at once dazed, stunned and inconsolably sad as she stood completely still in a local church before a silent audience of hundreds of mourners, recalling her sister's energy and spirit, and calling upon all of us to use Chanelle's death as motivation for fighting the hate.

I can't even imagine the bond between the two of them, or the loss she must have felt. It's such a unique bond. Since then, having become married to an identical twin myself and witnessing their unique connection, it hits me even harder.

Following the service, we walked in a slow, candlelight vigil to the nearby State House where Gabrielle helped us lay a memorial wreath to Chanelle's memory.

Christian Paige

In March, 1996, in Chicago, in an attack echoing Deborah Forte barely a year earlier, 24-year-old Christian Paige—a black transgender woman—was found savagely murdered in her apartment. She had been beaten, strangled and stabbed deeply in her chest over a dozen times. The murderer—apparently a young man she had met just days before through a phone dating service—then set fire to the crime scene, either to eradicate her or to destroy clues.

The murder was largely ignored by mainstream media, and not exactly given high priority by the Chicago PD, who (predictably) insisted on both referring to her as a "white male" while ignoring all evidence to the contrary and steadfastly refusing to classify her violent murder as a hate crime. So the following May, Tony and I flew in and the Menace held a vigil downtown. Also participating were It's Time Illinois, Queer Nation and the Anti-Violence Project (AVP).

Tony had already interviewed the detective assigned to her case. Again, I don't know how he does this—I guess it's the Brotherhood of the Badge. Nice to have if you're planning a career in activism.

On a clear, chilly winter morning, we started walking from the Baton Lounge where Christine had worked, and slowly marched the six blocks to Daly Center downtown, where the Police Headquarters and City Hall were located. Carrying posters with pictures of Christine that were headed *"In Memoriam,"* and *"Transpeople Are NOT Disposable,"* we distributed 1,500 leaflets. Timing our event for morning rush hour, we made sure that every single person walking into or out of the Police Station or the City Hall got one.

A M*A*S*H Tent

For the next two years, whenever another transperson was reported dead I'd call Nancy and Tony, and one of us, two of us, or all three, would plan to fly to another city and help the local activists hold a vigil or demonstration. Most times, Mariette would be there too, with her camera, thanklessly but determinedly documenting everything. Our only guiding concept was that murdered trans people *will* draw a response.

In many cities, this was a new concept. While some local activists had stood up to transphobic local politicians or LGBT leaders, few had any experience with street activism or protest. Our vigils turned into a good demonstration of the power of example to catalyze people. In every city the outrage and energy were already rife in the trans-community, but no one knew how to take the next step.

Yet once they knew that someone—even an outsider they'd never met—would be out on the streets protesting, they turned up in droves.

Sometimes, if Nancy or Tony couldn't come, I'd be flying into some city afraid that I'd be the only one standing around in a black T-shirt with an armload of posters and fliers. It never happened. One by one, a crowd of determined transgender people and supporters *always* showed up. People were just ready for it; all they needed was a hand the first time—they never needed you for it again.

For me personally, those two years often had an intrusive, coercive quality. I'd been programming trading systems for Wall Street banks, which paid enough so that I could indulge in trans-activism in far-flung cities.

So I'd be at home blobbing out in front of my favorite movie after working a 50-hour week. Then the phone would ring. As soon as I heard the voice on the other end I knew with a sinking feeling everything would go on hold, I'd be making phone calls and booking plane tickets, and soon I'd be flying someplace new where another one of us had just been violently murdered.

It may have been a bold move to say that from now on we would always show up whenever one of us fell. It did prove a great way to finally get media attention to the epidemic of violence. And it certainly proved a good way to radicalize people by introducing them to street activism.

But, beyond that, it was hard to notice that our efforts didn't have a lot of what is called "problem impact." Lines in the sand are just that—they may be dramatic in the moment, but they're washed away by every new wave of murders.

Eventually you wake up to the fact that the violence is not going to stop, and that nothing you're doing is really making a big dent in it. In other words, you can't stop a war from a M*A*S*H tent. For that, you need to go up on the front lines and fight a different war.

Gender is a systemic oppression, it requires a systemic response, which is a fancy way of saying we needed to build something, like a national gender rights organization. Although I didn't know it yet, at a transgender conference in the Midwest, that was about to happen.

Epilogue

On September 16, 1996, just as the murder trial for Deborah Forte was about to start, Michael Thompson took a plea bargain for Second

Degree Murder. He was sentenced to life with the possibility of parole in 15 years. He may have been released and out of prison since 2010.

In 1997, Abner Louima, an African-American Haitian man, was brutally and repeatedly sodomized with a broom handle by members of the NYPD in a precinct bathroom. Seeing this as a clear case where issues of gender, sexuality, race and class intersected, I reached out to members of the trans and gay community. Some 7,000 New Yorkers attended an enormous rally on a hot August 29th afternoon—as did Clare and I: two six-foot-tall, white trannies resplendent in Menace T-shirts, a tiny island in a sea of black and Hispanic marchers. We drew lots of stares, but little else but camaraderie and appreciation—except for a mile of NYPD cops strung out every 10 feet along the route, in 'at rest' position, hands in the small of their backs, heads straight ahead, but their eyes following the two white middle-aged folks like those of angry pit-bulls who'd love to be let off the leash. Gay and transgender organizations remained silent on the beating.

The Gay Games continued to struggle with how to impose its cisgender rules on transgender athletes. By Cologne in 2010, we were allowed to complete in the identity of our legal papers or if we presented doctors' statements attesting that we were on hormones and living in our preferred gender for at least two years. I mean, *really*! Nearly two decades later and *this* is progress? It probably also helped if we could show evidence that we'd had fantasies of crossdressing since we were three, could document that complete strangers had referred to us as "she" in the preceding week, wore rhinestones when we competed at events, and promised not to win and show up the "real women."

InYourFace!'s fifth and final printing was the issue for Spring, 1997. It was no longer tenable. Printing 600 hard copies and shipping them all around the country was getting very expensive. As more transpeople got into activism, the amount of news began to grow exponentially. And with the growth of the Internet, more of them began looking online for current news rather than depending on monthly or quarterly hard-copy publications. IYF then migrated to an online version, edited by Clare, that had a mailing list that included the *New York Times* and every LGBT outlet we could find. This version lasted until the early aughts.

Gwendolyn's "Remembering Our Dead" became the go-to source for tracking transgender victims. In 1999, struck by the similarities between the murder of Massachusetts transwomen Rita Hester and Chanelle Pickett, Gwendolyn and some friends held a Transgender Day of Remembrance in the Castro. Over the next decade, TDOR became a nationwide event, and today is observed in schools and local communities around the world.

In 1997, the newly-launched national organization GenderPAC would conduct a first National Survey on TransViolence. Complied by trans-activist and researcher Emilia Lombardi, in complied responses from 402 participants. This is a snapshot of its findings:

Street Harassment/Verbal Abuse 55.5%
Assaulted without a weapon 19.4%
Being followed or stalked 22.9%
Assaulted with a weapon 10.2%
Rape/Attempted Rape 13.7%

That same year, the Civil Rights Division of the US Department of Justice agreed to a first meeting with the transgender community to explore what could be done about the epidemic of violence. It was led by GenderPAC's Dana Priesing, and also attended by TOPS, the Task Force and Bi-Net USA.

In 2000, GLAAD and GenderPAC met with the Associated Press Stylebook, the industry standard for journalists. We asked them to update their standards for transgender coverage. Two old salts more used to enduring arcane arguments about dangling participles listened silently as we passionately made the case that the least murder victims deserved was to be identified by their proper pronoun when that was precisely what had cost them their lives. In the end, they agreed and updated the Stylebook guidelines so that victims were supposed to be identified by the gender in which they lived their normal daily lives. For the next 10 years the rule was more honored in the breach, although recently it seems most newspapers have finally caught on.

In December, 1995 an investigation into the death of Tyra Hunter was finally reopened after additional pressure from the Task Force, Gays & Lesbians Opposed to Violence (GLOV) and the *Washington Blade*. Evidence showed that had she had been properly treated at the scene and the hospital, her chance of survival would have been 90%.

Tyra's mother Margie was awarded $2.9 million. Over 2,000 people attended her funeral. No EMTs were ever disciplined.

Chanelle Pickett's surviving twin, transgender woman Gabrielle, eventually left the Boston area for New York City. She was found murdered in 2003, just seven years after Chanelle.

On July 4, 1996 President Bill Clinton signed the reauthorization of the Hate Crimes Statistics Act. It included "race, religion, sexual orientation or ethnicity" and once again excluded "gender identity" and transgender people.

On November 13, 2015 the House's Equality Caucus hosted Congress' first-ever forum on transgender violence, announcing a new Transgender Equality Task Force to develop legislation aimed at improving the lives and safety of transgender Americans.

Chapter 4—The Battle for The Rooms

There was a time in the 1990s when Twelve Step groups—named after the Alcoholics Anonymous (AA) program which recommended addicts follow a dozen guidelines or "steps" in order to recover—swept through the gay community. They even became a foundation of gay social life, and an alternative to the bars. It seemed everyone was in a 12-step program, and everyone needed one.

The NYC Lesbian and Gay Community Center on West 13th Street hosted dozens of "Anonymous" meetings each week on a variety of problem issues, both substance abuse (cocaine, narcotics, marijuana and alcohol) and behavioral addictions (sexual compulsivity, gambling, overeating and debt).

Attending was simply called being in "the rooms," as in "I've spent five years in the rooms working the Steps and believe me, recovery is no picnic." It was a huge thing in New York when the Sunday morning AA meeting was a highlight of the gay week, completely filling the immense ground floor of the Center.

One minute you'd be standing on a quiet street in the Village near the Center, and then, just as 9:00 a.m. chimed, 200 or 300 people would come streaming by at once, as if in a queue, inside the empty Center. Suddenly there would be standing room only for the next 90 minutes.

It was not *hip* or *cool* to be gay then. AIDS had detonated in the lives of gay men in most major cities, where you could also still get assaulted leaving a bar late at night, and by day you still couldn't walk safely hand-in-hand with your lover.

To survive rejection, discrimination, hate, and of course fear, many of us had developed one addictive behavior or another. I think 12-Step groups were one sign of a community coming to grips with the emotional toll of its experiences, and trying hard to recover from them.

And it wasn't just a fad. Even today, the Center lists dozens of such groups, with multiple meetings every day of every week.

On the Inside

My own family background was casually abusive. Neither my older brother (who turned out to be gay) nor myself (yes, folks, it does run in families) felt free to come out until decades after we'd left home. It's fair to say my parents raised three very dysfunctional kids. None of us have been the slightest bit normal, and all of us have had difficulties dealing with the real world.

We were not often physically abused, but I was struck enough to live in fear of my father's temper at all times. Since he was a true *rage-aholic*, the slightest thing could set him off, or just nothing at all. So we lived in a perpetual state of hyper-vigilance and anxiety. When he wasn't physically aggressive, he was verbally aggressive, constantly using sarcasm to ridicule and humiliate. We grew up with all our scars on the inside.

One time he mistakenly thought I'd back-talked him, and turned and slapped me across the face in one motion. He was bout 6'2", and I was about a bit over three-feet tall, and beyond the hurt and surprise it made my head spin. Another time he beat me so badly for some minor school infraction that I couldn't sit well for two days. My fear was constant, and I never knew when suddenly he would boil over.

I actually celebrated for three days when he died. The only ones who understood this were my 12-Step women, the ones from The Rooms, who had come from highly abusive backgrounds themselves. No one from a normal home can possibly understand what it's like spending decades in a family hell like that. No matter what you say your parents did to you growing up, they never really get it.

You can tell them, "When I was bad, my parents used to beat me and blindfold me and tie me down on the train tracks and then have a picnic waiting for a locomotive to come." And they'll look straight at you with those slightly wet, cocker-spaniel eyes and solemnly intone, "Yes… but they're your parents."

Other mantras folks seem to think are absolutely killer, "They're the only parents you'll ever have" and "You need to come to a place of acceptance." Well, some things can't be—and shouldn't be—accepted, ever.

So I knew it was unnatural to be celebrating the death of a parent and that normal people didn't do this. But I didn't care. It felt so good to live in a world he was no longer a part of and in which he could never, ever hurt me again.

Sleeping with Zombies

As hokey as it is, I credit the 12-Steps with bringing me back from crazy. I think up until I was 43 and started attending, I was pretty much nuts, but in a chronic, quiet, able-to-cope kind of way. What we called in my graduate psych program a few blocks away at The New School "sub-acute."

There's a saying in The Rooms that it takes the first five years to get your brains back, and the next five to figure out what to do with them. In my experience, that was about right. If you hurt a child enough, once they grow up and can do things on their own they inevitably start acting out in addictive ways with all kinds of things, just to deal with the pain: alcohol and drugs, for sure, but also things like money, sex and food. Especially food.

I'd finally dealt with a lot of my more addictive behaviors that were making me miserable, but I was still having nightmares every night. Pretty much always the same dream—someone big and overpowering and male was in the house and coming to attack/kill/rape me.

I'd attack them with all my might, over and over. But zombie-like, they'd just keep coming. It was like trying to fall asleep in a live episode of *The Walking Dead* every night. I'd wake up covered in sweat. Many mornings I was exhausted. Today we call that PTSD.

I'm neither religious nor into totems, but eventually I started surrounding my bed with holy books at night. Almost any one would do. I saw them as something stronger than my father, a sign of something positive and good in the world, that he couldn't touch. It's weird to admit it, but that actually helped me sleep better. But I knew it wasn't a solution. And I knew I needed help.

I had been in therapy for some time and my shrink was very good and understanding. But she didn't know what it was like from the inside and it wasn't doing me any good. I needed to be around women who had similar experiences growing up. I found there was a 12-Step women's group meeting at the Center (providentially right around the corner) for people just like me. It was called Survivors of Incest Anonymous, or SIA.

Although I had no "snapshot" memories of anything sexually inappropriate, fortunately they welcomed anyone who had been through any kind of abuse. They met in a big room with brick walls and few windows on the second floor. I stopped at the threshold, terrified to walk into the room. But I was more scared of going home and to bed, so I went in. I just sat and listened. My first two meetings were shattering.

You think you're an original, in some way unique. Then you hear every secret and detail of what you've been feeling and holding in, coming out of a complete stranger's mouth. And this happens many, many times. The meetings were incredibly emotional and deeply intense and it all was starting to be healing, except by the third meeting, when all hell broke loose.

There was always a break in the middle to handle group business: elect officers, collect donations that paid the Center for the room rental, announce upcoming meetings, etc.

A Man in the Midst

One woman took advantage of this break to raise her hand and announce, "There's a man in the room, and I don't feel safe." I actually got so physically nauseous, I almost threw up. I knew in my bones what was coming.

Everyone started peering around looking for a man. No one exactly looked at me. But no one exactly looked away either. At least two women in that room knew me from outside, and one was smiling slightly and looking just past me.

For the next half hour, they debated me in absentia, without once saying who was under debate. Every one of the 30 or so women attending took a turn on me.

We covered how I was invading women's space, how unsafe they felt with me there, how my presence activated people's rape fears, and whether the simple fact of my presence (since I was still too paralyzed to have actually said or done anything yet) was making some women feel violated and thereby "re-incesting" them... all the Golden Oldies.

All 12-Step meetings have rules, called the 12 Traditions, to keep order. In fact, to keep things like this very debate from happening. The 12 Traditions make no allowance for single-sex meetings. They also specifically say that meetings are to have "no opinion" on outside issues.

No matter. They decide to hold a vote on me, the Mystery Man haunting in the room. When they were all done, I announced that it was me they were discussing, and since I could no longer sleep at night, and in fact was having terrible nightmares I couldn't control, no matter how they voted I was not going to leave the room voluntarily because I needed it.

The vote went in my favor, but just barely. I didn't realize it then, but I was the first test case for trans inclusion in all the 12-Step groups at the Center. I don't know if the Center would have backed me up or not had I been voted out and refused to leave. I like to think they would, but who knows?

It sucked always being dependent on cisgender women to decide when and if I was welcome in places, and where I did and didn't belong. And even if you get voted in, you're still the only one who gets voted on, and so you're always a second-class citizen in a way no one else is. And, of course, they can always revoke your citizenship since it's contingent on them allowing you to keep it.

Everyone's Pet Trannie

It started occurring to me that transwomen (and men) needed their own space, and their own group, a thought that was shortly to take on even more urgency. Attending the group, I listened to countless stories and slowly healed through the healing of others. Eventually I was able to sleep most nights, and the nightmares began receding. Even when trans-phobic newbies showed up, over time I built a sufficient caucus of support that being voted out became unlikely.

Of course, there was always the possibility of someone calling for a vote on a slow night when only a few people were in the room. You're never entirely safe.

One night, when no one wanted to run for chair, I agreed to do it. I was a pretty good chair, too. I felt in some way I was also modeling a positive transgender presence. I finally felt accepted.

Heading the meeting like that, people kept asking me why I never told my own story, why I kept holding back. My 12-Step "sponsor"—a person more experienced in the program that is simultaneously a guide, a friend, and confessor—thought it was a good idea.

So, one week when they were asking who would be the opening person to "share their story," I hesitantly agreed. I was pretty scared by the whole thing. I wasn't going to be sharing a story exactly like anyone else's—no one knew the extra violation of being a girl forced to live a boy's life in a boy's body—and I wanted friends in the room.

So I invited two friends. Both of them, as it turned out, looked a hell of a lot more feminine than I ever did. I'm not too big on "passing," but if anyone ever did, it was the two of them. They sat quietly through the meeting, hugged me at the end, said nothing and left. But someone must have known them from outside. Because at the very next meeting, some woman announced a change in the rules. From now on, only "post-ops" would be allowed to attend women's SIA meetings. It was just the kind of weird occurrence that the "no outside opinion" rule was meant to circumvent.

We're right back at the Michigan Festival once more. Again, I immediately announced myself pre-op. *You don't understand*, they explained. *We don't mean you—they're the ones we want to vote out.*

I had succeeded so well, I was now everyone's pet trannie, the one they wanted to keep around. I wondered how many of them would feel the same way if I really *was* pre-op. I made it clear I would not change my status. As chair, I held the vote. They voted. I lost. I got up out of my seat and left without a backward glance.

A Lesson Learned

I don't know why I thought anyone would follow me in solidarity. I thought all the deep friendships I'd formed in that room, the mutual hugs and crying and late night phone calls over the past two years, were worth something. Even my sponsor of two years stayed put. We never spoke again.

I supposed I could have taken it up with the Center, which had a strict non-discrimination policy. I might have come under it. But they had no specific policies around transgender, and in any case, I didn't want to put them in that position. And, anyway, what would be the point? Forcing my presence into a meeting where people didn't want me?

Since the Center was around the corner, most Thursdays I would see all my old "friends" walking in to go to our meeting. It was extremely painful to watch. I felt angry seeing them all go in and also ashamed of myself for being different. I know some of them saw me too and were ashamed at what had happened, but they'd look away and go on in.

That's what identity politics and drawing boundaries and voting on other people's identities gets you: division, hierarchy, and hurt. It was a lesson I knew well from the women's groups back in Cleveland, from Michigan, from Camp Trans and now here. It was a lesson I never forgot.

It would inform much of what was to come, whatever I tried to build. But it would also eventually cause a deep and irreparable break between me and the trans-community leaders.

I realized that even this, even going into a 12-Step room to try to heal from a childhood of abuse was political, and politicized. There was no aspect of my life from which trans-hating feminists couldn't attack me or evict me.

A Room with a View

It was time that transgender people had their *own* support group. Perhaps, as that *other* Virginia would have put it (not Virginia Prince but Virginia Woolf) what we needed was *A Room of One's Own.* But this was more difficult than it sounded.

Even in as big and busy a place as NYC's Lesbian and Gay Community Center, there was nothing for transgender people, in fact, no support groups of any kind anywhere in the city. The Menace really hadn't started yet, so those meetings weren't happening. And to be honest, many of us kind of avoided each other. I'm not proud to say it, but I know I did.

I'd be in some lesbian bar in the Village, hoping and praying to maybe finally meet someone nice, and someone would come up and breathlessly point out another transgender women who'd come in.

So, there I am, looking tall, gawky and slightly masculine and totally self-conscious trying to blend in—and what I really, really want to do is go over and stand right next to *another* tall, gawky slightly masculine woman so we can talk "girl talk" and both stand out like sore thumbs together, and any woman who might have come over to chat me up will now probably stay away.

Or at least that's what I feared. Maybe there were women all over who really were attracted to tall, gawky slightly masculine lesbians and I never met them because I was so busy trying to blend in. I guess I'll never know. Like I said, I'm not proud of it. Internalized self-hate isn't pretty. But that's how it was. And it wasn't just me. I didn't notice any of those other transgender women making a beeline over to me either.

I wasn't sure what a transgender support group should look like: a therapy group with a facilitator, a transition support group, an organizing meeting? It occurred to me that the 12-Steps offered a dandy format that seemed to be pretty robust and worked across a variety of issues.

I sat down and re-wrote the original 12 steps and supporting materials (even my enemies will agree I've never lacked for *chutzpah*) passed down from AA founder Bill W. himself, but focused on around issues of shame and self-acceptance.

S.T.A.

I called it Survivors of Transsexuality Anonymous (STA), which was a terrible name but better than all the other ones I thought of. And, anyway, we really *were* trying to survive the experience and discrimination of being transsexual in a cisgender world.

I don't know who I thought would benefit from a meeting like this, but it would certainly help *me* to talk about all the shit I was going through. Somehow I convinced two friends to join me for the first meeting, and the Center to give us a space. Except there was no space. Every room was taken. So they gave us the old storage room off the main floor on Thursday evening at 7:00 p.m.

It was a small, windowless expanse of gray, cracked concrete with nothing but a bunch of old chairs and tables stacked up in a corner. It was a place you wouldn't want to spend five minutes in if you could avoid it—perhaps the most depressing place possible for first meeting of a new and untested group.

But we settled into several of those hard, gray, steel folding chairs, and for the next hour the three of us held the Center's first support meeting for transgender people. It was not an unalloyed success. We were very self-conscious going through all the meeting formalities—announcing our names, calling on each other, thanking each other for sharing, etc. With only three people, it felt very hokey.

But it was also, in a weird quiet way, very powerful. The 12-Step format allows you to say whatever you need to and know that you'll be heard by those who are most likely to understand, without them having to know you, without your worrying that they won't be interested, and without fearing that someone will interrupt to give you free unwanted advice or contradict your deepest feelings.

Just as Bill W. recognized, sharing your problems with other people, even strangers, and hearing them confess theirs to you, was very therapeutic. For a couple of months it was just the three of us. Folks would stop by to join us, stay for a meeting or two, and then drift off. But then some came for good. There were half a dozen of us. Sometimes there would be nearly a dozen. Within a year we had up to 40 transgender people attending, and the Center had promoted us to a real room, and then had to upsize us to bigger quarters twice.

And me? I'd gotten over my own transphobia. One of the best things about the meeting was that afterwards, nearly all of us would walk around the corner to a restaurant on Seventh Avenue and West 11th Street in the Village.

This was at a time when even a single transgender person would turn heads, even in Manhattan. In fact, there'd been a transgender hairdresser at the shop around the corner, and guys would stop by to point and make fun at her through the window. (She eventually had to quit.)

So you can imagine the stares we drew every night when 20 or 30 of us would pile in and take over the whole back room. There, many of us who'd never spent much time around another transgender person would sit over coffee and French fries and talk for hours. Moreover, the back room was ours.

Even those few straight males who made it clear they disapproved couldn't do anything. There were 30 of us, and we had each other's backs. It became such an event that people started attending STA meetings just to hang out afterwards for the solidarity and fellowship.

As I mentioned earlier, on some level I'd always wished I could pass, and was silently envious of those transwomen who could—even though I knew it was politically incorrect. Yet in STA, I learned to see things differently. People who could pass would come to a first meeting and then disappear. They couldn't stand being around other transpeople.

It turns out that passing is like a drug, and you can get hooked on it. Because you pass, you never have to deal with the realities of your life. But you're also living a lie—one always with the possibility that in the next relationship or at the next job, you get outed.

So, like hiding anything else—your religion or your race—it makes forging true self-acceptance impossible. Some of the most miserable folks I ever saw were those who attended an STA meeting and could pass easily. Many of us regulars came to realize that not passing was actually a benefit. It forced us to go through the crucible of dealing with the realities of cisgender hatred and rejection, to learn to accept ourselves and our bodies as they were.

We Need Our Own

It was around that time that NYC had its first Gay and Lesbian Health Conference, hosted by the Center, of course. The name said it all. We were still fighting for inclusion in the gay community, on every front, even at the Lesbian and Gay Community Center, which was very liberal. But we were not in the Center's mission, and we were not in the Center's name.

Even their medical insurance—chosen in part for its excellent HIV coverage—included the standard exclusions for any kind of trans-related medical care. So I approached the conference organizers to try to persuade them to include transgender.

Trans people had important and pressing health issues. With many of us in the early stages of transitioning (and more than a few of us addicted, self-cutting, or HIV positive), wondering about the long-term effects of hormones, trying to find good doctors, or struggling with the frequent and institutional transphobia of hospital and emergency room care, there was a huge need for accuracy on trans health and medicine.

But the organizers were adamant. Their position was that they had too much to cover with gay health issues. But that wasn't the reason. They could have easily made a modest gesture of inclusion—an information table, a few small workshops on transmen's and transwomen's issues.

But it was 1996, and we were still being routinely excluded almost everywhere and had to fight for inclusion in any event in the gay community. And the few times we weren't being actively excluded, we were still being sidelined as second-class citizens. That's the way it was. We simply weren't the organizers' demographic.

I ended up bitching about all this with Dr. Barbara Warren, Director of Social Services for the Center—a pretty dynamic individual who was generally smart, open-minded and a real ally. She was also straight, a fact for which she took a lot of shit, especially from people who'd just assumed she was a lesbian and thought every job in the Center should go to a gay person.

We were sitting on the front steps, discussing the stonewalling (pun definitely intended) by the health conference and I turned to her and said, "We need to have our own." You could see the gears turning, as she thought it through, including all the objections she was going to face for being so far out in front on a transgender issue. Then she more-or-less agreed.

Mental and physical health weren't really my big issues, but they were certainly hers. The next year a transgender health conference was organized, one of the first in the US. They added "empowerment" to the title, to give it a positive spin. To this day I have no idea exactly how she pulled it off—I really tried not to be in that loop, since my plate was full with other kinds of activism.

But I did stop by and it was packed. It was the first Transgender Health & Empowerment Conference in the country, and it was a hit.

Nice Jewish Boy Becomes Non-Blond Bombshell

It also gave me another idea. When I got my surgery in 1978, I was unknowingly part of the first big wave after Christine Jorgenson's groundbreaking 1952 change (*"Ex-GI Becomes Blonde Bombshell"*). By the late 1960s, Johns Hopkins University Medical School had started doing the surgery, legitimating it for the medical establishment. And by the 1970s, forward-thinking hospitals in many major urban centers followed suit.

However, in the early 1980s when a major transphobe took the reins at Hopkins, he commissioned a loaded study which (surprise!) suggested Hopkins withdraw from surgery, and the program ended. A few years later, no major hospital in the US was offering it either. Cowards—they all followed suit.

This meant that the kind of integrated, hospital-based program I took advantage of at the famous Cleveland Clinic, which combined psychiatry, social work, general surgery, endocrinology and plastic surgery all in one place—was unavailable to anyone else. Trans folks undergoing transition in the 1980s and beyond had to create their own networks of information, support, legal help and medical care from scratch, and from many different places.

It was a truly hellish proposition: trying to acquire and use a new wardrobe; change your name and your legal sex; identify a source of hormones; battle with your insurance company; save for surgery; find a good surgeon and get on their waiting list; and get in therapy with someone who would write "surgery letters" to various medical providers—all the while holding on to your day job (probably a lost cause anyway), your family, your partner and your kids (ditto); and suffering electrolysis sessions three of four hours a week that were so painful that you got through them only by rehearsing how you could kill your electrologist in as slow and medieval a manner as possible. (For her two-hour sessions, Clare needed three Percocets and two muscle relaxers.)

All of this hoop-jumping takes gathering and collating tons of new information, all of which you'd have to hunt down and check out in the spare time you wouldn't and didn't have. Of course, to survive the whole process you'd need lots and lots of emotional and psychological support—which you also wouldn't have the time or energy for, and, even if you did, would be in very short supply.

One day Barbara and I were discussing all this and I said, "The Center needs to launch a Gender Identity Program." She stopped and thought about that too. It was like the Health Conference all over. I tried again, "The Center needs to start a Gender Identity Program. There's nothing else out there, and everyone has to do it alone and reinvent the wheel. And if you don't do it, no one else will."

She agreed it was a good idea, but she'd have to run it past Richard Burns, the Center's President (a very effective and wonderful guy). And the Board of Directors would have to approve it. It was all very, very political, and would take a lot of management and lobbying and nudging along. This wasn't a one-day affair like the Health Conference, but an ongoing commitment by the Center to provide services and support to an extremely needy population. For some reason I never fully understood, because of internal politics, it was a big no-no to call it a "program." We had to refer to it as a "project."

Somehow, slowly but surely, Barbara got all the pieces into place and got it done. Within less than a year, the fledgling Gender Identity Project launched at the Center. For their first coordinator, they hired an incredible transwoman named Roslyn Blumenstein, easily one of the most kick-ass trans-women I ever met. She and Barbara were very dedicated to the GIP.

I attended some of their first support meetings—kind of like STA, but without all the 12-Steps and Higher Powers stuff. They had a special audience among trans people who were low-income or of color, which was wonderful since many of them were even more underserved than those of us lucky enough to be white and/or middle class.

Every time I'd check back in, Ros and Barbara had grown the program... sorry, the project... adding new services, taking on more staff, and having more and more people enrolled. Eventually it became a model program. They helped a lot of people transition and I'm sure saved a lot of lives along the way.

Both the GIP and STA helped provide for a broad population of transpeople who were out and socially connected with one another. This in turn provided a foundation for groups like the Menace, and much of what followed, at least in NYC.

Yet, as with the murder vigils, it had become more and more apparent to me that you couldn't stop the discrimination and carnage with direct services any more than you could with street protests. Gender was a systemic injustice; to fight it you needed to organize a systemic response. We needed an organization. But what, I wondered, and how?

Yo' in a HEAP o' Trouble, Boychick

It was around then that I happened to go on a (rare) summer vacation to Wrightsville Beach, SC.

Desperate for a 12-Step meeting, I attended the only one available: the local AA meeting held in a small hunting and meeting lodge (I am not making this up) right by a trailer park.

The proliferation of different Anonymous groups was strictly a Northern thing (along with liberal Western states). In the South, they still mainly just did AA and, boy, their meetings were straight up, traditional and by the book. Substance abuse wasn't my problem, in fact, it was perhaps the only addictive problem I *didn't* have. But AA rules allowed anyone to attend who didn't want to get drunk that day. I never wanted to get drunk. And anyway I really needed a meeting.

I'd been to this one the year before. It was all white and mostly male. I'd been deathly afraid to identify myself or say anything. I simply hid as best as I could, trying to pass. It was a lie of omission, born of shame and fear of what I'd face if I came out. I was ashamed of myself for doing it, and as a result I hadn't met anyone or made any friends and didn't know a single person in that meeting.

Having thought about it all year long, and coming off what had happened in New York, I decided I had to find a way to stop hiding. So at my first meeting back, during a slow point when no one else was speaking, I raised my hand.

It's a cliché by now that you start whatever you have to share by saying, "I'm so-and-so, and I'm an alcoholic" or, in my case, "I'm so-and-so, and I have a desire to not drink today." When the meeting chair called on me, I said the usual introduction, and then thinking I had to find a way to stop hiding and lying or it would be pointless, introduced myself by starting out (in my best STA voice), "My name is Riki, I'm a grateful recovering transsexual and…". Luckily, there was enough background chatter that no one really heard. The chair, a small smile on his lips, realized this and asked me," Would you repeat that?"

I was now mortified. Now everyone knew something was up, and was paying attention. About 40 strangers were all looking at me. The room was dead silent. I said it again. At the word "transsexual," the whole room seemed to go into slow motion. Everyone just stopped whatever they were doing and took that in. We were out in the woods a bit, and you could literally hear the crickets chirp in the ensuring silence.

I remember looking around and thinking, as with Falls City, "I am going to fucking die." While they all just sat, I said my piece, quickly, and then sat back. At the end, I made my way slowly to the door after everyone else was out, carefully not looking at anyone or trying to meet anyone's eyes. I found out later a few strong disagreements broke out afterwards. The pretext was that I'd brought in "outside issues."

But the real problem was that some of the guys didn't appreciate having an open trannie in their meeting. I didn't blame them. I didn't appreciate having a few redneck alcoholics in *my* meeting, but I guess we were stuck with one another.

At the next meeting, a quiet, blond woman who lived alone in a cabin up in the hills found me afterwards. For the first time I wasn't afraid to talk, to be read, to be found out because she might turn her back on me. All that was behind me. After some small talk, she inquired gently if I might need a sponsor while I was in town. Did I ever. I could feel myself spirally down again.

For the next two weeks I attended meetings, we talked regularly, and eventually became friends. It would never have happened if I'd stayed closeted. So maybe the one who got the most out of STA was me after all.

Epilogue

By the late 1990s Johns Hopkins Hospital, once a proudly cutting-edge Sexual Behaviors Consultation Unit, was in the deception business, attracting transgender people desperately in search of medical services who were unaware that Hopkins would intake and evaluate them, but then deny them surgery and hormones. By the time Laverne Cox was on the cover of *Time* Magazine for their *Transgender Tipping Point* article, Dr. Paul R. McHugh MD, Hopkins former psychiatrist-in-chief, was publicly denouncing transgender as a "mental disorder" and changing sexes as "biologically impossible."

In April 2017, fully 38 years after McHugh's transphobia wrought havoc in the field of transgender care, Hopkins finally reopened its transgender surgical program. By then his one-sided research and intransigent and anachronistic statements had come under increasing public fire, including being denounced by a half-dozen colleagues at Hopkins's Bloomberg School of Public Health. Commented the head of the Hospitals' Plastic and Reconstructive Surgery Department, "It took an exceptionally long time…too long."

The Trans-Health Conference has been held annually in Philadelphia since 2001.

The Gender Identity Program at NYC's LGBT Center is still going strong. It and the Center now host a variety of transgender support meetings, including one for transgender Latinas, for Trans Masculine and for Trans Feminine support, a legal clinic, a Trans Beauty Clinic, Trans Poets, groups for Trans Partners and for Trans Families. As they say on their website, "If you are looking for powerful role models, trans-friendly resources or support from your peers, The Center is here to help."

Dr. Barbara Warren now serves at the Director of LGBT Health Services at Hunter College, where she is also an Adjunct Assistant Professor of Women and Gender Studies. In 1995, the GIP became the first community-based program serving transgender individuals to be government funded. In 2016, it will mark its 25th anniversary. Thousands of transpeople have passed through its doors and attended its peer support group... including Laverne Cox.

STA was tried in a few other cities but never really caught on outside NYC. However, the NYC meeting remained strong for another year or two, until I stepped down as chair.

Chapter 5—Mr. Smith Goes to Washington (In Sensible Heels)

The "Be All You Can Be" conference, affectionately known simply as "The Be-All" was a major conference—not quite the level of Southern Comfort or IFGE's—but a big annual get-together with a Midwestern focus. As the name implies, the Be All is about learning to be your best self, featuring workshops on applying makeup, self-acceptance, marital problems from crossdressing, etc.

It wasn't a place where I was well known, or knew a lot of the participants. But in June 1995, I decided to fly down to Cincinnati, walk around in my black Menace T-shirt, and generally try to look either cool or subversive—preferably both. It may have worked too well, because I was invited to address the conference. I had nothing special to say, but I went on stage anyway.

I realized the last thing I wanted to do was give a speech to the several hundred crossdressers and smattering of transsexuals in the audience. In fact, I hate giving formal speeches of any kind. What I wanted to do was to be *with* them, to talk *with* them, not *at* them. Handing someone back the mic, I jumped down from the stage, but kept talking.

This caused a big intake of breath (you don't see a lot of athleticism at transgender conferences—and anyway it's hard to jump around in 4-inch heels).

At one point, pointing to all the latest actions by Menace chapters, I encouraged folks to get involved, declaring that the T-shirts came in styles for both females (here I pitched my voice higher, and stood in the classic one-legged feminine "stork pose") and also for males (lowering my voice to a gravelly baritone, and striking a wide-legged, double-biceps pose).

I didn't think it was an especially great bit, but the audience went wild. I think part of it was the gender-fuck aspect—you don't see transsexual women publicly proclaiming their masculinity at these conferences, nor much switching from one gender to another. Part of it may just have been me: Short haired, makeup-less, blue jeaned, and very clearly not trying too hard to do any gender at all—was not how any other male-to-female transsexual at the conference looked, and certainly not how any crossdresser *wanted* to look.

Emboldened by the reaction, I launched into a very angry and at times funny speech completely off the cuff about the need to organize, to fight back and to stop meeting privately in out-of-the-way hotels, however nicely appointed. The room erupted again. From then on, it was a love-in. There's an old saying, "Never give a trannie an open mic." For the next 20 minutes I proceeded to show why this was wise advice.

When I was done I was rewarded by a standing ovation, pretty pleased with myself, and thought nothing more about it. Unknown to me, later that day, folks began walking up to Allison Laing, one of the dearest people in the trans-community, a long-time crossdresser, and the current head of IFGE, and pressing unsolicited cash and checks into her hand for whatever organization I was announcing… or perhaps running.

A Small Start

But I wasn't doing either. Yet, later that night, she came to the room Lynn Walker and I were staying in to offer me the money. Basically, she dumped it all on one of the beds. We counted almost $600 in small and large donations. It would have been easy to take the money as a one-off donation to "the work" and let it go at that. But clearly something had shifted. It didn't take a genius to realize there was a lot of momentum built up.

It was an opportunity, but for what? How do you turn that into something concrete like an organization, one that could begin doing political activism for gender rights? Lynn and I sat there discussing it late into the night. First, we needed a larger amount. I agreed to contribute to the amount, bringing it to a barely respectable $1,000.

Second, we needed a way to jump-start things. It would take years to recruit a decent membership, time we didn't have. Plus there was already an excess of affiliative and educational organizations in the trans-community with their own memberships. In fact, they were practically all we had. Why reinvent the wheel and recruit the same people?

It made more sense and would be quicker to get the organizations involved, to pitch whatever new political group was about to take shape representing both them and the community-at-large. But they were distinctly non-political. Politics wasn't something any of our organizations were pursuing or expressing any need for—at least not yet.

It wasn't like their members were knocking at their doors, demanding they launch a political or an advocacy arm. Quite the contrary, a lot of folks preferred the community to stay non-political—just as it was.

We needed to put the organizations in charge of something. Nothing engages people faster than putting them in charge of something they have control over. I came up with the idea of "endowing" our $1000 for a fund to launch a new political group, with the major trans organizations in charge of it. In effect, they would be a Board of Directors, they wouldn't have to do much, and yet would have final say over how the funds were to be spent.

This worked. We pitched it to each of them, beginning with IFGE, Southern Comfort, AEGIS, Renaissance, etc. And they all agreed. We needed something short and punchy. I wanted a name that wasn't bound by identities, and that was short, catchy, and punchy. Someone suggested GenderPAC and it caught.

We decided to use the following Southern Comfort as a first fund-raiser. There were almost a thousand attendees, and it would have gone great—except that no one gave anything. I stood like a statue by the steel donation bowl which had maybe $20 or $30 in it. I thought money would just magically appear, as if it were the Be-All.

Not having any experience in non-profits, I had no idea what to do. But Atlanta's own Terry Murphy, dressed to the hilt for the big Saturday dinner knew, and did it. She grabbed the bowl and—as I watched in amazement—walked up to every single person waiting to go into dinner and told them, "I'm sure you'll want to generously support GenderPAC tonight."

It was a bravura performance, one I never could have pulled off. I think she even accosted several perplexed members of the hotel kitchen staff. In the end, she collected an additional $1,000. It wasn't a big amount for an operating budget, but the good news was everyone gave. And, for the first time, the transgender community was being asked to give to support national political activism.

It was a start. But it was also a sign of the financial problems to come. Funding would continue to be a challenge for us and every other transgender rights groups for decades. Most were doomed to be almost entirely dependent on foundation support from the tiny, fragile ecosystem of gay funders (at that time, there were only two gay foundations of any size at the national level). This was not only because we were not a rich community. There was and is real wealth among transpeople. But we were not a *unified* or *giving* community. There was none of the sense of unity and belonging that made people give generously to HRC or NOW, and that made even some state gay groups able to support a substantial amount of their work through personal donations.

If we lacked a sense that we were in it together, perhaps it was because almost all of us had had to go through our own traumas and struggles alone. There is no unifying "trans ghetto" where we live in proximity to one another and form neighborhood institutions, and (except for a few major cities) no "trans bars" where we hung out together regularly. Our numbers were much too small for that.

In fact, even with all the conferences and (now) the Menace demonstrations, we were still less of a real community than a series of flash mobs of strangers thatwould come together for specific occasions but didn't live together or see one another in-between. So, transgender was more of a private experience, not a real, place-based community you could live in and belong to.

The idea of unity and loyalty to a community and its structures was still largely foreign—as was donating money to our own political struggle (a very new idea indeed). There was (and still is) no tradition of philanthropy in the community. Even our few big donors worth hundreds of millions, and, in a few cases, billions of dollars, give little or nothing, or only give to pet causes which are mostly vanity projects that don't improve the community as a whole.

The Launch

We had enough to hold a meeting. We needed to get people involved beyond just the main organizations, to create a sense of ownership and buy-in. We decided to hold a launch meeting to formalize the new organization the following November 1996 in King of Prussia, PA, near where crossdressing pioneer JoAnne Roberts operated the Renaissance Education Association.

In a long day of constant meetings, articles describing the new organization's activities and mission were cobbled together. Key signatories at the event included AEGIS (American Educational Gender Information Service), FTM International, IFGE, It's Time America!, Renaissance, Tri-Ess (Society for the Second Self), Intersex Society of North America (ISNA), all of whom signed.

The new organization's activities would be public education, combating hate crimes and employment discrimination, public education and Congressional advocacy. Attempting to tie together gender identity, sexual orientation and racial oppression, its mission was to be pursuing "gender, affectional and racial equality." We didn't know it then, but over time, the last one of these would get lost, and the second would cause the organization and the community to split.

"Transgender" had started out as an umbrella term, a grab bag for anyone who wasn't clearly transsexual or a crossdresser. But with all the new political energy and attention, it was quickly becoming an identity in its own right that included all of us who were profoundly gender non-conforming. In other words, a non-identity created to hold all the gender rejects like me was in the process of hardening into another identity, with rules, walls and hierarchies. It happened quietly, and without any discussion, but it happened. I remember precisely when it struck me.

One was a young transman. He had been pushed out of a trans support group after being accused of not "really" being transgender, because he didn't want to take testosterone or get surgery. I remember thinking with amazement, "Transpeople are evicting people from groups?" There was a time when we were so desperate for company us we would have taken anyone. Now we had boundaries and rules—just like every other identity.

Then, there was the middle-aged butch lesbian, resplendent in a starched white Oxford and pressed blue jeans, who pointed out to me that she only considered herself "lowercase-T transgender not capital-T" because she didn't want to change her body in any way. She meant it to show that she recognized and honored my identity as a *real* transperson. It was meant as a sign of respect, but I just found the fact that *trans* now had hierarchies of legitimacy profoundly depressing.

I still do. As lawyer-turned-activist Dana Priesing would put it (more about her later), "*Transgender* used to be a whole cross-section of communities. But once people got their own identity, they tended to use it as a hammer." And, as the saying goes, if all you have is a hammer, everything looks like a nail.

I understand both the need for and the strength of identarian movements. But I remain completely opposed to their frequent need to create rules of identity, impose hierarchies of "real-ness" and police their boundaries by rejecting anyone whom those higher up in the hierarchy find wanting.

Those are exactly the same tools used against me. I wasn't about to be a part of them being used against anyone else. Still won't. In many ways, this was a sign of progress. We were taking ourselves seriously. Unfortunately, in some ways we were busy reinventing another gender regime similar to the one that had led to our need to organize in the first place.

Cisgender regimes valued real-ness and biology in the service of binary genders. The transgender regime that was emerging privileged changing your body (surgery, hormones, etc.) to make it fit one of those binaries. In time, it would be partly replaced by a youth-led regime that would privilege genderqueerness and *not* changing your body in the service of being *beyond* gender binaries.

But all that was still in the future. Before it came to pass, we needed to start somewhere. Being good Americans, of course the first place was our elected representatives.

Priscilla, Queen of the Capitol

For some time I had been mulling over the idea of Congressional lobbying. I don't mean the kind where you make donations and push for votes—more along the lines of visibility, advocacy, and education. If we had to start somewhere, why not start at the very top?

From a practical standpoint, we certainly didn't have the numbers or the organization to mount a state-by-state fight. But if we could concentrate our efforts together at a single point, we might be able to have a significant impact. I had actually put up a poster at one

Southern Comfort conference promising a Transgender March on Washington, and invited people to sign up. About a hundred did, but nothing came of it.

I had heard that Phyllis Frye, her wife Trish, and trans activists Karen Kerin and Jane Fee had been visiting Capitol Hill offices, talking with Members of Congress. It was typical of her that Phyllis had not only thought of this, but started doing it before anyone else. An Eagle Scout, She was a true straight-arrow, intrepid and unusually fearless.

I reached out and asked if I could accompany them on their next trip. I was a little intimidated by the whole idea. And I hadn't been in DC since my parents took me as a kid, and I certainly had no ideas about how to talk with a Congressional office.

I took the train down from NYC to DC's Union Station in Spring of 1994. It may sound hokey—I'm sure it *is* hokey—but there was something about walking out of the train station and seeing that big white Capitol dome rising in the sunlight over the cherry blossoms that made my chest swell. And still does, even after living in DC for a decade and a half.

I walked towards the dome—I wasn't going to rush the experience with a cab ride—all the way over to the immense Rayburn Building cafeteria where we'd decided to meet and where pretty much everyone who's not a Member of Congress or a major lobbyist eats between meetings.

I didn't know what was involved in calling on a Member of Congress, who to ask for and what to say to them about our issues. I was a complete blank. Luckily Phyllis and Jane already had a bunch of appointments set up (they would give you an appointment?) and let me trail them through a series of meetings.

There is a ritual and a tone to visiting Congressional offices, a certain formality, very like a business meeting, and I started picking it up. By our third visit, I asked if I could do part of the presentation. After the fourth, I asked if I could take a couple of the appointments on their list and do them solo. At the end of the day, we sat again in Rayburn reviewing the day's events, and digesting what we'd learned. Almost everyone we'd met with was a liberal Democrat, so you'd think they'd be inclined to be friendly. And they were, but that didn't necessarily mean they were supportive.

The idea of transgender rights, even the idea of transgender people, was still not in the public domain. Even the *New York Times*, the nation's newspaper of record, "all the news that's fit to print," had never run a story about transgender politics. And neither had anyone else.

In fact the only coverage the *Times* had run was typified by articles that referred to the movie *Priscilla Queen of the Desert* as a "Transvestite Musical" or coverage of an encampment of homeless transwomen as "A Shantytown of He-She's." And remember, this was the country's leading *liberal* newspaper.

(On the latter article, at least they ran a Letter to the Editor which criticized the coverage "for focusing on the squalid and degrading aspects of their lives and [ignoring] the bigotry and hatred with which they must cope every day.")

In those pre-Caitlyn Jenner days, changing sex was considered bizarre and repugnant, and the idea of men dressing up in women's clothes was considered perverted as well. So it's safe to say few Congressional offices really knew anything about our issues. Their staffers met with us partly I suspect out of curiosity, partly out of policy interest, and also partly simply because it was their job to talk to constituents.

I found that just sitting in a Congressional office, talking about our issues, about *transgender issues*—hate crimes, job discrimination, insurance exclusion—was incredibly empowering. In many ways it was the antithesis of what I'd once thought transgender was about—being accepted, passing, blending in. I had a voice. I had opinions. And important people in our nation's capital—our elected leaders—would listen to me, if I talked seriously about the problems we faced.

Uncle Samantha Wants YOU!

I think it's the first time since starting my transition almost two decades earlier that I started to feel again like a civilian instead of a combatant in the gender wars. It felt like being a normal person, not some perpetual *gender outlaw* confined to the outskirts of civilized society. I mean, talking with your Congress Member was about as civil and mainstream as you could get.

I felt immensely proud. It was a profound and intoxicating feeling. I realized that we could make it available to everyone. Hell, we *should* make it available to everyone. Every single one of us who was busy *woodworking,* every one of us who was trying to pass, every crossdresser who felt ashamed, every struggling transsexual who felt they had no rights should have the chance to experience that immense sense of legitimacy and validation I'd just had. It was like Camp Trans—it could definitely scale, if only we invited the whole community in.

On an impulse, I suggested to Phyllis, Jane and Karen that I wanted to announce a National Gender Lobby Day and invite the whole community to show up. Would they support that? In doing anything new, I've always tried to get partners. Sometimes inspiration is just simply misguided. You can end up chasing your own visions. I always figured if I couldn't get at least one or two other people to support an idea, it probably wasn't a good one. They thought it over for a minute, and agreed. We were on. I posted the first announcement—*"Your Uncle Samantha wants you!"*—on the last page of the first *InYourFace*!

TEXICAN DEMO:
IT'S TIME TEXAS led a peaceful protest in Austin on April 2 at a large gay rights rally to protest their exclusion by the LesBiGay organizations from the Hate Crimes bill currently before the state legislature. More in-depth, totall fabricated details in the next issue.

☞ A NOTE FROM YOUR EDITRIX ☜

The fight against gender oppression has been joined for centuries, perhaps millennia. What's new today, is that it's moving into the arena of open political activism. And nope, this is not just one more civil rights struggle for one more narrowly-defined minority. It's about all of us who are genderqueer: diesel dykes and stone butches, leatherqueens and radical fairies, nelly fags, crossdressers, intersexed, transsexuals, transvestites, transgendered, transgressively gendered, intersexed, and those of us whose gender expressions are so complex they haven't even been named yet. More than that, it's about the gender oppression which affects everyone: the college sweetheart who develops life-threatening anorexia nervosa trying to look "feminine," the Joe Sixpack dead at 45 from cirrhosis of the liver because "real men" are hard drinkers. But maybe we genderqueers feel it most keenly, because it hits us each time we walk out the front door openly and proudly. And that's why these pages are only going to grow. We're not invisible anymore. We're not well behaved. And we're not going away. Political activism is here to stay.

So get out. Get active. Picket someone's transphobic ass. Get in someone's genderphobic face. And while you're at it, pass the word: the gendeRevolution has begun, and we're going to win.

Your Uncle Samantha wants you!

Yes, it's true. Your Uncle Sam wants you up on the Hill, deep in the bowels of our nation's capital, Washington DC (smile when you say that) for **the first ever National Transgender Lobbying Day**, *Monday & Tuesday, Oct. 2-3.*

Our past 2-day trip to DC was amazingly successful; 4 of us met with the staffs of House and Senate leaders like Senators Jeffords (VT), Moynihan (NY), Kennedy (MA), Rockerfeller (WV), Mosley-Braun (MI), Wellstone (MN), Hutchinson (TX), as well as Rep's Frank (MA), Studds (MA), Rangel (NY), Foley (FL), Luther (MN), and many more.

What was our biggest hurdle? Most of them had never even met a transperson, never thought of us as constituents, never considered our rights and concerns. We've been invisible as citizens.

Now YOU have the chance to change that, once and for all!

Your Uncle Samantha wants You! Instead of 4 of us, National Transgender Lobbying Day is going to put 54 of us up on the Hill. That's right: **5 dozen transpeople and friends**, from every state and territory in the union, all lobbying for inclusion on issues critical to *you and your loved ones* like job discrimination (the ENDA bill), veteran's affairs, child custody rights, and the national health care and insurance.

But we can't do it without YOU: We need YOU there!
Seize YOUR chance to make a little American history...
Stand up! Be proud! Be a United States citizen!

Registration flier for first National Gender Lobby Day from InYourFace.

I showed up at every transgender conference I could to promote it. I sent emails and made phone calls. I helped arrange for people's transportation, got people to share rooms with anyone who couldn't afford their own, and answered tons of questions from people who were just as scared and intimidated as I'd been about talking with Congress. Perhaps, most importantly, I helped people make appointments with their own Congressional representatives.

I thought getting in to see a Member of Congress was a heavy lift. I was totally wrong. One of the big secrets that I learned that first day on the Hill is that anyone can request a meeting with their Member to discuss their issues.

If you live in Allentown, PA, and represent the left-handed Jewish pastry-makers, you can get to see your Representative. You just have to call and make an appointment. Unless you are a big donor or have lots of political pull, you end up seeing a junior staffer, which sounds like a bit of a disappointment.

But chances are, the Member knows absolutely nothing about your issues anyway. The staffer that meets with you will probably be the only one in the office who is actually knowledgeable about left-handed Jewish pastry-makers, as well as the one responsible for telling your Member what positions they should take on the issues. So they're actually the best person to meet with.

I suggested folks make several appointments within their state's delegation to maximize their opportunities, and also with any Members' offices nearby in contiguous states bordering on there's (these will often listen to you as well, since communities span state borders). They should also have a list of other nearby offices they could try with random drop-ins if they had time (Congressional staffers will often see you without an appointment if it's a slow day). There are several great guides to Capitol Hill offices and we made sure to buy a bunch.

I booked a ton of rooms at a Quality Inn in College Park, MD, out on the Green Belt, in the hopes that "National Gender Lobby Day" would draw many from throughout the country to our casue. It was across from Fraternity Row at the University of Maryland. It was one of the few hotels within a couple Metro stops of the Hill that had clean rooms at reasonable prices, good food options nearby, and a conference room we could get for next to nothing.

Of course I flooded the media with faxed press releases. This was going to be a great news story; it had everything: Congressional intrigue, political struggle and men in brassieres. Who could resist that?

Moreover, it would finally be a hard news story about transgender, one that would show us pursuing our civil rights. That could help shift the way we were covered forever, if only people would show up. I thought it would take the earth being destroyed by a meteor to push transsexuals on Capitol Hill off of front pages and the CNN airwaves.

Unfortunately, there was something even bigger coming. But I didn't know it then. All I prayed for was that people would come, and it wouldn't be half a dozen of us answering reporters' embarrassing questions about why no one showed up. I sat back and waited. Every few days I'd check with the hotel on the number of room reservations that had been taken in our block. I was going to release all the unused ones so I didn't get charged. I needn't have bothered. We completely exhausted the room block and had to take more.

I took Amtrak down early Sunday, unpacked, and spent the whole day watching the troops arrive. It was a blast. People I knew—and plenty I didn't—kept arriving all throughout the day. We'd just get one group checked-in and settled when another would show up.

Can't You People Take a *Joke*?

That night, we all converged on the conference room for the main briefing. When we walked in there were 104 people. I know because I counted every one. It was an amazing turnout. Easily three or four times what we could have hoped for. Without a microphone to reach such a large group, I stood on a nearby chair, looked at them all and shouted, "It was a JOKE! We were kidding—can't you people take a JOKE?"

Once the laughter died down, we got down to business. We went over the main issues to cover: hate crimes and employment discrimination. We discussed the status of the bills pending on these: the Employment Non-Discrimination Act (ENDA) and the Hate Crimes Prevention Act.

Going through each one, we introduced all the piles of papers laid out on a long table at the rear: talking points, how to speak with your member of congress, topics to avoid, overviews of each of the bills and their numbers, and lots of "leave-behinds" documenting the terrible rates of hate crimes and unfair job termination among the trans community. These leave-behinds were important, because those are the things that the staffer you met with will keep in the file on your issue, and maybe even show the Member.

We asked for volunteers to help assemble lobbying packets, and a dozen people leapt forward, lined both sides of the table and began stuffing 200 Lobby Day kits in order, passing them hand to hand so every kit had the same papers in the same order, until the last one was assembled.

Then came my least favorite part. Before the meeting, one of the other co-hosts and I had had a major disagreement about the tone, tenor and schedule. She wanted to lower the boom on people for not being more politically involved. I thought this was just plain nuts for a number of reasons.

Yes, the larger trans-community was politically disengaged, but these were the people who had come to our call. Many had taken off time and traveled great distances—some even putting their jobs at risk—simply to be here today. Almost all of them had paid their own way for a chance to make some trans political history and move our community forward.

Second, going up to Capitol Hill for the first time was pretty intimidating, especially for the crossdressers. It could be pretty daunting, as I knew first hand. Plus, although I was careful not to talk about it and maybe spook the crowd, no one had ever seen a hundred transsexuals and crossdressers out together publicly—let alone traipsing across the Capitol grounds in a group and pouring through the Congressional office buildings.

I had no idea how that would play out, none at all. I actually thought at least a few of us would end up arrested—especially the crossdressers and perhaps some of the transwomen who were pre-op. Because, at some point during our eight or ten hours on the Hill, they would each have to use the restroom. If they walked into the Congressional Men's Rooms, they could get arrested for public indecency, disturbing the peace... whatever charges the Capitol Police wanted to think up.

If they used the Women's Room, they might have been in dresses and sensible shoes, but they were still legally males under Federal law, under which the Capitol operated (*and* local law too). Just think of all the fun charges the Police could bring for *that* situation. What they were doing was still borderline illegal in many other places as well. Miami and San Diego had passed laws in the mid-1960s specifically banning crossdressing (not just restroom use). Oakland had a similar law on the

125

books until 2010 and the State of New York *still* had a law prohibiting "impersonating a female" on its books as late as 2011. Living full-time as a woman and being pre-operative (or non-operative) was still a dangerous and hazardous business; it took guts.

So it was especially brave for crossdressers and pre-ops to be there at all. In these circumstances, you keep people's energy up, applaud their bravery and build e*sprit de corps* for whatever is to come. What you don't do is upbraid them for what they're not doing or have failed to do in the *past*.

In the end, it was resolved by all agreeing to have a DC activist that the co-host was close with address the whole group. (This was the same activist who had hysterically predicted that I was coming to Atlanta to "destroy" Southern Comfort.) It was not a good compromise, but it was the best I could get. Neither of them ever spoke to me again.

The DC activist used her time to launch into a passionate 20-minute harangue about how transpeople needed to get more politically involved (presumably like the two of them). Well, who would argue with that? She seemed blissfully unaware that she was preaching to the choir, that these were the people who had come running when asked.

The room had been jumping with laughter, good energy and anticipation until the moment she started. Then suddenly it was like all the air went out of the room. People's smiles disappeared, they stared at the floor or off into the distance. The discomfort and dismay were palpable. It was crazy. But there was nothing I could do. As the tongue-lashing wore on, I felt bad for them, but I was still proud of every damn one of them.

Afterwards, we went over the now-assembled Lobby Day packets, toddled off to numerous late-night conversations, and awaited the morning.

Yes, We're Here for Your Children

All of us got up early, and assembled near the hotel's front door where they were serving a continental breakfast. There was lots of shuffling and nervous jokes.

Then we headed off in an immense, straggling group towards the Metro entrance three blocks away, packing several cars. The stares from the early morning commuters—probably imagining they were suddenly trapped in Gender Hell, or among an extremely large and well-behaved transgender biker gang (Film at 11!)—were priceless. A photographer from the *Times* who accompanied us was already taking pictures. Unfortunately, they would turn out to be the wrong ones.

We all got off at the Capitol South Metro station near the Library of Congress, and headed over towards the main Capitol dome. We'd sent out a number of releases, and hoped to hold a press conference.

Monday, October 2nd was a beautiful sunny DC fall day: the temperature hovered around 70, there was a slight breeze and a blazing sun. The Gender gods had smiled; after today, we would no longer be silenced or shamed into political passivity. Sure enough, there was a press gaggle waiting for us. I made a beeline for the podium. You may not know it, but it's the same one you've seen in countless public statements by Senators and Representatives, with the Capitol dome right over their shoulders.

I found out that it's left there all day, for just such occasions—but not for civilians like us, as I was soon to learn. With cameras rolling and flashes going off in front and all 100 or so of us arrayed around behind it, I stepped up to the mic. I began, thanking everyone for coming and announcing the event, knowing as I said it that, whatever happened next, we were making history.

I began with a statement I'd memorized: "We are here today to talk with our elected representatives, because we've been harassed or beaten on the streets, or we know someone who has. Because we've been fired from our jobs, or we know someone who has. Because we've been refused medical care we desperately need, or we know someone who has…"

I spoke for only a few minutes. Then Phyllis took over and gave a longer speech. Several others then spoke. About 20 minutes in, I stepped forward and asked if there were any questions from the gathered press group. A number of networks showed up to film the event. I spotted ABC, Fox News, CNN and Reuters.

One I didn't recognize was a group of exceptionally clean-cut young people smiling ferociously, and their reporter was the first to raise his hand. All this should have set off alarm bells, but I was way too distracted to process the information and called on him, waiting for a softball question about the groundbreaking nature of this gathering I could knock out of the park.

"I'm from the Family News Network and our viewers want to know why you think teachers that try to change their sex should be allowed to into elementary schools to teach our children."

Welcome to politics.

After a few more questions, someone tapped me on the shoulder. It was the Capitol Police. It turned out the podium was for Members of Congress only. Everyone else had to apply in advance and get a permit. Did we happen to have a permit? Welcome to Washington, DC, our nation's capital.

Cafeteria Activism

We wound down the news conference, and headed off to the Capitol. Mariette took pictures of all hundred of us standing proudly together behind Phyllis' 30-foot long "Transgendered and Proud and We Vote" banner.

The first two parts of that were great. I was never sure the prospect of a couple thousand transpeople voting was really enough to strike fear into the heart of politicians. But it gave us something to rally behind.

Although I expected at least a few of us would get arrested that day, as we all walked off together with the media in tow, I remember thinking that whatever happened, this was the right thing to do. And off we went, the group breaking into groups of twos and threes heading determinedly across the plaza to their various buildings and first appointments.

Dana Priesing, a DC lawyer, had helped set everything up was with me when we set up a kind of command center in a corner of the Rayburn Building cafeteria. Dana was a smart, quick, hardheaded litigator armed with a vodka-dry sense of humor and a Georgetown law degree. She had worked at a prestigious DC firm but was soon "constructively terminated" once she transitioned.

Dana and I met shortly after she left the firm. She reached out to me and I promptly invited her to a Menace picketing. Short, wiry and plain wicked in her head-to-toe black leathers when riding her BMW (which was seldom far away), she was easy to pick out. We bonded quickly.

We were short on level-headed and unflappable lawyers, and I soon found myself asking her if she would become GenderPAC's main voice and strategist in everything involving the Hill, legislation and the courts. It was less an offer than a plea, since at the time I couldn't offer her any salary, but she agreed.

On Lobby Day, Dana stayed at our command-center table in Rayburn, coordinating the action, tracking everyone's appointments, making sure no important Members were overlooked or duplicated. Karen and some of her It's Time America folks helped, ensuring we met with or dropped in on almost every one of the 500 House and Senate offices. It makes my arches hurt just thinking about it.

(Getting to see your House Representative, who is one of over 400, is about as easy as getting an appointment to see your doctor. Getting to see your Senator—who is one of only 100—is like getting an appointment to see the Pope, only harder. They are as gods: they never, ever meet with mere mortals (like constituents). And they never, ever allow themselves to be spotted out "in the wild" where someone could just walk up and talk with them.

Dana debriefed participants on their Congressional office's stands on our issues and the pending legislation, eventually creating a tabulation of who stood where on what issue. Having spent a lot of time on the Hill, she could also answer all their questions about the status of particular bills, their co-sponsors and likely votes.

It was fun watching Congressional staffers doing classic double takes (WE control your horizontal. WE control your vertical. WE control your hormones) as they came by the Rayburn Cafeteria around noon for a quick bite and spotted three or four tables of transsexuals and crossdressers quietly having lunch.

It was also fun getting off the underground Congressional subway going to the House, only to watch a carload of transgender activists boarding the other side going to the Senate. Hey! Just your average day in Congress, no?

By the end of the first day, it had already become blindingly obviously that there was a lot of sympathy for our cause on the hate crimes issue, but Human Rights Campaign (HRC)'s staunch opposition to including "gender identity" to ENDA, the big Employment Non-Discrimination Act, was a huge obstacle.

Members' staffers (not a small proportion of whom were gay themselves—even in Republican offices) saw HRC as *the* litmus test on queer issues on the Hill. Most of them lined up behind HRC's argument that "gender identity" didn't belong in ENDA and would never fly if it were added. And these were the liberal Democrats who should have been our friends. We were going to have to confront HRC. That would come next.

In the meantime, from our commandeered tables in the Rayburn cafeteria, we provided fresh kits and papers for those who were out, and suggested drop-by appointments for those who had extra time, and went out on appointments for those who got cold feet and wanted more experienced help.

At some point, I became one of the latter. About halfway through the morning, the last week's tension got to me and I suddenly felt totally exhausted. I didn't want to make the effort to think my way through talking with another Congressional staffer and I was so tired of being "on" all the time, I feared I'd say the wrong thing anyway.

Instead, I excused myself, walked outside to the Capitol Hill grounds, sat on a bench until lunch in the quiet shade, looked out at the sun and the trees and the big white dome and smiled.

Epilogue

The first Lobby Day attracted transpeople from 20 some states—just under half the country. It marked the first time the trans-community had raised its political voice in national politics. Before Lobby Day, almost none of the Congressional offices had met and spoken with a transgender constituent, considered their rights or answered to their concerns. After Lobby Day that would no longer be true. Moreover, it was closely followed by all the national gay rights groups (and endorsed by some of them). It announced to the gay rights movement that our days of the "conference culture," with transpeople voluntarily confining themselves to dress-up events along the interstates while our political interests were consigned to the tender mercy of HRC's lobbyists were over. As Dr. Barbara Warren accurately observed in the *Times* article about the event: "The fundamental building block of the whole movement is the willingness of transgender folk to put themselves out there and be visible." We were politically active, we were coming in numbers and we wanted our rights. We were out for good.

The New York Times ran a lengthy article inexplicably titled, "Shunning He and She, They Fight for Respect" (to my knowledge, none of us avoided pronouns). Equally inexplicably, the photo editor picked a picture of Jamison Green on the previous morning's Metro ride to a Tyra Hunter demonstration to illustrate Lobby Day. *Times* readers were no doubt completely baffled as to why an article about transsexuals was accompanied by a picture of a bearded businessman taking the subway on his way to work.

But it was the lead story at the top of the National page, inaugurating the *Times'* long run of finally covering transgender as a civil rights issue and giving it the "hard news" coverage it deserves, instead of providing the intermittent stream of "human interest" puff pieces it had been running in the Culture or Arts sections on how one of us had transitioned, what the neighbors thought of living next to a transgender person, or the latest off-off-off-Broadway musical comedy featuring a crossdressing character. (This was just seven years after the *Times* agreed to stop insisting on the word "homosexual" in its stories and finally agreed to start using "gay.") Other major newspapers slowly followed suit. By 2007, the *Times* hired trans author Jennifer Boylan as a regular opinion columnist, and by 2014, its op-ed page came out with a ringing editorial favoring full recognition of transgender rights. It had taken just about 20 years.

At the end of the day, October 2nd, we sat glued to news waiting for all that coverage by CNN, Reuters, ABC and Fox to hit the airwaves and announce our presence ("Transsexual Mob Invades Nation's Capital—Film at 11!"). The coverage—and perhaps even the backlash—would be huge. Alas, it was not to be. That evening, the OJ Simpson jury let the judge know they had reached a verdict. Even though the verdict could not be announced until the following day (Tuesday October 3rd), even though no one knew the outcome, and even though it could only be one of two things, endless hours of speculation pushed every other news story off the airwaves... including ours. In effect, OJ was the earth-destroying meteor that swallowed our event. By Wednesday, we were yesterday's news, and by the second National Gender Lobby Day we were also old news. Welcome to journalism—if it bleeds, it leads—even if men in dresses invade the halls of Congress.

In 2000, I hired a boyish, short-haired, very high-octane lesbian who had been Action Vice President of NJ/NOW (more on NOW later) and then single-handedly put what became NJ Equality on the map.

Gina Reiss attended that year's Lobby Day, and afterwards we discussed the need to move GenderPAC to DC, where the nation's political power was concentrated. By then I was semi-retired in sunny, beautiful South Beach, enjoying the year-round sun and some very long over-due rest. But Gina informed me bluntly that if I ever wanted GenderPAC to be a real organization, I'd have to quit my job, move to DC and work on GenderPAC as a full-time job. It wasn't fun, but I did it. It took us over a year to get our first grant in the door. But in five years we had incorporated, moved into a nice, donated office in Dupont Circle, and hired a staff of two full-time and two-part-time on a budget of $150,000 for staffers. In five more years, we had grown to a staff of 12 and a budget of about $1,250,000.

Following HRC's lead with their "sexual orientation pledge," beginning with the second National Gender Lobby Day in 1996, participants began asking their Members to sign a Congressional Non-Discrimination Pledge that affirmed they would not discriminate based on individuals' "gender identity or expression" (this was the legal "term of art"). In August 2006 Republican Senator Rick Santorum of Pennsylvania—a notorious homophobe—became the 170th Congressional signatory when students from Muhlenberg College asked him to sign it during Lobby Day. After a GenderPAC press release lauding the Senator for his embrace of diversity—followed by a furious right-wing outburst—he quickly rescinded his signature. But, by the end of the year, we still had almost 200 Congressional signatories on a transgender pledge, including a dozen Republicans (!) and as many Senators. This was a tide slowly shifting. The following year, HRC finally reached out to incorporate our pledge and "gender identity" into theirs. However, they kept ENDA strictly limited to "sexual orientation."

In July 1997, as part of a broad coalition of progressive national groups, GenderPAC was invited to the White House to participate in its upcoming Hate Crimes Conference.

In 2000, the Gill Foundation of Denver CO, then the largest gay foundation, gave GenderPAC their first grant of $15,000. It was the first grant from any of the gay funders to trans issues. In 2003, philanthropist Tim Gill invited me to address OutGiving, the Foundation's annual gathering of major gay donors. Later that year they added "gender identity" to their mission. The other two gay funders—Jon Styker's Arcus Foundation and the David Bohnett Foundation—soon followed suit, making transgender gifts and expanding their mission statements.

132

As of this writing in 2015, National Lobby Day is in its 20th year. In 2003, another political organization launched with a more specific focus on transgender identity than GenderPAC, which was fine with us. Alas, each year it would wait for GPAC to announce National Gender Lobby Day, then announce their own exactly one week before. Members of Congress always seemed completely baffled as to why the world's smallest, most marginalized and most dispossessed minority would split its efforts and call on them twice in two weeks. But then again, so was I.

For more than a decade, the Hate Crimes bill failed to pass Congress. In 2006, GenderPAC published, *"50 Under 30: Masculinity and the War on America's Youth."* For the first time, it examined every known gender identity murder over a ten-year period from 1995-2006. Except for the National Center for Transgender Equality and the Task Force, the report was unanimously adopted by the Hate Crimes Coalition of major civil rights groups that meets in DC. HRC made sure that every Member of Congress was provided with a copy before the 2007 vote on the hate crimes bill.

In 2009, GenderPAC ceased to operate, and both it and its Lobby Day ended. *"50 Under 30,"* was upgraded and reissued just two years later with 20 additional murders as *"70 Under 30"* and was taken over in 2009 by the National Coalition of Anti-Violence Programs (NCAVP). It has since become a much-cited part of their annual report on LGBTQ violence. When GenderPAC started, none of the national gay organizations embraced "transgender." Today all of them have. Our Workplace Equality project in 2000 started with six Fortune 1000s that had "gender identity" in their non-discrimination policies; when we closed our doors over 200 did, and today such policies are near universal. New national transgender non-profits like NCTE, the Transgender Law Center and Sylvia Rivera Law Project bring in an estimated $3 million annually, and are supported by all the gay foundations, and many mainstream ones as well.

In 1998, gay male Matthew Shepard was killed near Laramie, WY. The same year, James Byrd, Jr. was tied to a truck by white supremacists and dragged down the road until he was decapitated. The hate crimes bill was formally renamed the Matthew Shepherd and James Byrd, Jr. Hate Crimes Prevention Act. In September, 2007, for the first time both houses of Congress passed legislation that included transgender and "gender identity" protections. But President Bush threatened a veto and the provisions were stripped from the underlying legislation. The bill was finally signed into law October 2009 by President Barack Obama. In December 2014, for the first time, the FBI released its annual Hate Crimes Statistics tallying gender identity attacks.

On May 9, 2016 Loretta Lynch, U.S. Attorney General and an African-American woman, went on national television to declare to transgender Americans: "We see you. We stand with you." Later that December, for the first time, the Department used Federal law to bring criminal charges in a transgender case. Alabama gang member Joshua Vallum was charged with murdering 17-year-old Mercedes Williamson. He was charged under the Matthew Shepard and James Byrd, Jr. Hate Crimes Prevention Act.

Chapter 6—HRC and the Fight for ENDA

"Life Is Harsh—She's a He"

If hate crimes was a big issue for transpeople, employment discrimination was even bigger—perhaps *the* issue for the gay community. Unlike many gay people, most of us had no closets we could recede into. We didn't get jobs, and when we did, we were fired for transitioning.

As I mentioned earlier, the only job I could get once I started my transition was tutoring English at a tiny community college where many of the staff refused to talk to me or even meet my eyes, and I ended up needing Valium to cope with the daily harassment by students whenever I stepped beyond our small tutoring room.

Even Tony the Transgender Cop, who founded TOPS and was initially backed by his Sheriff with much positive publicity, found himself suddenly written up for ridiculous infractions and then eventually, inevitably, forced out of his job.

Dana's separation from the high-priced law firm that had employed her (and her launch into trans political activism) wasn't an exception, it was the rule. Many of us became politicized because employment discrimination against transgender employees was a given, even in major cities.

And we were the "lucky" ones: middle class, white people with educations. It was much, much worse for many transpeople who were of color, lacked advanced degrees, or both.

Moreover, a substantial number of our hate crime victims *became* victims because they had been thrown out of a job (and often a home) and had no other choice but to engage in "survival sex"—picking up random johns in order to eat that night, or have a place to sleep—the most exposed and vulnerable kind of commercial sex work.

It wasn't just HRC's steadfast opposition to adding "gender identity" to ENDA that had to be confronted. It's hard to imagine now, but this was a time when the major gay organizations at the state and national level simply refused to "add the T." *Everything* was "Lesbian and Gay."

New York's (very inclusive) community center was still the Gay & Lesbian Community Gender; the very progressive Task Force was still the Gay & Lesbian Task Force. But the battle for trans-inclusion had broken out and was now being joined on numerous fronts: medicine, law, psychiatry, media—everywhere.

For instance, in February, 1996, the Gay and Lesbian Medical Association (GLMA), one of the nation's oldest and most prestigious organizations for queer physicians, decided to "better define its mission"… by removing all references to transpeople from its letterhead and mission.

Forty members of the Menace and other groups promptly picketed GLMA, chanting *"Hey doctors / Get a clue / Some of us / Are some of you,"* and carrying signs imploring them to, *"Keep all stripes in the rainbow."*

Faced with the public backlash and negative publicity, three months later, that May, "transgender" was reinstated, but only after the Executive Director declared that GLMA's focus would still remain gays and lesbians. That was the political environment in which we operated, and the depth of the animus towards trans-inclusion that we confronted on every front.

That same year, the Civil Rights Roundtable, the national coalition of groups engaged in "queer law," began openly considering adding trans, composed of groups including Lambda Legal, the NY Center for Lesbian Rights, the ACLU, GLAAD and others. Local chapters had long resisted representing transpeople, arguing that their focus was "sexual orientation."

Lambda Legal to Butch Lesbians, Fairies, Transsexuals & Crossdressers:

GET LOST!

Did you know... Lambda Legal Defense & Education Fund, the US' largest gay & lesbian law practice, **still refuses to take on transgender and transsexual cases**?

Did you know... LLDEF **still refuses cases of gender non-conforming gays, lesbians, and bisexuals?** Yet studies show 38% of G/L/B people are discriminated against in at least *partly* due to gender expression.

Did you know... LLDEF says that **"gender is NOT A GAY ISSUE"** ??? Didn't they ever hear of drag queens, butches, fairies, diesel dykes, or transpeople? Those who hate and attack us certainly have!

Hey Lambda: You're Taking Our Money, Why Not Take Our Cases, Too!!!

We're not quiet. We're not well-behaved. And we're *not* going away.

A public service announcement from your local Transexual Menace chapter: *We're here. We're genderqueer. Get used to it!*

Flier for Lambda Legal protest.

This was a step forward for Lambda, which had refused to handle any transgender cases, again arguing that they were a gay and lesbian organization. We would talk regularly with their E.D. who was very smart and very cordial and very tough and still wouldn't take a single case. Eventually, we picketed their headquarters nearby at Manhattan's Wall Street.

One of the more bizarre struggles over trans-inclusion broke out that September at GLAAD (Gay & Lesbian Alliance Against Defamation), consistently one of the more trans-sensitive organizations, over our representations in the media.

GLAAD/NY's new Managing Director had been spiking trans-related stories, including one about Safe Space, which helps queer and trans teens, and the disgusting *"Life is harsh - She's a he"* campaign for Sauza Tequila ads featuring outed transgender super-model Tula. What made this ad doubly depressing was that life WAS harsh, but for us, not for the kind of trans-and-homophobic middle class white males who were the ads' target audience.

What happened next was instructive. GLAAD's new Director reportedly stated that: a) GLAAD did not endorse a "laundry list" of identities; b) that GLAAD's focus was gays and lesbians; c) that the Sauza ads were not offensive (??); d) and that if they were, they were not GLAAD's responsibility but the transgender community's (note the distinction).

Interestingly, in a sign of solidarity, GLAAD/SF's MediaWatch led with the Sauza story anyway. Responding to mounting pressure and public outcry, GLAAD/NY agreed to start a caucus to discuss transgender issues, beginning with the Sauza ads. Accordingly, a meeting was called, reportedly by the Associate Director, Donald Suggs, and over a dozen local activists responded.

However, soon after, Donald, Cathay Che, and three other long-standing and trans friendly members of GLAAD staff were fired, reportedly following a series of disagreements with the Managing Director. So being trans-exclusive or even openly trans-hostile wasn't limited to HRC—it was just one prominent example among many.

While many local grassroots communities leaned at least gently towards inclusion (they hung out with us and knew us personally), at the national level organizations tended to be as conservative as their major donors and the crossover straight moderates they needed to succeed. Thus they studiously avoided taking any positions that might seem extreme (I'm looking at YOU, trannies!) in order not to risk alienating their dreams of going mainstream.

It was common to read op-eds in major gay newspapers questioning why transpeople were trying to horn in on the gay movement, pointing out that sexual orientation and gender identity were very different, and none too subtly suggesting we go build our own movement and leave theirs alone.

We Are All Transgendered

One outstanding exception that deserves special mention was a December 1996 article by director/journalist Gabrielle Rotello in the *Advocate*. Titled, "Transgendered Like Me," Gabe not only made the case for trans-inclusion as incisively as any of us had ever done, but it came from a high-profile gay man.

His analysis of the confluence of sexual orientation and gender identity prefigured positions that would eventually come to be recognized by the larger gay community as well—arguments that would eventually win the day in legal circles, too.

"Homophobes don't merely hate us because of how we make love [but] because it violates our expected gender roles. We are hated for gender transgression. When I was 10 and was taunted for throwing a ball "like a girl," those schoolyard bullies didn't suspect me of sleeping with men. They bashed me for not being boy enough. That goes for almost all of us. Whether we face prejudice for being too butch or too femme... or being perceived as gay or lesbian, we are all ultimately disliked for the same basic reason: transgressing our expected gender roles. Sexual transgression in the bedroom is just one aspect, although a very important one. All gays are in a basic sense transgendered." You SO rock, boyfriend. But Gabe's insights were then far outside of mainstream gay opinion.

HRC's continued opposition to our trans-inclusion in ENDA was a problem. But in a larger sense it was also symptomatic of a movement that remained defiantly "gay, lesbian, and bisexual," didn't represent us, and didn't see itself *as needing* to represent us.

Moreover, HRC's leadership was great at slipping punches on our exclusion from ENDA. When confronted by media, they'd murmur something comforting about cooperating with the

139

transgender community, understanding our concerns and how they were making progress on including us in the hate crimes bill, etc. In other words, everything except the obvious, which was that they didn't support our inclusion in their mission and they didn't support our inclusion in ENDA.

This "I feel your pain" strategy worked fine with the gay media, but was so blatantly exclusionary that it pissed off nearly everyone else, and instantly politicized the issue and the entire transsexual wing of the transgender community. What we needed was a way to make this exclusion visible and immediate, in a media-friendly way, with good visuals that would result in media coverage.

In the chapter on the murder trial vigils I said that street activism is only good for focusing media and public attention, not making actual political change. There is an exception, however.

If you can get an organization where it is stuck in the public eye, particularly in front of its donors and supporters, it is vulnerable to a confrontation campaign by a relatively small group of highly-motivated activists acting in concert.

Every year, HRC sponsors huge dinners in dozens of major cities. In fact, they are a hallmark of the organization, black-tie events with celebrity speakers that are well-attended and highly publicized. Big-money donors show up regularly and they raise a substantial portion of HRC's annual budget.

All of which is to say they need to run smoothly, to be—and *be seen to be*—successful, happy events that are an expression of the community coming together: making them practically the perfect political piñata for a sustained public protest by those who were being quietly shunted to the sidelines.

The problem was, we had no idea when or where they were. The HRC website listed the upcoming cities, but with no times, dates and places, I assume so no one (like us) would be tempted to crash them.

Wracking my brains for how to get the information, I decidedly to the direct route was best: lie. I would simply call up HRC and ask for the Membership Department. I identified myself as a Federal Club member who traveled a lot and wanted to attend dinners while on the road. I then asked if they could they tell me when and where the Chicago meeting was? Or the Dallas meeting, since I hubbed through DFW airport a lot and would have time on my hands.

Each time I'd get a couple of cities, and then hang up. I'd wait a few days, and then call back and get someone new, and get a couple more cities. In this way, I was able to compile a complete list of all the HRC dinners for the coming year.

Then I started recruiting. In cities where I knew people, I'd call them directly and explain the plan. In cities where I didn't, I'd try to get one or two friendly emails and outreach that way. Eventually I had two or three willing activists in every one of 16-18 upcoming cities with dinners.

It was touchy politically, because on one hand, HRC had been supportive of Lobby Day, providing information and training and occasionally doing joint visits with participants.

DC is a small town: as GenderPAC's ED, I had to regularly interact with them and cooperate on a number of gay community projects. So I couldn't do street activism any more, or be seen to be fomenting insurrection towards HRC. My hand couldn't be obvious.

The plan was simple: every time HRC had a dinner, we'd make sure there were trans-activists outside protesting, putting a public face on exclusion, and making the case for inclusion. What I was counting on was that, unlike at the national level, in local communities protesters would be personal friends and probably hang out with many of the attendees. They would have worked closely together on local campaigns or frequented the same bars.

It's hard to walk past someone you know or are friends with, who is telling you they're being excluded at the event and their issues are being thrown under the bus. *Thrown under the bus.* This was a really resonant phrase that many trans activists used when describing our being left behind. But in another way, it avoided the real issue.

In the early days of Gay Liberation, radical queer groups like Gay Liberation Front envisioned a grassroots struggle by the masses against heterosexism and homophobia. But as the movement gathered momentum and power, the frame had shifted from Gay Liberation to Gay Rights, from liberating people from strictures of mainstream heterosexual society to another civil rights group demanding inclusion and rights within that society.

So the real question was, *whose bus was it?* The resolution to this question would convulse the queer community and color nearly every gay political initiative for the next 20 years.

Let's Get This Party Started

Kicking things off, in August 1995 Alison Laing, the head of IFGE—which was then the oldest and largest national transgender organization, issued an open letter to Elizabeth Birch, ED of HRC, calling on her to reverse their two-year-old policy of excluding transgender organizations from their ENDA coalition. This was important because, for years, HRC had long used the coalition as a fig-leaf, maintaining that all decisions about ENDA were the result of a "broad coalition" that included the NAACP, ACLU, National Council of La Raza, etc.

While this may have been technically true, they held considerable sway over the bill, and they certainly had the first and the last word on its LGB-but-not-T provisions. Moreover, HRC— who thought they had everyone fooled—was notorious for this kind backroom maneuver.

It was not unusual to be invited to HRC headquarters for a big meeting of all the queer groups to discuss some pressing major issue confronting the community... only to discover later that HRC had already reached a decision.

As my critics will confirm, I'm not exactly a stranger to *hubris,* but sometimes HRC's sheer arrogance took even my breath away. For instance, when Elizabeth Birch retired, an HRC staffer called me repeatedly to get my input on her successor. I found this surprising, but was still somewhat gratified to think my opinion mattered and they cared. They didn't. At the end of our 20-minute conversation, I asked the friendly young man when HRC would be making their selection. He informed me it had already been made; they just wanted to make sure everyone felt consulted. That was what it was like trying to work with them, and why some of what followed... followed.

Riki's Rules for (Quiet) Riots

That summer in June HRC once again introduced ENDA without "gender identity." The office of Senator Jim Jeffords, a Senate sponsor who was friendly to our issues, publicly confirmed that HRC had specifically asked for a "sexual orientation" only bill. This was pretty galling, since Phyllis Frye and Karen Karin of It's

Time America! had worked hard with Sen. Jeffords' office to create an amended, inclusive version.

Shortly thereafter, we put out a new release from the Menace announcing a nationwide protest. HRC had upcoming fundraising dinners or Gay Pride events coming up in New York, Boston, Washington, Baltimore, Tampa-St. Petersburg, Dallas, Houston, Indianapolis, Seattle, Chicago, Atlanta, San Francisco and Los Angeles.

I aimed to have us hit them all, and we had the activists already lined up. I mean, it wasn't like there was exactly a shortage of volunteers. The big stumbling block was that nobody knew how to picket. I mean, what exactly do you do? What are you not allowed to do? And what should you never ever do? And perhaps most importantly, was it legal and what could get you arrested?

I started teaching folks Riki's Rules for Riots. To begin with, you always let folks know you're going to picket them. I'd already made the mistake of going after folks who were ready to concede the point, except no one had ever really asked them.

Also, you're going to have to work with the folks you picket, so while you want to force their hand, you want to do it as cordially as possible (this would not be true of some groups that followed like The National Transgender Advocacy Coalition (NTAC), which apparently believed in burning the bridges to the people they were trying to change).

As a nice side-benefit, telling the target of your protest in advance helps build their paranoia. They might show up and find only you there, but it's far better for them to agonize for weeks beforehand about a sea of black Menace T-shirts at their event. Finally, you also want to inform your local constabulary.

Police hate anything that smacks of public disturbances; it looks like things are out of control, which makes them look silly. They also don't want to end up sending a bunch of mobile units (like our *Village Voice* vigil), only for them to discover a bunch of middle-aged men in dresses demon-strating peacefully. That stresses them out, and also makes them look silly.

Far better to identify the local precinct, ask for the desk sergeant on duty, and tell them what you'll be doing, when and where. I often left my name and number and told them to have the Officer-in-

Charge ask for me when they arrived on the scene. And they *always* arrived.

And last but not least, the rules for exercising your rights (memorize these or write them down because you're going to recite them to the Office-in-Charge when they tell you that you have no right to be there and must disperse immediately):

1). You are on public property (make sure you actually are before you say this)
2). You are not blocking the sidewalks (ditto)
3). You are not blocking pedestrian egress to or from any buildings (also ditto); and,
4.)You are not creating a disturbance but are peacefully informing the public of your views, which is your right under the First Amendment (you know, freedom of speech and all that).

Also make sure that all posters are of fiberfill poster-board, which stands nicely in a high wind (it's always windy). And make sure none of them have handles like wooden sticks or poles that could be used as a weapon, since these will give the po-po an excuse to confiscate them and/or accuse you of carrying a weapon (if they really want to be mean).

You are also advised to make sure that no one carries a pocketknife of *any* kind (please see "carrying a weapon," above). We suggest you have the name of a friendly gay lawyer (easy to find) who will be on call during the demo, just in case the worst happens. And make sure your friends know where you are going too, just in case.

With these rules, and a bunch of fliers we emailed a few days before which could be customized with the local city name, trans activists were ready hit HRC's dinners—as were any number of others at Pride Parades and festivals, acting on their own.

Let's Get This Party Started

In Cleveland, Emilia Lombardi and friend leafleted HRC at the Dancing in the Streets carnival.

At the National Lesbian & Gay Law Association, Phyllis and Sharon Ann Stuart (who had gotten them to pass an ENDA inclusion resolution the previous year, one of the first national ones) got a time slot to address the full group.

In New Orleans, trans leadership called off their planned leafleting of the HRC fundraiser. And no wonder: the keynote speaker, film producer and HRC board member Dee Mosbacker challenged the 500 attendees by asking, 'Who do we think we are, as we go about obtaining our rights, to exclude others from obtaining those same basic rights? Who do we think we are to exclude the transgendered, the drag queens and the dykes?...[I will] not be part of an organization that denies the transgendered their rights."

In Atlanta, trans activists publicized the exclusion of ENDA during Pride, engaging hundreds of supporters (the local HRC public policy coordinator actually offered to display copies of their flyers at their booth!)

Riki Wilchins

Hey HRCF: Can You Spell
E-N-D-A I-N-C-L-U-S-I-O-N?

Did you know... our national queer lobbying group, the Human Rights Campaign Fund (HRCF), actively ***worked to exclude transpeople*** from the Employment Non-Discrimination Act ("ENDA") when it was introduced in 1994?

Did you know... HRCF's own ENDA lawyer, Chai Feldblum, **acknowledged** to the Transgender Law Conference that transpeople were ***purposely omitted*** from ENDA because **HRCF thought *inclusion because it might cost them 20 votes*** .

Did you know....after transactivists worked their tooshies off to get ***back in*** ENDA, **HRCF again *insisted on omitting transpeople*** when they re-introduced it last Friday? Gosh HRCF: If you're not going to work for us, *at least stop working against us*!

Are you comfortable with HRCF's strategy of jettisoning *radical fairies, butches, diesel dykes, drag queens and drag kings, crossdressers, SM queers, intersexed, and transgender people,* so the "acceptable" queers can "get theirs?" Are we disposable?

Gay Pride celebrates people who rioted at Stonewall like **Marsha P. Johnson, Sylvia Rivera and Yvonne P. Ritter -- the kind of transpeople *of* HRCF** says it can't longer "afford?" Is this "Pride?"

HRCF: GenderQueers deserve rights, TOO!

We're not quiet. We're not well-behaved. And we're not going away. The Transexual Menace: We're here. We're queer<u>er</u>. Get used to it.

Flier for Human Rights Campaign Fund protests used around the country

In San Antonio, Tere Fredrickson and two friends leafleted 200 attendees at the HRC dinner where Candace Gingrich, half-sister of former House Speaker Newt Gingrich and one of their key lobbyists on the Hill, was a keynote. (Candace is now the proud owner of a black Transexual Menace T-shirt. She thanked us.)

At the NYC Pride Parade, Clare and I leafleted in front of the HRC tent at the terminus of the march near the Christopher Street Piers—in stifling heat—to the surprise of some lesbians whose gawking laughs of derision were meant to get our attention, while the majority of the Menace members were far back in the parade, marching behind the Menace banner.

When I began leafleting, one young man took extreme exception to our fliers critical of HRC. He decided to stop me by invading my personal space, standing right up to my face, so I couldn't give any out. I countered by reaching around him. He responded by snatching any fliers I handed out from people's hands the moment I handed them out.

I countered again, by turning first one way, then the other, reaching out in every direction, so he couldn't predict which way I would hand out a flier. Being sneered at from a distance is par for the course, but it's intensely threatening having someone, openly hostile, standing quite literally in my face preventing me from taking an action.

I am totally non-violent, yet I had this overwhelming urge to hit him. But I realized that if we got in a fight, he would win not only the fight—because he was bigger—but he would win politically as well, because he would have succeeded in preventing me from doing what I was there to do.

The urge came up again and again, strong, like nausea and an increasing need to vomit. And I kept fighting it down. Our street demonstrations and leaflet campaigns were all done with a resigned sense of having to be strong and positive, which we inevitably were, but, still, we are human and the accumulation of petty griefs like this register in the soul.

In Philadelphia, JoAnn Roberts and Renaissance handed out fliers at the University of Pennsylvania, where Candace Gingrich was again a featured speaker. In the hot auditorium, people fanned themselves with the fliers, which many took and read, thinking they were programs (sometimes you just get lucky). Nancy Forest of Renaissance made a speech demanding to know who would fight for her as a transgendered woman and protect her job.

147

In Chicago, Debbie Johnson and Stephanie Young coordinated a leafleting at the HRC dinner, trudging down to Navy Pier and—working in groups of twos or threes—passing out nearly 1000 fliers in just two hours. The Chicago Police were very accommodating and even read the leaflet, and Elizabeth Birch came out to talk with them. ("We pressed a flyer into the hands of two of the wealthiest guys in town, in elighted to get it. One said he was thick with the leadership back East, and shocked at the exclusion.")

But Five-Oh wasn't always so accommodating. In NYC former Massachusetts Gov. William Weld was keynoting our dinner, and security was tight. The two cops who showed up were not friendly, and they didn't like trannies at all either. The lead officer—a sergeant no less, I guess we were that dangerous—decided to throw his weight around, immediately announcing "This is MY city and it's MY sidewalk and you will stay where I tell you or you will be arrested."

Where he told us to stand ended up being two parking spaces about 100 yards from the event—nearly useless. I started arguing with him that we were on public property and we had a First Amendment right to air our views, etc. etc... But he just reiterated that if we moved out to the box we were going downtown.

Our Menace group debated it, but it was hard to see what it would accomplish if our goal was to get fliers into the event. So the dozen of us in our black T-shirts stayed inside the small boxed area. I told them about half the people attending would have to come past us. If they were on our side of the street, we leafleted them. If they were on the other, we'd have to beg, cajole and charm them into coming over.

So we worked it. We leafleted anyone who came by. Some of the groups of well-dressed men and women just passed us by, ignoring us entirely. Others stopped by to talk. If they were across the street, we'd yell out and smile and explain piteously that the police would arrest us if we moved, begging them to please at least come over and talk with us.

Any person who took a flier or expressed interest, we asked to take a handful inside and share them with their friends since we weren't allowed to get near. In that way, hundreds of fliers got inside the event and were passed around.

The second officer watched us work with undisguised disgust. In fact, he made a point of leaning across a pickup truck, with his chin in his hand, and looking directly at me the whole time, as I joked and danced and begged people to stop by, with a look of complete contempt that was supposed to embarrass and humiliate me.

And the intimidation did hurt. But it wasn't going stop me, either. After about an hour, we were low on fliers and it was time for the event to start. The river of upscale gays and lesbians had dwindled to a trickle. I took a last long look at my nasty cop friend, gathered everyone around, and called it a night.

Asymmetrical Warfare

If there was a dinner, we had people there, making sure our fliers got inside and the issue was raised in conversations and Q&As. The behind-the-scenes dealings in Washington were finally getting communicated to the grassroots. They were also getting into the news. Public spats were good for readership, and the gay media was only too happy to give us lots of free publicity.

Plus, the gay press always loved anything that stuck it to HRC. We offered them a strong story, along with good visuals—pictures of transsexuals in black shirts handing out fliers to men dressed up in tuxedos on their way into expensive downtown locations. It was perfect.

Except the press wouldn't do their job. They loved covering the fight; not so much the details. So I would get one phone call after another, and explain the exclusionary policies in detail and why we were picketing. Then the reporter would talk to HRC. They would repeat all my carefully-phrased quotes to HRC's reliably and unfortunately duplicitous national spokesperson.

He would sing them eight to 12 bars of all the wonderful ways HRC was working with the trans community (although they were still excluding us from their mission), how they were partnering with us on Hate Crimes (but excluding us from ENDA), and how a litigation strategy in the courts was the "best avenue" for securing our rights (which weren't really their problem anyway, which they had no intention of helping to pay for or participate in, and which would conveniently wash their hands of us for the next 20 years while we all waited for our case to work its way up through the appeals process to the always-sympathetic Supreme Court).

In city after city, the press would run his BS, without comment, and without asking a single follow-up question. It was infuriating. I got so frustrated that, in new cities, when reporters called, I started *prepping* them on what HRC would say in response, and then I would *give them* the follow-up question that would puncture those deceptions. It never happened. HRC may have been totally deceptive, but they was simply better at this job than the press members were at theirs.

At least HRC was finally being forced to stop doing business as usual and start defending its stands in public, even if it had to keep dodging obvious truths (and us, and the press) to do so. And they were slowly losing ground. There were several forces at work here.

First, the dinners were where the money flowed and bigwigs came together. We were demonstrating that we could adversely impact their fundraising or at least the community goodwill that oiled its gears.

Second, we were showing that we were prepared to confront them for as long as it took, any and every time they tried to hold a public event. So we were slowly raising the costs of exclusion.

Third, and perhaps most importantly, trans people were answering in the most visceral way possible that underlying question, *Whose bus is this?*

By showing up, by putting their names and faces to the exclusion, by visibly being part of the gay community (as they had always been), these brave activists—many doing their first public protest—were challenging HRC's narrative that "our community" was gays and lesbians.

Bad Day at Black Rock

After six months of demonstrations in 18 cities, a group email came from Phyllis saying that HRC wanted to meet with a group of trans leaders. They even offered to pay for travel to DC.

So on Sunday, September 17, I took the train down to DC again. With members of the American Boyz, the Transgender Law Conference, It's Time America!, It's Time Texas! and Transgender Nation, I trooped into the conference room at HRC's headquarters in a large, dark building in downtown DC.

Since it was unlikely they would go to all this trouble simply to underscore our exclusion, I assumed all this meant we had won. I was wrong. Arrogant as always, they had gone to all that trouble to see if they could convince us to go away. Nothing more. If they'd told us in advance, they could have saved themselves, and us, a lot of trouble.

A half dozen of us sat around the table with a half dozen of them, including key ENDA lobbyist Nancy Buermeyer, and Georgetown law professor and HRC legal and legislative advisor, Chai Feldblum. I gathered Chai was supposed to be the final word here. She began patiently explaining how the courts would be a natural avenue for us to work for our rights.

The phrase "because of sex" contained in Title VII of the Civil Rights Act of 1964—if read in its plain, black-letter meaning—should obviously cover those of us suffered employment discrimination because we had changed *from* one sex *to* another.

She explained that the phrase had since been interpreted to apply to discrimination against employees who didn't fit "gender stereotypes"—which had us all over it. She made a very logical case, which fell on totally deaf ears.

First of all, transsexuals—particularly male-to-female—are classic cases of what are known as "unsympathetic plaintiffs." Meaning courts would (and did) twist themselves into judicial knots to avoid extending new rights to us. In fact, back then it would have been exceptional for a federal circuit court to so construe the law.

But even if they were sympathetic, taking a trip through the federal appellate system was a time-consuming task that would cost hundreds of thousands of dollars, and take at least a decade or more. Even if we won every step of the way—which was highly unlikely in itself—the issue would likely be ultimately decided by the Supreme Court, not exactly a friend to gay issues.

And that was if we were lucky. We could also lose in the federal appellate courts and the Supremes could refuse to hear our case, in which case all that money and energy and time were for nothing. All of this was academic anyway, because HRC wasn't offering to pay for a penny of this litigation, and the budgets of all the trans organizations added together wouldn't pay for the first set of briefs to be drawn up. They might as well have suggested that the best way to secure our rights was if we could build a rocket to the moon.

What went unmentioned was that there was already a bill pending in Congress that could easily be adapted to include "gender identity," which had strong sponsors and co-sponsors in both houses, and which, moreover, would help cover gay men fired for being "effeminate" and lesbians fired for being "too butch" (as Gabe's article had pointed out).

Yet, all the while, no one had mentioned ENDA, which was conspicuously absent from the conversation. It was the original "dog that didn't bark"—but boy, was it growling in the corner. So while Chai was working hard, and making logical points, being the honest broker that she's always been, everything she was saying was received on our side of the table as a brush-off, basically a slap in the face, and just making all of us angrier.

We refocused the meeting on ENDA. HRC was adamant that "gender identity" wouldn't work in ENDA, and moreover trans people weren't in their mission. Also that they couldn't get the votes. (To be fair, they also explained that the sun was in their eyes and the dog ate their homework.)

Better to pass what could be passed now, and secure employment rights for gays and lesbians, than risk indefinitely delaying passage, all the while exposing many gay people to discrimination from which they might otherwise have been protected.

"Gender identity" would have to wait until a later date. That argument was a non-starter too. The idea was that ENDA should pass now as is, and later perhaps we could all come back to add "gender identity." No one on our side of the table believed that would be the case. Again, it was classic HRC misdirection. They weren't actually offering to *do* all the heavy lifting and years of lobbying this strategy would require.

And they knew was well as we did that a stand-alone national bill to benefit transsexuals and crossdressers would have politicians on *both* sides of the aisle just salivating for a chance to vote it down. The approach would generate about as much political lift as a flying brick.

In fact, in most states that have tried this strategy, it hasn't worked. Once legislatures pass bills on an issue, they typically don't go back to revisit it until years, or even decades, later. And so do organizations. Even for those with the best of intentions, events have a way of overtaking their plans. For instance, once a hate crimes bill passed, the community expected to pivot to ENDA.

But gay marriage court cases stepped in, and sucked all the oxygen and energy out of the room politically, philanthropically and media-wise for the better part of the next decade. So the *"Wait-we'll-come-*

back-for-you (really)" gambit was a complete non-starter also. Again, pretty much a slap in the face.

Not thinking very clearly, I let my temper go making all these points, and a few more. HRC's Executive Director responded by asking me, "Why us, why don't you go bother NOW?" (Actually, we had— more on this later.) Yelling back, I asked her, "No! No! The *moral* question is not: Wh*y are we bothering HRC?* The *moral* question is: *Why do we have to!"*

Things kind of rolled downhill from there. It was good moral outrage. It may even have been good political theater. But I'm not sure it was the most effective tactic. The distance between our two visions of what constituted the gay community was striking. It once again brought us back to trans-inclusion's central question: *Whose bus is this?* Through all this, I keep making eye contact with Nancy, and she's looking at me, and neither of us is looking very happy.

At one point, she excused herself to go make some photocopies. Sensing an opening, I followed her to the copy room. Looking her in the eye, I asked, "Why don't you guys *like* us?" There followed a very intense and intensely personal 15-minute conversation over the Xerox machine.

When we returned, the HRC folks asked for a break and went and caucused among themselves, with Nancy obviously taking a lead role. A truly good-hearted person, and one who cared about individual people as well as issues, Nancy functioned, as the head of HRC declared several times, as "our moral conscience." Over many years of working with her, and her organization, I was to repeatedly find this was true. But it also was kind of amazing.

Unlike the Task Force, HRC had no Policy Institute. I don't think they even *did* policy. They simply did what they thought was politically necessary.

After a marathon four-hour negotiation, they agreed to issue the following statement:

- *HRC has made a commitment to work with representatives of a spectrum of the transgendered community with a specific focus on hate crimes.*
- *HRC has also committed to assist transgender representatives with **an amendment strategy in the context of ENDA.*** [emphasis added]

153

- *The strategy does not include re-introduction of the current ENDA; the language of the current bill remains as is.*
- *Both groups will work in good faith to continue dialogue and to build coalition in the context of ending violence and discrimination against this community.*

The Right Side of History

No one knew what the key phrase, "an amendment strategy in the context of ENDA" meant. It was another fig leaf, something to postpone, rather than resolve, debate. I suspect that to us it meant, "HRC will craft and propose an amendment and work to get it passed." To them it probably meant, "We will craft and propose an amendment and work to get it passed; but don't expect us to lift a finger until ENDA has passed without you in it."

Yet it was still a big step forward, and a major concession. Chai started working with Dana and others to draft an amendment. (To her credit, and after conferring with transgender lawyers she liked and respected, she also rethought her position in a highly public series of papers and statements. Not everyone has the intellectual courage to do this.)

Just to provide a sense of context, HRC at that point was about a $34 million organization, with 70 full-time professional staffers. We were a few dozen grassroots amateurs, with no budget, and no staff. But as Archimedes once famously said, "Give me high heels and a place to stand, and I will move the world."

We had found our point of leverage, and we'd been able to move one of the biggest and best funded civil rights groups in the country on a core political stance in under a year. For the first time trans-activists had coordinated a concerted, sustained and ultimately successful nationwide demonstration on behalf of their political rights.

It was a far cry from the "conference culture," or for that matter the green woods of Michigan or even the empty flatlands of Falls City. The fact that we were able to succeed with what would today be termed "asymmetrical warfare"—few troops and fewer resources—should have told them something: they were on the wrong side of history.

Their traditionally very conservative donor base no doubt backed their trans-exclusive position, but the community at large didn't. The tide was running out. The narrative and the tide of history was steadily swinging, as it almost always does, towards inclusion. The fact that there had to be a "tide" at all on this issue was remarkable in itself, an artifact of identity politics.

We'd not only been *in* the movement, the drag and transpeople like Sylvia Rivera and Marsha P. Johnson who rioted at the Stonewall Inn *were* the movement back in the 1970s. But then we were whitewashed out, as the movement redefined itself narrowly around sexual orientation and mainstream acceptability.

Identity politics forces you into this awkward positions of telling people whom you see in the bars, go to events with, who are sitting in your office and feel that you are one movement that ...umm... no, we're not. You're on your own.

But it would take HRC another two decades to realize that. In the intervening years they would repeatedly shoot themselves in the foot on this issue, until finally arriving at a conclusion that was obvious to nearly everyone else.

In retrospect, the issue of trans-inclusion turned out to be more than a matter of practical politics. It was one of the great moral questions the movement faced over the last 30 years.

It was one that became practically inevitable from the moment the movement narrowed its focus to securing sexual orientation rights for gays and lesbians. Adding "bisexual" later came relatively easy, because it fit the existing frame. But addressing issues of gender identity was much, much more challenging to the whole model.

Movements of oppressed people often start out with the moral high ground. As they begin accumulating power and legitimacy, they begin facing their own moral dilemmas. Especially in identity-based movements, this often comes in the form of what to do with those excluded or marginalized bodies seeking inclusion, or with more complex bodies that don't fit neatly within defined identity lines.

If gay rights has faced at least two great moral issues, one has been trans-inclusion. The other has been race. It's past time to finally solve the other.

Epilogue

In the summer of 1996, the head of HRC inserted testimony about Brandon Teena's murder and transgender violence into the hearings for the Hate Crimes Statistics Act reauthorization. It wasn't exactly a public statement before Congress, but it did fulfill a promise made in our meeting.

Barely two years later, in September 1997, Executive Director Kerry Lobel of the National Gay and Lesbian Task Force announced a new and expanded mission of "gay, lesbian, bisexual and transgender." It was one of the first national organizations to do so, and a key weathervane that the era of LGB-but-not-T was at last coming to an end. Along with former ED Urvashi Vaid, Kerry had always been very progressive on trans issues, in 1999 personally leading 1,500 attendees out of its annual Creating Change conference to protest the abuse of a transgender woman by Oakland police on the street outside.

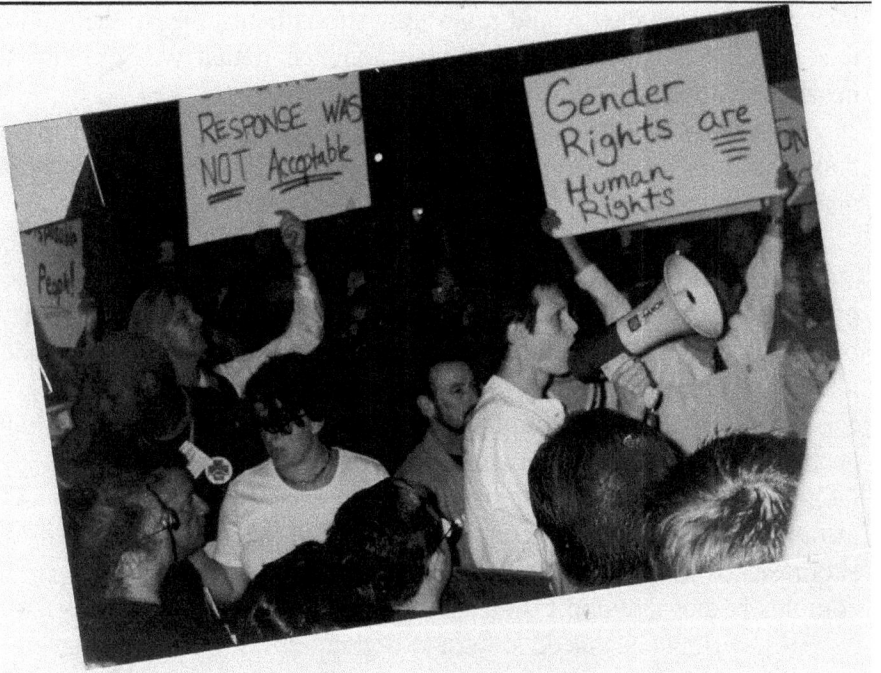

Riki addresses marchers at 1999 Creating Change to protest Oakland police abuse of a transgender woman outside the conference hotel

In 1998, HRC, GenderPAC and the National Center for Lesbian Rights (NCLR) sponsored a "Gender & the Law" meeting of all the leading legal groups (Lambda, NOW Legal Defense Fund, ACLU, etc.)

to discuss a litigation strategy for gender identity rights, but no clear conclusion was ever reached. What did become clear was that none of the organizations present was prepared to fund a long and expensive litigation strategy, leaving ENDA as the only viable path for achieving workplace protections.

Nancy Beurmeyer ended up working closely with GenderPAC's Dana Priesing on the successive Lobby Days, providing advice, training participants and providing briefing papers on pending bills. It was Nancy who suggested GenderPAC start its own "gender identity" Congressional Diversity Pledge, like HRC's on "sexual orientation," as a way to track support on the Hill and also as a good "ask" for Members who wanted to be known as supportive.

In 2005, Lambda Legal finally expanded its mission to include transgender. GLAAD would follow suit in 2007. Today (particularly as the right targets transpeople in dozens of states) transgender cases now make up 25% of its docket.

Sometimes life is stranger than fiction. In 2009, the then head of HRC met my partner's identical twin sister, and they fell in love. I attended their commitment ceremony (they have since separated). This taught me another key lesson of Washington: it's a very small town. So watch out who you yell at in meetings. One day you will either end up dating them or else they will end up one of your in-laws.

Working with HRC—practically a requirement for getting anything done in DC—had its downside. Dysfunction was not uncommon in the trans community, combined with the outrage and near-paranoia about HRC that was never far from the surface. In 1999, Nancy, Dana and I visited some of the friendlier Congressional offices prior to Lobby Day. ENDA was not even coming up for a vote that year, but Hate Crimes was moving, and we had significant support from everyone we visited, so we decided to focus Lobby Day's firepower on that. But one grassroots group prone to conspiracy theories and wild hyperbole (a toxic combination common in the online trans-community) portrayed this as GenderPAC "pre-lobbying" our own event in order to destroy and undermine the highlight of our own political calendar, which had cost thousands of dollars and hundreds of hours to convene.

The presumed motivation was that we were "in bed with HRC" or "had been bought off by HRC"—probably both. One dim bulb, hearing that I had bought a postage stamp size condo in South Beach, put two and two together and got 22—proof that I had been "paid off" by HRC. With this kind of hysteria, Nazi analogies can never be far behind. Sure enough, a posting went up on their website comparing the head of HRC to Adolf Eichmann. One keyboard activist even complied a 35 page (!) "forensic report." This was a more impressive achievement than it might appear, considering it documented something that did not exist. In a way, it was a preview of today's right-wing sound chamber, in which online media allows people to create their own alternative reality, and then to blog and interview each other about it endlessly. Of course, this didn't faze HRC, but it played hell with our work for years.

In 2000, the head of HRC was invited to give a speech to the Democratic National Convention, mentioning the "gay, lesbian, bisexual and transgender" community before a primetime audience of tens of millions. Doubtless, for many it was the first time they'd heard the word, or that four-part description of the community. It was a small, long-awaited step. But HRC continued to stumble over ENDA. In 2004, their Board voted to support only an ENDA that includes "gender identity." Following that, they recruited well-known activist Donna Rose to be the first openly transgender member of their board, and she eventually became national co-chair for Diversity. Retired DC eye surgeon Dana Beyer joined HRC's more community-based Board of Governors. In 2007, at Southern Comfort, HRC's new President Joe Solmonese pledged before an audience of 900 that it would support only inclusive ENDAs and oppose any legislation that left transpeople and others who suffered because of their gender expression behind. In doing so, he was also bowing to the reality that 400+ national, state and local groups had organized United ENDA, launched by the Task Force, that had declared it would actively oppose a sexual orientation-only bill. So we had won...

... But not really. Less than a month later, citing "the fear about having a bruising discussion on the floor—what about transgender people in workplace, in schools, what about this, what about that?"— Rep. Barney Frank pulled an inclusive version and replaced it with the sexual orientation-only bill. (Barney was known to be obsessed with the issue of trannies in the showers as the ultimate vote-killer. Once Gina and I walked into a meeting with him, and before we were even seated, he started yelling at us about transpeople, ENDA and bathrooms. His opposition was a huge obstacle because few Members were prepared to get to the left of Barney on gay rights.)

HRC, perhaps not wanting to turn its back on the opportunity or piss off Barney, announced it would not support the bill... but it would not oppose it either. Joe confessed to "misspeaking" at Southern Comfort (probably similar to Janet Jackson's Super Bowl now-infamous "wardrobe malfunction"). The trans-community more or less exploded—this being the slow-motion consummation of all the fear and distrust it already had about HRC. Donna resigned. Dana was kicked off the Board of Governors after publicly supporting Donna. ENDA never became law.

With ENDA permanently stalled, the struggle over employment non-discrimination rights and the inclusion of "gender identity" moved to the states. Many local gay rights groups adopted the *Wait-we'll-come-back-for-you (really)"* strategy. The owner-editor of the *Washington Blade* and other gay newspapers put the case succinctly in print, "[the] trans-or-bust strategy... would take "the most politically palatable form of protection (the workplace) but saddle it with the least politically palatable category (gender identity)."

He went on to accuse community leaders of "'trans-jacking' ENDA and the whole movement." However, most LGBT activists now consider the strategy of "sexual orientation now, gender identity later" to be discredited. For instance, New York State adopted "sexual orientation" only protections in 2002; trans groups were told the bill would be amended. Yet, although "gender identity" amendments have been introduced every year since 2003, they have failed each time. And New York is a classically Blue state that votes reliably Democratic in national elections. Finally in 2015, Gov. Andrew Cuomo directed the State Division of Human Rights to issue regulations reinterpreting a 1945 law banning discrimination "because of sex," (reinforcing Chai Feldblum's theory). However, the policy is vulnerable to being overturned by any future governor.

On 2009, President Obama nominated Chai Feldblum as Commissioner of the EEOC (Equal Employment Opportunity Commission), a federal regulatory body which interprets and enforces federal laws against discrimination. She was finally in a position to put into effect her long-held belief that laws forbidding discrimination "because of sex"—*i.e.*, because of gender stereotypes—included transgender people. In an historic case in April, 2012, she had her chance. Mia Macy had successfully applied for a job at Bureau of

Alcohol, Tobacco, Firearms and Explosives. However, when she transitioned to female, her job offer evaporated. Macy sued, and the EEOC agreed with her. (EEOC rulings are followed by the courts, but do not have the full effect of law.)

As *Huffington Post* columnist and activist Dana Beyer has repeatedly declared to everyone within hearing, the Macy decision meant that "transgender Americans are protected against discrimination in employment in all 50 states under federal law." Yet, presumably because it weakens the argument for passing Congressional legislation, most national gay and transgender rights groups continued to ignore Macy, and made little effort to inform those transpeople suffering from or in fear of job discrimination of it (the Transgender Law Center remains an outstanding exception). Following the highly unusual event of Chai Feldblum publicly chastising the Task Force in print for this omission, most gay and trans groups have come grudgingly around. At this point, one could argue that transgender employees and their gender non-conforming LGB brethren have *better* federal-level workplace protection than many regular gays, lesbians and bisexuals.

In September 2014, President Chad Griffin became the second HRC President in ten years to keynote at Southern Comfort. He began by explaining that as he attended HRC's Columbus gala, the annual TransOhio Symposium was going on two floors up. "They" were upstairs, and "we" were downstairs... HRC has done wrong by the transgender community in the past, and I am here to formally apologize. I am sorry for the times when we stood apart when we should have been standing together." He then committed HRC to inclusive non-discrimination, starting with a new comprehensive, LGBT civil rights bill that included employment, housing and public accommodations. Specifically addressing Barney's bathroom fixation, he added, "I want to say something here today. Whenever the inevitable chant about 'bathrooms' begins, they're not just attacking you, they're attacking me, they're attacking us. We must hold the line. We will tell the truth. Because these are our lives, and this is the moral thing to do." Almost exactly 20 years after our first meeting, a President of HRC had finally asked the *moral question,* and then answered it.

Chapter 7—Feminists, Leatherqueens and Intersex Activists

The Skunk at the Picnic

When HRC's Executive Director had asked why we didn't go bother NOW (National Organization for Women), she'd unintentionally echoed my own thinking. In fact, we *had* been after NOW for some time. I thought it was important to bring feminists along. Anything relating to tearing down gender walls should have engaged feminists and our struggle with rigid binaries should have dovetailed with theirs.

Plus, gender non-conformity challenged core values about what it meant to be a man or woman, ones that were nearly primal in nature. And we were going to challenge all this and create a new world order with what... maybe a few hundred activists? We needed all the friends we could get.

NOW was an obvious first stop. Why women's rights and gay rights had ever been separated had always been a mystery to me. You'd think lesbians would have been an obvious point of intersection. But not really. Gay rights had always been more about gay (white) men, and feminism about straight (white) women. And they went off in different directions to fight the same gender system and seldom spoke. Lesbian rights, alas, ended up marginalized in both movements.

But, on an issue like gender non-conformity, feminists should have been natural allies. A woman who aspires to masculine roles and privileges was frequently mocked or dismissed as mannish, overbearing, unfeminine or simply a "bitch"—particularly if she eschewed high heels, long hair and make-up.

And let's face it, historically, American feminism has had more than its share of strong, independent lesbian butches, many of them movement leaders. As we used to say in the 70s, "Feminism in the theory, lesbianism is the practice." It wasn't right, but it wasn't far off either.

So feminists should have been natural allies, but they weren't. In fact, gender non-conformity and NOW had a long and troubled history. It began with butch-y dykes who wore short hair, flat shoes and mannish clothing—and sometimes even suits and ties—who were tailor-made to set off every gender alarm bell a middle class feminist had about Nature, nurture, motherhood and the role of women.

And the crossdressers only made matters worse. A very small number showed up at NOW events and conferences, hoping to find a sympathetic space. To them, of course, NOW made sense. They saw their issue as a feminist one. And it was.

Feminism was based around a deep commitment to challenging traditional binary gender stereotypes and the system of privileges that went with it, one that kept women and all other feminine people (crossdressers, transwomen, effeminate gay men) subordinate.

What could be more revolutionary than a man in a dress? This is still true today. In practice, however, the sight of crossdressing men gave most feminists a sense of the galloping "icks."

As with transsexual women later, feminists tended to interpret a man in a dress not as a challenge to gender norms or a profound subversion of masculinity but as aping the worst parts of femininity (all those heels and corsets and rhinestones you know)—and doing it badly. Most feminists didn't want their men in dresses, they wanted manly men who would simply give them their frickin' rights. So crossdressers were seen as almost as bad as drag queens, who were openly making a burlesque of femininity and women for entertainment.

So, rather than seize on crossdressers as potential allies, or something at least worthy of closer feminist examination, they tended to tolerate them with the kind of tight-lipped smiles women get when they'd prefer you leave and hope you won't use the Ladies Room on the way out (I get these all the time).

What the 'F' Stood For

Transsexuals were still a new thing for many feminists—there were hardly any of us in the 1980s—but we did not exactly expect to be welcomed with open arms. And we weren't. My future partner, Gina, who had been Action Vice President of NOW/NJ, suggested I try for the position of Action VP of NOW/NY, which was vacant. With my political background, this seemed a good fit. However, the head of NOW/NY quickly informed me that I was welcome to participate only as a male ally, nothing more.

Since she insisted on addressing me as a man, I responded by putting on my deepest masculine voice. Our meeting went downhill from there, with a lot of yelling, none of it by me. I thought this was interesting—apparently I could be mis-gendered and told I *was* a man, but if I actually *sounded* like a man in response, I was being disrespectful of women and displaying my deep-seated, much dreaded Male Energy. On our way out, she asked me for a hug. For me, that was American feminism in a nutshell.

A few of us, however, wrangled an invitation to a national presentation in NYC on women's rights. Who should turn out to be the lead presenter but NOW's smart, unflappable new President who lately seemed to be everywhere: on the network news, getting quoted in the *Times*, going head-to-head with O'Reilly on Fox News.

On our way out, one of our group asked why we'd bother to fly in and what we'd accomplished. I snapped back, *"She* was what we accomplished—that was *Patricia Fucking Ireland."*

Indeed it was. Years later, hearing this story, Patricia would respond, "I always wondered what the 'F' stood for." I pushed my way through the crowd afterwards and managed to stick my hand out and introduce myself and our issue. She gave me a card and encouraged me to keep in touch. More than anything it was Patricia's openness—ahead of her time and her movement—that encouraged us to keep trying.

WE NEED YOUR HELP!

N.O.W. has been historically committed to inclusion, to the right of all people who are gender oppressed to freedom from employment & economic discrimination, and most importantly, to freedom from violence.

BRANDON TEENA was a transman man from Lincoln, Nebraska who was raped and beaten to "prove" he was a women. When he went to the police, they failed to protect him. Five days later, his assailants returned and killed him. *Brandon's murder was part and parcel of the system of gender oppression*.

MARSHA P. JOHNSON was one of NYC's best-known drag and trans activists over 20 years, dating to the days of the Stonewall Rebellion. She was last seen being harassed by teenageers near the Christopher Street piers, then later found floating dead in the river nearby. Police refused to investigate, stating there was no reason to suspect a bias crime, or *even* any crime at all. *Marsha's murder was part and part of the system of gender oppression.*

LESLIE FEINBERG was a self-identified "stone butch" and growing up in the working-class bars of Buffalo. Leslie's story is told in Stone Butch Blues: the queerbashing, police rousts, bogus arrests, beatings in police back rooms *Leslie's vicious oppression was part and parcel of the system of gender oppression.*

Gender oppression strives to keep _all of us_ in our place. As transgender people, we have paid with our lives and our loved ones for daring to contest that system. The same gender hierarchy which says "Biology IS destiny" will go to any lengths to keep _all of us_ imprisoned and powerless.

The heart of a feminist politics is the struggle against gender oppression.

We Need Your Help. We're asking NOW to address the needs & concerns of its transgender members. Help us generate this dialog. Talk to us. Ask your chapter about its trans policiy. Remember those of us who have fallen in the same struggle.

Flier for NOW National Convention trans-inclusion effort

Be It Resolved

The problem with going after NOW was they did everything by resolution—with national leadership only considering resolutions after they'd been passed by several of the state chapters. This meant there was no central point of attack, no leadership you could engage and hope to win over as with HRC. You had to start at the bottom and work from the grassroots up.

So it was that in the Spring of 1995, I found myself in Jersey City, New Jersey, huddled with Terry McCorkell of Monmouth Ocean Transgender Alliance, NOW/NJ Lesbian Rights Task Force director Wendy Berger, and NOW/NJ's newly-minted Action Vice-President Gina Reiss (who would later become GenderPAC's first paid staffer bringing that organization to life).

Terry was one of those brave transgender people in NOW's orbit then. Equally at home in the feminist, gay, and trans communities, Terry was a quiet, determined grassroots activist who always seemed to show up just where they were needed and never said "no" to a plea for help.

Wendy was an old friend: an accomplished chef, wicked smart, always ready with a smile. She was an old-style lefty organizer and activist—a true *bleeding-heart liberal*, just like me.

They proposed to introduce a two-part resolution into the NOW/NJ State Convention affirming the rights of transgendered and transsexual people. They also introduced me to two of the most astonishing people I'd ever seen, two identical twin sisters who were so bright, so sparking, I could hardly tear my eyes away. One was Gina. She was then Wendy's partner. It would be five long years until their relationship burned down and they separated as friends, when I could tentatively approach her for a date. (Today she is my life partner and the mother of my daughter, DJ.)

(left-to-right) Riki, Gina Reiss, Leslie Feinberg, and Wendy Berger at NOW Convention after successful Trans-Inclusion campaign

After a lot of discussion, our resolution was passed, almost unanimously. But it was a two-part resolution. Always thinking ahead, they decided to bypass other states and had written the second part to call for our resolution to be introduced at NOW's upcoming National Convention in Columbus, OH.

That summer, a horde (a pride, a dread, a covey?) of Menace activists and friends descended on the Convention to educate, run around in black T-shirts and carry petitions calling for a trans-inclusion. In a sign of things to come, one of the earliest signatories (thanks to Tony of TOPS) was none other than Ellie Smeal, a past-president of NOW.

Smiling brightly, we swarmed anyone we could as they rushed between meetings, or headed off to meals, explaining our issue and asking for their support. It was especially important that Tony was there. I don't think many of them had seen a transman or even considered the masculine side of the issue. There were about 700 attendees, and we got almost half to sign our petition.

NOW being NOW, the conference never got beyond debate on the first few resolutions, and the remainder were tabled for the National Board for a later date. Ms. Smeal and several key national staffers pledged privately to work for passage, and the National

Membership Coordinator requested a trans-inclusion information packet be mailed to all 50 state chapters, which was progress.

On the last day, NOW attendees staged a march to the State Capital Building. Our small contingent made sure to enter the square early and mount the steps facing the Capital Building. Phyllis Frye unfurled her ubiquitous 30-foot "Transgendered and Proud and We Vote" banner.

If the last part of that sentiment was not particularly compelling, there was no doubt it made a great visual, and her timing was perfect. Entering marchers, seeing trans-activists standing in solidarity in black T-shirts behind the banner with our right fists high in the air, raised a spontaneous cheer. Our support was definitely growing, particularly among young women.

WHEREAS,
 gender discrimination is at the heart of feminist politics;
WHEREAS,
 the transgendered and transexual communities confront the same gender system that oppresses women, and therefore are the target of marginalization, loss of medical care and economic and civil rights;
WHEREAS,
 there is a lack of understanding and information on the issue;
WHEREAS,
 this resolution was introduced at the 1994 New Jersey NOW State Conference by the Lesbian Rights Task Force and unanimously passed therein,

THEREFORE
 let it be resolved that NOW adopt a policy that supports the lives and identities of transgendered and transexual people;

LET IT BE FURTHER RESOLVED
 that NOW chapters examine current policies and practices that discriminate against the transgender and transexual community.

***Resolution passed at NOW national conference
on transgender inclusion.***

But we were not out of the woods yet. For the next two years NOW chewed on our issue, but refused to take a bite. The resolution was reintroduced over and over, but never got voted on. I finally came to the realization that this was no accident. The National Board tended to schedule those resolutions that would go through quickly at the head of the queue.

Contentious issues, like trans-inclusion, would get put in the back of the long list of pending business, and never make it before the convention attendees to an open vote (which we now believed we could win).

The Future is Men with Vaginas?

In the meantime, Wendy, Gina and NOW/NJ President Bear Atwood worked hard to get other state NOW chapters to pass trans-inclusion resolutions, both to build consensus and to build pressure on the National leaders to finally call for a vote.

NOW Lesbian Rights Coordinator Kimberlee Ward was also working for us on the inside, bending ears and arms and growing support. The breakthrough came with the invitation from Bear Atwood to activists from GenderPAC and other groups to address the NOW State Coordinators Conference in San Francisco.

As more State Presidents got behind us, Patricia began putting her weight behind the resolution as well, personally pushing for passage. This was not as easy as it sounds. Although she was President, NOW's board was huge and unwieldy, with many factions and a lot of old stalwart feminists. To say they had minds of their own would be a huge understatement.

Unfortunately, this took the form of inviting me to address the full board during one of its annual meetings. For reasons which now escape me, I thought it would be in good taste to remind them of NOW's purges of lesbian and bisexual women in 1969 and their confrontations with the Lavender Menace.

So I wore my black Menace T-shirt, with its blood-dripping red letters. I had short hair, absolutely no make-up, and probably looked about as much like a man with bosoms as possible. The fact was, I was getting very tired of pleading with one group after another for our inclusion. You showed them all your wounds and pain. You tried to work their guilt and goodwill. And you tried to show how your issues were really their issues. All these identities arguing with one another about who belonged and who would represent whom. And I wasn't going to plead my woman-ness before a room of old-line, national-level feminist leaders, damn it.

Patricia introduced me and then sat down, looking tolerantly and encouragingly up. As I wrote in *Read My Lips:* "There were only two ways to go about this. Way One relies on liberal guilt coupled with earnest appeals to good old-fashioned liberal values like tolerance and acceptance, i.e., you should include us because it's the moral thing to do, we're so hated, and transwomen suffer many of the same oppressions of the patriarchy.

"Way One depends on your listener's goodwill and well-honed consciences, and it often works—but it's no fun. Who enjoys feeling guilty? I'd much rather feel bitchy. So let's choose Way Two.

"Way Two consists of building a post-modern argument that is so insubordinate and hopelessly perverse that it undermines the paradigm that created the issue of trans-inclusion and made a presentation about it necessary in the first place. Way Two is a lot more fun.

"Looking around the room at all those powerful, serious and intimidating women, I said, 'Many of you are no doubt wondering why a man with a vagina is standing here lecturing you on where American feminism should go...'—I looked down at Patricia then and noticed she was now searching vigorously for a good vein in her wrist to open— 'but consider for a moment that men with vaginas are what gender looks like when it's de-regulated, and so my presence here today is a sign of your success and not your failure.'"

I don't know if it was a winning argument, but I sang them eight-bars of Judith Butler straight out of out *Gender Trouble,* with a chorus in four-part harmony thrown in: rigid gender regimes oppressed *all* women, gays, transgender people, crossdressers, effeminate boys and lesbian women—and were intricately connected to issues like race and class.

Let's talk about that first, and then trans-inclusion will be beside the point. As I said, I don't know that it was a winning argument, but it was worth trying. I got a decent round of applause on the way out but couldn't really gauge if I'd had any impact or not. At least for once, however, I had challenged people's minds rather than pled for their sympathy.

A few months later, we finally had enough grassroots support from state chapters to get our resolution in front of the next NOW National Convention in Memphis, TN. We used the measure originally passed unanimously at NOW/NJ's State Conference that had languished through two Conferences. It was finally passed and became a NOW national policy.

This was July, 1997, only months before Kerry Lobel and the Task Force became the first major national gay organization to expand its mission—more than a decade before HRC, Lambda Legal or GLAAD would do the same.

However, unlike HRC, NOW wasn't expected to actually *do* anything with the change; it was just a policy they passed. They never put any energy behind it or any action on it. They were like that—a lot of policy but very little through-put. In many ways, almost the direct opposite of HRC. But I always wondered if it wasn't the presence of a strong feminist analysis that allowed them to grasp inclusion so much sooner than most national gay groups.

The gay rights movement, while I rejoice in its strengths and progress, long ago abandoned being analytical and self-reflective. There are reams written on queer theory—but none of it is absorbed by the gay leadership, who see themselves as engaged in an entirely political struggle for civil rights that is not, and need not be, informed by a theoretical framework. (The Task Force's Policy Institute is an outstanding exception to this.)

This is also, I fear, why the mainstream national gay movement continues to lack any real strong engagement with issues of race and class. A grounding in theory combined with a strong intersectional analysis that comprehends the interlocking nature of these oppressions would have saved them that major failing. It is a mistake the old radical lefty founders of the early Gay Liberation Front did not make, and would not make today.

LeatherQueers & Sex Radicals

In fact, once you start thinking about gender theoretically as a social regime that constrains what we can be or do, you also start thinking about sex, which is closely aligned. For gender displays are how we communicate not only our sex, but our sexual desires, our availability to fulfill them, and our desired role. There's a reason it's called "gaydar."

I had been working on writing my first murder mystery around this time and desperately needed help. Having written only nonfiction, I found myself stymied by strange things like plotting and dialogue. A friend suggested I might talk with sci-fi writer Susan Wright—a supersmart and accomplished sci-fi author—and her long-time husband Kelly. We got to discussing how the trans community was finally breaking out politically, and a recent article in *The Economist* that had drolly noted that in Germany, even the S/M community was a recognized and respected voting block (oh, those Germans!).

I told her the BDSM community here needed to do the same. If men with sex changes could organize, practically anyone could. Perhaps more seriously, many of the strictures and punishments S/M folks faced were the same, and for the same reasons.

Anything the shrinks and the medical establishment didn't like they called abnormal, and made a disease. Then laws were passed against it, and employment discrimination came along in the bargain. Because of this, there are laws against entirely harmless if somewhat unusual activities that consenting adults do for pleasure in their own bedrooms. Thus consenting adults assume a number of serious risks, including being labeled with a sexual pathology and/or prosecuted under ancient "obscenity" laws many states still have.

In fact, simply being outed means automatic job loss in most jurisdictions, where alternative sexualities are still considered perverse and shameful. The logic seems to be that you had to be some kind of mega-deviant to get off on someone hurting you, or on hurting someone else (even if it was all totally consensual and sexy and safe).

Perhaps because of this, in some communities, S/M triggers a kind of sex panic on the part of authorities. More than one couple has lost access to their own kids when accused of practicing S/M and a divorcing parent who can accuse their spouse of practicing S/M is still likely to be awarded full child custody on that account alone. Remember, America's second most populous state still enforced a law against owning more than six dildos until a court overturned it in 2004 (Texas' Attorney General appealed the ruling).

Nature clearly loves diversity—only bio-diverse ecosystems are stable. But our medico-psychiatric establishment clearly fears and loathes it, and is ready to pathologize anything that moves, if it threatens their cherished ideals of total gender and sexual uniformity.

So Susan agreed to form a new organization, but wanted to call S/M community leaders together to discuss it. I just wanted to announce the darn thing. Leadership and innovation hardly ever happens by committee. Someone always has to take the first step. Then (if you read the situation and the timing correctly) people come running.

But big steps into the political unknown never come out of a big caucus of people—in fact, quite the contrary. We went back and forth like this for several weeks. Finally she reluctantly agreed... but only after checking with her own group—NY SM Activists. In the end they helped us bring on board BDSM groups in the coming months.

I was overjoyed. But, as two writers, we both were stuck on what language to use in our announcement. Any term that actually mentioned sadism or masochism was a complete non-starter that would make possible allies in legislatures, courts, and the civil rights community go running for the hills at the first mention.

What we needed was a soothing phrase that said everything while saying nearly nothing. I suggested "alternative sexualities," which some folks had begun using, and we went with it. The second problem was the name. Something like Americans United for Kinky Sex, or the National Center for Whips & Chains was probably not going to fly.

In fact, we needed to avoid anything about sex *per se,* and focus on civil rights and the principle of keeping the laws out of consenting adults' bedrooms (just how early gay rights advocates had pled their case). I suggested the National Coalition for Sexual Freedom.

national coalition for sexual freedom inc.
Logo of the National Coalition for Sexual Freedom

We had some cards and stationery printed up with Susan as the Executive Director, and we put out a press release announcing the formation of this new group. In it Susan declared, "We are people who lose our jobs, our children, and sometimes our lives because of our sexuality or our sexual preference. All we are seeking are equal rights." And we were off.

Well, *they* were off. In 1997, the first six groups that joined this new organization were many of the community lynchpins: New York SM Activists, National Leather Association—International, Gay Male S/M Activists, The Eulenspiegel Society, Black Rose, and the Society of Janus.

But while I had always found S/M—sorry, "alternative sexualities"—interesting and racy, and fully supported practitioners' political rights, it was not my kink. (More about that later. Actually, no: nothing about that, ever, at *any* time).

Granted, I was probably missing out on something. But being transsexual created more than enough complexity in my bedroom, without my having to go import additional wrinkles. After the first meeting of other S/M organizations I quietly receded into the background.

Although GenderPAC continued to cooperate with NCSF whenever we could, and we even shared some major donors, it was not a fight my board would be pleased to see us taking on. But I always kept tabs on the organization and watched its growth with a certain pride.

One in Every 1,500

The same year that Susan and I were thinking of launching NCSF, I met Cheryl Chase. She was kind of a legendary figure—I'd heard a lot about her, but there had been few sightings of Cheryl in the wild, and I kept thinking one day we'd run into one another.

One night I was doing a reading at a bar in New York, and she walked up and introduced herself. I was fascinated. We started talking, kept talking, ended up sitting on the stoop of a brownstone into the darkening evening and talked some more.

Cheryl Chase was her nom de guerre. She had been born a healthy little baby. But as she puts it, "they freaked out continuously for three days (keeping my mother sedated the whole time) because they could not determine my sex." Finally they decided to label her a boy. Until, that is, when he was about 18 months old, his doctors decided that his penis was too small—whatever that meant—and that he was "really" a girl.

As Cheryl put it eloquently and succinctly, "Intersexuality is a psychiatric emergency on the part of the doctors, treated by cutting into the body of the patient." So Charlie's small penis (or, if you prefer, enlarged clitoris) was surgically removed in its entirety to make her better resemble a "normal" female.

Then they hid all evidence of the procedure, and told Cheryl's mother she must always lie and say nothing ever happened, even if and when Cheryl confronted her with the facts—again following medical protocol. The wholly unnecessary surgery also removed a lot of erotic sensation along with her ability to orgasm.

By the time she was grown, Cheryl found herself catastrophically depressed. She knew something major had happened to her physically and that whatever is was was wrong, but she couldn't find out what.

Cheryl is one of the smartest, most accomplished people I've ever met. Attractive (in any gender), a very talented programmer, someone who learned Japanese so she could code in two cultures, she told me it was while on assignment in Japan that she came close to killing herself: depressed, alone and convinced she was the only one who had undergone such experiences.

So she decided to go looking for others who might be like her. In 1993, she announced the first advocacy organization of its kind—the Intersex Society of North America or ISNA—hoping that by doing so others of her kind would see it and come running. They did. She found that she was not alone, and also that almost single-handedly, she had started a new movement.

Only two years later, she gathered everyone who was able to come for what must have been the first gathering of intersex people ever. It was filmed for a remarkable documentary in which they shared their stories. It's called, *Hermaphrodites Speak*! It was an amazing act of courage, political theater, and street activism, all rolled into one.

Intersexuality (which some people now refer to as those with "Disorders of Sex Development") had been around forever. It was one of the many diverse things that Nature came up with. Perhaps as many as one in every 1,500 or so births could be classified as intersex. While some fraction do have abnormalities with medical implications, most of the rest do not.

In fact, the vast majority of infants historically diagnosed as intersex are otherwise unremarkable babies who happen to have extra-large clitorises. But in the 1950s, like so many things related to sex (I'm looking at you, Gender Identity Disorder), intersexuality was pathologized.

Pediatric doctors suddenly decided it was a "medical condition" that should be "cured" through surgery. This meant cutting down the organ so it more closely resembled a "normal" female clitoris. (Up until the 1950s, as with Cheryl, they just cut off the organ entirely. Regardless of the procedure—and surgery has advanced in this area—these are all still entirely cosmetic procedures inflicted for the comfort of cisgender society.)

Needless to say, extra-large penises are never, ever presented for cutting down, because unlike large clitorises they're not... well, yucky. Not much was cured, but one unexpected consequence has been tens of thousands of traumatized kids.

And, since doctors instructed their parents to deny their children's medical and gender history forever to help their new gender identity solidify, many of these kids had disturbing memories (not to mention physical scars) that even their parents denied to their faces (Something which DSD advocates are quick to point out is done out of love for their own good).

So a second consequence for many people with DSD was a consuming sense of shame, a fear that they were crazy and a conviction they must be isolated freaks—all of which in some ways was even worse than the original physical injury.

Possessing the Secret of Cheryl

ISNA set out to change all that. This may not have been strictly a transgender issue, but in many ways it paralleled issues of gender identity and the enforcement of binary genders. I proposed an alliance.

So far most of ISNA's work had been reaching and recruiting new people, and talking to the medical establishment. But arrogance is like a mental blindfold, and the medical establishment seldom changes anything without being pushed, hard.

For that we needed two things. First, we needed publicity. The public knew nothing about this issue. Hell, I hardly knew about the issue, and gender activism was my life. So a lot of public education was definitely going to be needed. Second, to get publicity, we needed an easy name for what we were talking about.

This was around the time that the campaign around Female Genital

Mutilation (FGM), was taking off, led by author Alice Walker and detailed in her groundbreaking book, *Possessing the Secret of Joy*. For the first time, Congress had passed legislation outlawing FGM. (Sadly, female anti-FGM activists tended to dismiss intersex issues as a "distraction." (Is identity politics fucked up or what?)

I reasoned that, if what they were describing was "Female Genital Mutilation," then what we were describing must be "Intersex Genital Mutilation." I tried the phrase out on Cheryl, she agreed, and once we began using it, the phrase caught.

The issue of publicity was a thorny one. While it was mostly a dark corner of pediatric medical, there were already a number of academic and medical articles on IGM. But these did nothing to inform the general public.

We didn't want some yawner of an article buried deep in a peer review journal, or some soppy human interest story ("Hermaphrodites— Just Like You and Me, Only Better") in the Times Style section. We needed news coverage—hard news that would help launch intersex into the national debate. I responded with my customary answer to nearly every political problem: go picket someone.

her·maph·ro·dites
WITH ATTITUDE

Hermaphrodites With Attitudes logo

Hermaphrodites With Attitude!

In the winter of 1994, acting mostly alone, Cheryl launched a unique newsletter, cheekily titled, *Hermaphrodites With Attitude!* It simultaneously mocked pediatric medical anxiety around intersex bodies, informed intersex people about their situation, and moved to instigate others to action.

We agreed that HWA would also make a dandy name for a street action group. We used the newsletter design for the T-shirts and all we needed was someone to picket.

In 1996, on Saturday, October 26, the American Association of

Pediatrics obliged by hosting their annual national conference. The AAP was a primary target because they continued to promote IGM as the standard treatment for intersex kids. We immediately put out a release calling activists to come protest.

Twenty-six showed up. I blush to admit that at that first HWA protest, I think there were only one or two intersex folks actually represented—the rest of us were from the Boston chapter of Transexual Menace.

Cheryl herself couldn't make it—so I was in charge, which wasn't entirely comfortable. But, in the end, it came off beautifully. We yelled at doctors going past—who looked spooked at the controversy—waved placards and handed out hundreds of "Keep Your Scalpels OFF Our Bodies" fliers to attendees.

The AAP even helped us by responding (a good sign that you are getting traction) with their own press release, defending the practice and declaring that IGM was in the child's best interests because it prevented future psychological and social trauma.

An AAP spokesman even declared that surgery was by now so improved, that the activists were working from old facts, because IGM had virtually no adverse consequences, comparing it with cosmetic surgery to remove a facial deformity. (I know, I know—the medical arrogance is just breathtaking, even now.)

This was part of the pediatric urologists' and endocrinologists' standard defense—whenever a lone intersex person emerged to contest the terrible and unnecessary things done to their body, doctors would claim that that was then but now, we have much better techniques today (for unnecessarily cutting your genitals, that is).

A Perfect Storm of Gender Disempowerment

These statements by the AAP and their spokespeople got to the root of the problem of IGM. Transsexual individuals can ask for and consent to treatment. Infants diagnosed with Disorders of Sexual Development cannot. This means their doctors must speak for them.

These doctors are overwhelmingly rich, straight, white males who live lives of highly binary privilege—and who are naturally averse to the "messiness" of Nature's natural and predictable gender non-conformity.

This does not mean they are bad people. Quite the contrary.

Most doctors who perform IGM consider it compassionate surgery, and some even charge little or nothing for the procedure. Most of them believe they are doing good (largely because, as with transsexuality, they can't imagine gender non-conformity as anything but debilitating).

They enjoyed the luxury of thinking this because their patients cannot speak for themselves. The parents—naturally terrified when told that their child's genitals are "deformed" and they will suffer a lifetime of gender trauma and confusion—eagerly agreed to nearly anything.

By the time intersex infants were old enough to figure out what happened to them, offer their own input, and, you know… consent to irreversible surgery on their genital area, there's little they can do. As adults, many of them flatly declare that the surgery harmed them terribly, physically, and psychologically. Moreover, knowing that their parents and doctors lied to and deceived them for decades was far more traumatizing than having what Cheryl called "unexpected genitals" ever could be.

Medical malpractice statutes prevented any of them from ever suing over what was done to them decades ago as infants, because their doctors were following the prevailing standards of practice.

It was virtually a perfect storm for complete gender disempowerment. Pediatric surgeons never having to hear from their patients about the harms their procedures inflicted was a crucial part of the problem. Cheryl, by showing up in the flesh to talk about it, along with the first brave group of grown, surgery-survivors to follow her lead into ISNA, slowly began puncturing this model for good.

As did 26 obstreperous genderqueers in black T-shirts yelling slogans outside the conference. At last there was a voice—a counter discourse (a dynamic we were shortly to employ with psychiatrists and Gender Identity Disorder).

This is how a few dozen amateur street activists were able to move an extremely well-funded national organization, representing thousands of doctors, to issue a wholly unnecessary and defensive press release justifying a practice no one was aware they were engaged in—thereby providing much-needed visibility and legitimacy for a protest and an issue that otherwise would have gone completely ignored.

This is what effective asymmetrical street activism looks like.

Even so, we were largely ignored. Media showed up, even camera crews, but there was very little coverage. I think they just didn't know how to deal with the issue yet. And the absence of a substantial intersex presence didn't help.

There's an old PR saw that the first time you pitch a story, a reporter learns the issue. The second time, they get interested. The third time, you're a trend and they finally write your story. Of course, this probably doesn't apply too closely to a World War or Manhattan being struck by a giant meteor. But still…

Pediatricians to Intersexed: ## Drop Dead!

> Pediatricians cut into 5 intersexed infants daily to make their genitals cosmetically "normal." Most lose genital sensation, some will later commit suicide.

Did you know... Pediatric surgeons admit they cut off our genitals to make them *"look better,"* not for any medical reason. Intersexed Genital Mutilation (IGM) is not medicine!

Did you know... Pediatric surgeons operate on *non-complaining intersexed children as young as 2 weeks to 2-3 years of age*? Have they ever heard of "informed consent?"

Did you know... The AAP cravenly takes no stance on surgical removal of infants genitals because a clitoris is *"too large"* or a penis *"too small,"* and it is our bodies that pay the price.

HEY AAP! Get Your Scalpels Off Our Bodies!!

Hermaphrodites With Attitude: We're here. We're queer. So stop cutting into our goddamn bodies!

American Academy of Pediatricians protest flier for Hermaphrodites With Attitude and the Menace

Picketing Intersex—Film at 11!

But it apparently didn't apply to picketing hermaphrodites either. I had been pitching the rise of trans activism to a *Newsweek* reporter. He had written a long breakthrough article and then photographed folks all over the community for a cover article. And then, of course, we got spiked by a senior editor who decided at the last moment that the country wasn't yet ready for trans.

I was furious. And I still had an interested (and very frustrated) reporter. I love talking with these folks—they get all my in-jokes about current events, and I'm such a news junkie myself that I know where the national dialogue is and how to pitch them something that will have traction.

So, I pitched him the hermaphrodites. We had a chance to picket Columbia Presbyterian Hospital in New York City, which was a leading center for IGM and a prestigious high-profile supporter of the practice. I told him the story had everything: infants, tragedy, sex and (most important of all) strong visuals. Plus it would be the first story any national print news outlet had done. How could he resist?

He didn't. I had new HWA T-shirts printed up and overnighted in the day before so they could be photographed, otherwise you just see a groups of folks in street-clothes wandering about. *Newsweek* sent a photographer and my friendly journalist uptown.

ISNA members flew in and the Menace NYC organized. But unlike Boston, the Menace was to stay in the background. This had to be strictly an intersex event—it was their show, not ours.

We ended up with a striking three-page spread in *Newsweek*, complete with one ISNA activist whose surgery had been done at Columbia sobbing on their knees as they laid a memorial wreath at the hospital entrance. The writing was unexpectedly strong too—the reporter really nailed a difficult new issue. Also, CBS had a camera crew there and did a moving piece on Cheryl and our vigil in front of the hospital.

Suddenly everything broke in a rush over the new, ISNA-inspired debate over IGM. On June 17, *Dateline NBC,* a top-ten news show seen by 25-30 million viewers, featured an interview with Cheryl. Included in the segment was footage from the August 1996 demonstration at the American Academy of Pediatricians (AAP) conference in Boston that had never been run.

Following the *Dateline* report, *the San Francisco Chronicle* also ran a piece highlighting IGM. *The New York Times'* excellent science and health writer, Natalie Angier, had run a brief, earlier "trend piece" in 1996 on ISNA and Cheryl. In 1997 she wrote a long news piece titled, "The Debate Over Surgery on Genitals." It opened by directly comparing intersex surgery to Female Genital Mutilation.

Then things got weird. In September, *ABC's Primetime Live* ran a segment titled "Boy or Girl?" Unfortunately, it focused almost entirely on pediatric talking heads, in particular one pro-surgery genital surgeon from Johns Hopkins Hospital (apparently now intersex-phobic as well as trans-phobic)—and virtually no intersex people whatsoever.

He would show Diane Sawyer (and us) slides of intersex infants' genitals, while she tried to guess their "real one" hiding underneath which he "knew" them to be: Here's how I described that surreal exchange (from *Queer Theory/Gender Theory*):

Diane: *That's a male, right?*
Doctor: *Nope. A female. This one?*
Diane: *A female.*
Doctor: *No, a male.*
Diane: *Now this is certainly male. That looks like a small penis.*
Doctor: *Sorry, another female. This one?*
Diane: *Female?*
Doctor: *Male. This?*
Diane: *Male?*
Doctor: *Female.*
Diane: *Shee-it!*

Intersex issues surfaced at Creating Change, and other queer youth-oriented conferences with thousands of annual attendees. The issue, and Cheryl, and the whole community of people with DSD, had come out into the open to stay.

It was an amazing testimony to how one person's vision and desperation could begin to shift a national social dialogue on this most obscure corner of medical malpractice that pathologized a human being's natural physical and sexual development.

Columbia Presbyterian does Intersex* Genital Mutilations

US hospitals cut into 5 intersexed children every day to make their genitals look "normal." Most lose genital sensation. Many are cut at Columbia Presbyterian.

Did you know... According to the American Academy of Pediatricians' intersex children are genitally cut to minimize "**emotional, cognitive, and body image** " problems, and **not for medical reasons**. These children need counseling, not cutting.

Did you know... Columbia cuts *non -complaining children 2-3 years of age.* Ever hear of "informed consent?"

Did you know... Female Genital Mutilation is *not* confined to "primitive" cultures; its alive and well here at Columbia.

Hey Columbia:

Get Your Scalpels *Off* Our Bodies!!!

her·maph′·ro·dites
WITH ATTITUDE

We're not quiet we're not well-behaved & we're *not* going away.

A public service announcement from your local chapter of *Hermaphrodites With Attitude*

Flier for Columbia Hospital protest by Hermaphrodites With Attitude and the Menace

Epilogue

By 2001, Patricia Ireland had left NOW. We stayed in touch and eventually I asked if she would join GenderPAC's Board. She agreed, and the year after that she became co-chair. We had the chance to work closely with her for many years. We remain friends.

The following year, 1998, Susan executed and published the first-ever survey of Violence & Discrimination among members of the SM-leather-fetish communities. It found that 36% had been victims of harassment and 30% have been victims of discrimination—with about one quarter of those losing their jobs and three percent losing custody of their child/children.

Since then, NCSF has continued to flourish, growing from the original six organizations to a network of 50 and successfully forming alliances with mainstream rights groups like Task Force and the ACLU. Susan Wright is now the director of Media Relations. She continues to be a successful author (she has special expertise in Star Trek books), and has her own page on Amazon.

Also in February 2012, the American Psychiatric Association announced a change to the Diagnostic and Statistical Manual (the DSM-5) that governs who is and is not considered mentally disordered. In May 2013 it finally formally changed the diagnostic criteria to differentiate between sexual behaviors (called "paraphilias") and psychiatric disorders ("paraphilic disorders") which are sexual behaviors that are inflicted on non-consenting people and constitute a mental illness. In effect, the shrinks were saying being kinky in itself was no longer a mental disorder—as long as it involved consenting adults and didn't cause them distress or impairment.

Presto! Millions of kinky Americans found themselves cured. As Susan noted in a personal email: "It's had a huge impact on discrimination in child custody. We instantly saw a change when the proposed DSM revisions were announced in February 2012. [BDSM] parents immediately started introducing the proposed changes into their child custody disputes. Here are stats from our Incident Reporting & Response requests from parents who were in court facing a partner and/or the state Child Protective Services, because they were accused of being kinky and the kids should be removed because of it:

2009—132 parents, 2010—125 parents, 2011—115 parents, 2012—87 parents, 2014—37 parents, 2015—19 parents. We've had a dramatic decline. Child custody is no longer one of our biggest issues."

In February 2013, BDSM finally got their "breakthrough" article in the *New York Times*, running over three pages. (My favorite part was the "safe word" one woman used to alert a partner that sex play had gone too far; a diehard NY Mets fan, it was "Yankees Rule!" which her partners knew she would only utter under extreme duress.)

Intersex issues continue to advance. Pediatric surgeons and departments in American hospitals have slowly, and reluctantly, been yielding to the painful truth that decades of procedures have injured countless children. However, IGM is still widely practiced on infants with no issue other than that their genitals are unexpected.

By 2000, Cheryl was invited to be the plenary speaker at the Lawson Wilkins Pediatric Endocrine Society, whom she had once protested against. It was the first time an intersex activist addressed a major medical conference.

In 1999, Colombia became the first country to place significant legal limits on doctors performing IGM. In November 2013, Germany became the first country to allow a third gender designation of "X" for indeterminate gender, in part so infants won't be forced to undergo IGM just to fit the binary (some intersex activists still object to this because the determination is an arbitrary one imposed by doctors). Australia followed suit in July 2014. In April 2015, Malta became the first country to outlaw IGM. In January 2016, Chile suspended all IGM procedures until children are old enough to consent.

Reparations lawsuits are starting to appear. Christiane Völling, in 2011, won a four-year-old lawsuit in Germany. Her surgeon was ordered to pay €100,000 in damages, nearly three decades after the surgery. In May 2013, in the US, Advocates for Informed Choice and the Southern Poverty Law Center brought a reparations case against South Carolina's Department of Social Services and the doctors who recommended and performed IGM on a plaintiff only identified as "M.C." which is still pending in the courts.

ISNA, were it still around (it closed its doors June, 2008), would no longer be a lonely outlier: today there are several such groups in the US alone, and—from Zwischengeschlecht in Switzerland to Intersex South Africa—dozens of rights groups around the world. And October 26, the date of that first public protest demonstration outside the American Academy of Pediatrics conference in 1996, is now observed internationally as Intersex Awareness Day.

Chapter 8—ID, the Shrinks and the Struggle to Depathologize Gender

Let Men in Dresses Carry That Banner

When transsexuals wanted transition and gender-related medical care, they had to get a psychiatric diagnosis, both in order to get treated and to have any (slender) chance of their insurance covering it.

The diagnosis psychiatrists used was Gender Identity Disorder—also known as Gender Dysphoria—which was a medical classification found in the third giant compendium of all known mental illnesses put out by the American Psychiatric Association (APA) called the DSM-3 (Diagnostic and Statistical Manual).

You'd have to get letters from a couple of psychotherapists and/or doctors attesting to that fact that you really had GID and thus were an acceptable candidate for SRS and other care.

With some illnesses, DSM stands on a firm diagnostic foundation, with biological or chemical markers, etiology (underlying causes), and pathogenesis (how a disease develops). In many other cases, like transsexuality and what it called "transvestic fetishism" (as with homosexuality before them), it simply pathologizes feelings or behaviors that are different or make psychiatrists uncomfortable.

No one who seeks body-altering surgical procedures like a tummy tuck, breast enlargement or nose job has to undergo the indignity of getting psychiatric approval or accept a diagnosis of mental illness. But transpeople do for their body-altering procedures, because sex is a category in which society is deeply invested. In this, as in so may other non-diseases, the DSM and the psychiatrists act as agents of social control rather than deliverers of medicine and healing.

GID had even been considered for inclusion in the Americans with

Disabilities Act as a disabling condition, but arch trans- and homophobe Senator Jesse Helms of North Carolina personally made sure that language specifically excluding transpeople (along with pedophiles) was inserted.

Increasingly, many of us were trying to cast trans rights within the traditional narrative of other civil rights struggles like black civil rights, gay rights and feminism. Yet a medicalized narrative of disability and disorder kept predominating. To me, the two narratives were clearly incompatible, or, as I've told many trans leaders, "It's impossible to wage a civil rights struggle from within the confines of a mental disorder." This is one reason that gay rights had worked for decades to get homosexuality—considered a mental disorder until 1973—removed from the DSM.

The response I often got was that our work would solidify the stigmatization of those with mental illness. I got that mental illness needed to be treated like any other illness and de-stigmatized. My response was that I didn't think that men in dresses who wanted to grow breasts were the ones to carry the banner in that particular fight. Moreover, you can pick your fight. But you can't pick two or three fights at once, especially when there are only a few hundred or a few thousand of you in an entire country of 350 million.

It's simply hopeless messaging for a small, largely unknown, marginalized movement just starting out to say, "Yes, maybe wanting to change sexes is a mental illness, but, a) it's no different from a physical illness, b) mental illnesses shouldn't be stigmatized, and, c) you should grant us our civil rights anyway." In a just world that message should work, but in the real one it doesn't.

Always Bring a TransCop

Keeping the diagnoses intact so that a small minority of us could have surgery paid for—even if it meant accepting an 'illness' none of us believed in—seemed to me like the wrong way to go. We would pay for this acceptance in the court of public opinion every time we tried to make it the topic of our civil rights struggles.

I had a series of conversations with Kelley Winters, who had been working on the issue of de-pathologizing GID before it was on anyone else's radar, often quietly in far-flung meetings of committees and organizations little known outside the community and barely familiar even within it.

I even wrote and tried to meet with members of the APA, but (as Cheryl found with IGM) they only wanted to hear from other MDs, not actual (yuck) patients who might have disagreeable opinions or (gasp!) talk back. They were completely impervious to dialogue. But not to protests.

So, we looked for an opportunity to picket. The APA's annual national conference in New York provided it. On May 5th, 1996, about a dozen members of Transexual Menace Connecticut and NY along with Transexual Menace Men and Tony from TOPS demonstrated outside the annual APA meeting, calling for an end to diagnosing transsexuality as a mental disorder.

We handed out over 1,000 leaflets, while holding up signs reading "Keep Your Laws OFF My Body" and "Gender Euphoria NOT Gender Dysphoria." The demonstration continued for several hours while attendees arrived, many of whom stopped to chat with demonstrators.

Perhaps the most interesting part of it was Tony's interaction with the cops. We clearly were not supposed to be anywhere near the NYC Convention Center. It was designed to keep people like us away, with a small area off in the distance to which demonstrators were supposed to be banished. Yet we got right up to the building, because of Tony and his badge.

Different officers guarding the convention kept looking at him, and coming up to explain that they wanted to move us and were supposed to move us, but they couldn't, because it would involve forcing a brother officer. And since we were with him... we stayed. I certainly wasn't about to disagree with them.

A Solution in Search of a Problem

The protest generated news coverage—mostly within the gay community—and a lot of discussion within trans political circles. As I explained to one interviewer, "GID is a solution in search of a problem. Gender variance is good."

I was immediately denounced for my class-ist presumptions, on the grounds that only people like me who had already had surgery, or people well-off enough to pay for it, could afford the luxury of trying to shut down GID.

It was true that the diagnosis has enabled many transsexuals to obtain insurance reimbursement for the $10,000-$40,000 cost of SRS, without which they could never have been able to afford it. Yet this reimbursement was accomplished at the expense of pathologizing an entire category of people, including non-complaining crossdressers and transpeople who had no desire for surgery.

GID had other problems as well. It gave angry spouses a nuclear option during adversarial divorce proceedings. They could claim that the trans parent's "chronic mental illness" was harmful to their children and thus they should be denied custody and visitation rights. In a distressing number of cases, this kind of legal scare tactic worked.

Once homosexuality was no longer considered an illness, homophobic shrinks simply shifted to diagnosing kids as having GID in order to legitimize inflicting "treatment" on kids who were considered "pre-homosexual." These included gender non-conforming children as young as three—as well as "butchy" adolescent lesbians and "nelly" teenage boys—whose parents were simply uncomfortable with their gender non-conformity or possible gayness.

And this medically-sanctioned torture was often paid for by the federal government. Author Phyllis Burke's book, *Gender Shock*—fortuitously published right after our protest—documented that for decades the government had provided millions of dollars to pay for a network of hospitals and institutes that sought to "fix" genderqueer kids. And it was all made possibly by a GID diagnosis that made every gender non-conforming child ill.

Prominent among the doctors was Dr. Kenneth Zucker, notorious for trying to prevent homosexuality and transsexuality in kids, and Dr. Richard Green, from UCLA's feminine boy project, whose work was detailed in his 1987 study, *The Sissy Boy Syndrome*.

"Treatment" could include round-the-clock behavioral modification and even forcible institutionalization on a psych ward—sometimes complete with psycho-active drugs. One prime example was Daphne Scholinski, who as a child was involuntarily committed to a treatment center at 14, after being diagnosed with GID.

After the first three months, she attempted suicide by drinking Sea Breeze, a facial astringent. She would not be released until four years later, when she turned adult at age 18. And Daphne was one of many.

There was an entire network of underground centers operating in states like Utah and Idaho, where religious fundamentalism ran strong and communities were disinclined to question the commitment of a terrified queer kid into a locked ward by parents who were seeking to prevent their child from becoming a homosexual.

Explained Daphne at the time, "Most people die after they get out. The recovery from the system is what gets people in the end. Life expectancy of my friends is pretty low. Most of my friends are dead."

The Task Force Comes Out

Later that year we looked for another opportunity to protest and grow the controversy. Since there was no upcoming conference, we needed another target. On November 8, 1996, I found myself again back in DC with a broad coalition of national queer groups that had come together to picket the national office of the American Psychiatric Association (APA) in downtown DC during rush hour.

This effort was jointly sponsored by the Transexual Menace, the National Gay & Lesbian Task Force (NGLTF), Hermaphrodites With Attitude (HWA), Bi-Net USA and the International Gay & Lesbian Human Rights Commission (IGLHRC).

NGLTF's support was crucial, and a sign that the wind was shifting our way. In fact, the main reason we got such a diverse turn-out of protesters was that the demonstration was held as part of NGLTF's huge annual youth-oriented conference, Creating Change. And that turnout itself was yet another sign that the dialogue was shifting.

Our protests were met by a representative of the APA's Public Relations Department... along with five uniformed members of the DC Police Department (who no doubt envisioned *"Enraged Transsexuals Demolish and Burn Police Cruisers!!!"*). But like all our protests, it was largely a friendly affair on all sides, and the cops soon withdrew.

As a nice coda, that same month, the San Francisco Human Rights Commission passed a groundbreaking proclamation against the use of GID for genderqueer youth. It would prove to be a sign of things to come.

Folks who had no problem whatsoever with grown genderqueers like me being diagnosed got really squeamish about doing the same thing to an effeminate four-year-old boy. (In one of the baroque ironies of this situation, forcing treatment on children to prevent them from becoming genderqueer kids was routinely reimbursed by insurers, while medical treatment to help transgender adults was routinely denied. Yet another sign of how the diagnoses were about politics, not medicine.)

Declared NGLTF's Media Director, Robert Bray, "NGLTF is very sensitive to the differences of opinion within the trans-community on GID. Thus, instead of supporting wholesale GID eradication, we support GID reform. 'Reform' means another diagnosis—possibly physical—which does not pathologize transpeople or genderqueer youth, plus increased funding for research, and full participation by transpeople in policy decisions that affect their lives.

"The struggle of transpeople in 1996 is similar to the struggle of gay and lesbian people in 1973, when we removed homosexuality as a mental disease," continued Bray. We were clearly getting somewhere with gay rights organizations, media coverage, and the larger community dialogue. What we weren't getting was anywhere with the APA, whose support was critical for making any sort of real change on the issue.

Later that year, 40 of us showed up outside the APA's annual national conference for hospital administrators and managers at the downtown Chicago Marriot on the Magnificent Mile. We were a remarkably diverse group, including members of Transexual Menace (NYC, Chicago, Los Angeles, Tampa), It's Time America! (Illinois, Wisconsin), Queer Nation, the Lesbian Avengers, Transgender Officers Protect and Serve (TOPS), various leatherboys and at least one intersexed person.

We held up signs to flustered attendees rushing past us into their conference that read "Hey APA! How Many GAY KIDS Did You Treat TODAY?" "Get Your Laws OFF Our Bodies," and handed out over a thousand fliers to participants, hotel guests and passersby alike.

FLASH! American Psychiatric Association Discovers Its Members Have New Disorder:

GenderPatho-Philia

"unnatural desire to pathologize any person whose gender makes you uncomfortable"

Did you know... APA uses Gender Identity Disorder to inflict "corrective treatment" on non-complaining "sissy boys" and "butchy girls" as young as 2-3 years old?

Did you know... Daphne Scholinski, in locked wards from 14-18 with GID: "Most people die after they get out. Life expectancy is low. Most of my friends are dead."

Did you know... GID sustains the stigmatization of gender-difference as *deviant* and *abnormal* which fuels hate.

HEY APA!: Get Your Diagnoses *Off* Our Bodies & *Off* Our Kids!!!

We're not quiet. We're not well-behaved. And we're *not* going away!

Transexual Menace: Your average men in dresses with poor impulse control & really bad attitudes

Flier for Menace protest of Gender Identity Disorder at American Psychiatric Association annual conference

Gender-Patho-Philia

The flier we developed was actually something I was very proud of. Instead of just defending our own position—hard to do effectively when medical doctors asserted that you're not in full possession of your faculties—it sought to reverse the discourse by turning the tables and focusing on their deep need to pathologize any kind of gender behavior that made them uncomfortable.

We termed this problem Gender-Patho-Philia (a philia is a strong or even unnatural attraction). It was a joke, but I suspect it was closer to the mark than many of them would like to admit. An illness ought to have significant distress associated with it. But most of our distress was because of intolerant doctors and a deeply transphobic society.

There really wasn't much of a hook for a medial diagnosis *except* the fact that genitals were supposed to be sacred and our desire to change them gave shrinks a case of the willies. Similar to intersex, transsexuality was a psychiatric emergency on the part of the doctors, treated by diagnosing and pathologizing the patient.

The flier's tagline showed we were in on the joke, declaring the Menace as "just your average group of guys in dresses and women in pants with poor impulse control and really bad attitudes." It's a lot harder to pathologize someone who has mastered the discourse being used against them.

In a nice bit of guerrilla activism, some protesters managed to insert the flier in hundreds of the APA program guides… so that they were the first thing attendees saw when registering. Surprisingly, this time we were invited inside, and for the first time, all 40 of us held a passionate hour-long discussion with APA representatives.

Perhaps it was the contribution of Urvashi Vaid and her constant focus on getting policy right, or leadership like Kerry Lobel's deep commitment to social justice, but the Task Force has always seemed to be in the vanguard of policy disputes generally, and trans rights specifically.

On December 12, 1996, the National Gay & Lesbian Task Force sent a statement to the head of the American Psychiatric Association urging that Gender Identity Disorder be eliminated as a mental disorder. "We believe no one—whether gay, lesbian, bisexual, transgender or intersex (hermaphrodite)—should have to accept being

pathologized as mentally ill in order to attain wholeness, completeness and civil equality."

NGLTF's statement also went out to the APA's Gay & Lesbian Issues Committee, and requested meetings between NGLTF, trans rights activists and the APA. The action immediately brought to mind NGLTF's ultimately successful struggle with the APA 25 years earlier to remove homosexuality as a mental disorder—so the announcement had very special resonance and was widely noted.

De-pathologizing homosexuality enabled the modern gay civil rights movement to emerge and move into the mainstream. We could only hope that this was a sign that the burgeoning transgender movement might one day do so too.

NGLTF's statement also helped finally shine a bright light on the use of GID to pathologize and treat genderqueer kids. GID had kept the door open to homophobic doctors who would seize any available opportunity to change genderqueer kids, and this would be the focus of our final demonstration.

Why Can't Jimmy Be a Girl?

It happened almost by accident. Someone emailed me a flier for a meeting of the prestigious New York Academy of Medicine. Psychiatrist Judith Chused, MD, was (presumably proudly) presenting her paper on the "treatment" of a five-year-old gender non-conforming boy identified only as "Jimmy," who (naturally) had been diagnosed as having a Gender Identity Disorder.

It was a meeting of IPTAR, the Institute for Psychoanalytic Training and Research. Psychoanalysts, coming from a strict Freudian framework with deeply-essentialized binary genders, were probably an ideal audience for this message.

In this, IPTAR was far from alone. Transpeople were like a professional "freebee" for shrinks and researchers. We're different in profound ways, there was a hint of the perverse in our desire to cross-dress, and a flavor of the sexual in our feelings about our genitals, and you could pick almost anything to write up about us and get professional attention.

So we would show up (always silent and in absentia, of course) in seminars, workshops and clinical papers all over. And the best part was, there were few of us and we wanted so desperately to just get treatment and be accepted by cisgender society we never, ever fought back. We were the perfect demographic.

But not tonight.

"The Analysis of a Boy With Gender Identity Disorder: The Search for Why Jimmy Wants to be a Girl," was well-attended by three dozen psychiatrists and medical doctors. No doubt they looked forward to a quiet evening of professional dialogue while they picked over the bones of Jimmy's "illness."

But, this time, to enter the meeting they had to pass through a gauntlet of demonstrators. Our flier was headed, "The Search for Why Judith Wants to Enforce Gender Norms." It described the case of Judith C, a psychiatrist in private practice, presented with complaints of an irrational fixation on other's gender displays, complicated by uncontrollable urges to police gender norms and an obsessive need to "fix" gender-variant children.

Some attendees were flustered, several stopped to engage with us, and many reacted with bemusement to our flyers, which were formatted to look exactly like those advertising the meeting. (Less amused was Dr. Barone, an IPTAR representative. Although the program announcement stated, "No Registration Required, All Are Welcome," Dr. Barone refused to let us attend the meeting, despite polite assurances that we intended no disruption.)

So it was especially welcome when shortly thereafter the National Center for Lesbian Rights (which had provided the GID information kits that were distributed) issued a declaration that the use of GID to pathologize gender non-conforming kids had to stop.

The practice, it declared, "hurts children as young as three and as old as 18 across the country. Psychiatrists must stop using GID as a weapon against gender-variant children and youth, and start responding to the genuine needs and concerns of the transgender community."

NCLR's Kate Kendell sent a letter to that effect to the president of the American Psychiatric Association. It was one of the first gay organizations to do so, and was soon joined by Julie Dorf's International Gay & Lesbian Human Rights Commission (IGLHRC).

It was yet another sign that transgender rights were finally coming into their own—leaving the confines of medical pathology, moving away from being freakish or bizarre, and heading decisively towards the

American mainstream. And like so much we had accomplished, we had raised an issue no one was thinking much about and then quickly moved much larger forces and organizations to act upon it.

For me, it was the beginning of the end of street protests and grassroots activism. I would shortly disappear totally into GenderPAC and begin trying to build a structured organization that was more formal and durable.

But for three short years a small, dedicated group of transsexuals, crossdressers and genderqueers had taken on gay rights, feminism, mainstream media and the shrinks, in succession, and moved them all. It had been terribly anonymous and scary and sometimes totally futile work. Certainly it was thankless. But it also turned out to be the most productive time of my life, when more of me was brought to bear and put to work than at any time before or since.

It was a time when, if you knew where to look, all the pieces were right there, waiting to come together and be energized into a raw new movement for gender rights. It was a time when almost everything remained to be done, and when it seemed almost anything could be done.

It was a time when the forces of the world seemed arrayed against us, and yet we could sense deep down—however briefly—that one day we were going to win.

IPA
GC

Institute for the Psychoanalytic
Abuse of Gender-Variant Children

~ A Scientific Meeting ~

Analysis of a Transphobic Analyst with

GenderPatho-Philia

"an unnatural need or desire to pathologize any
gender behavior which makes you uncomfortable"

The Search for Why Judith Wants to Enforce Gender Norms

Judith C, a psychiatrist, presents with complaints of an irrational fixation on
other's genders, complicated by uncontrollable urges to police gender norms.
As in advanced cases of GenderPatho-Philia, her symptomatology included an
obsessional need to "fix" gender-variant children. Tonight's presentation by
psychiatrists from The Transexual Menace will focus on the etiology,
pathogenesis, and treatment of Judith C's condition, as well as her overall
prognosis (which, we might add, isn't all that rosy). Refreshments and a
healthy dose of gender-tolerance will be served following the presentation.
(Donations to the "Save Judith C!" treatment fund welcome.)

Did you know... That Gender Identity Disorder (GID) is used to inflict "corrective treatment" on "sissy boys" and "butchy girls" *as young as 2 or 3* years old?

Did you know... The only thing "wrong" with most gender-variant children is parents who are uncomfortable and psychiatrists fixated on "correcting" them; the problem isn't the kids, it's gender-intolerance.

Did you know... As with the "disease of Homosexuality," psychiatrists are again pathologizing sexual difference and trying to "treat" it. Don't you guys ever learn *anything* from your mistakes?

Hey Judith! Get a Life! Better Yet: Get Your Diagnoses *Off* Our Bodies & *Off* Our Kids!!!

The Transexual Menace: Just your average group of genderqueers
with poor impulse control and *really* bad attitudes.

Flier for Menace protest of IPTAR

Epilogue

A plethora of organizations eventually joined NGTF, NCLR, and IGLHRC in endorsing GID reform, including NOW, HRC, PFLAG and the Gay & Lesbian Medical Association. GLMA, which consistently rejected all attempts to get it to add transgender to its mission, was perhaps the most remarkable addition to this list.

GLMA originally offered the trans community a declaring that there was no demonstrated connection between childhood gender non-conformity and adult homosexuality, and so psychiatrists should not use GID to prevent homosexuality in children. This proposed stance would have actually made things worse, in effect legitimizing the use of GID on kids, so long as it was used solely to prevent transsexuality.

After five years of picketing their annual conference, the APA continued to refuse to meet, or have any kind of dialogue, with any organization or individual. (And you thought *your* doctor was arrogant?)

For decades, Dr. Kenneth Zucker still ran perhaps the largest, best known and most notorious facility for "treating" gender non-conforming children—the Centre for Addiction and Mental Health (CAMH). In February 1998, an *In the Life* segment on its work featured a surreal moment in which Zucker sat across from the PBS's openly gay, short-haired, slacks-clad journalist, Katherine Linton, and explained how masculine appearance in girls can be diagnosed and treated early so they don't grow up to become lesbians.

In 2015, in response to continuing outcry, CAMH announced that its child gender identity services would undergo a six-month independent review. Shortly thereafter it announced it would end its gender identity practice, after treating 650 unfortunate children over the 30 years since its founding in 1975. Dr. Zucker was reportedly called in and dismissed by CAMH, a leading Canadian mental health center. CAMH subsequently apologized for his work.

As of 2016, only California, Illinois, New Jersey, Oregon and the District of Columbia had banned therapists from offering the treatment to minors. However similar legislation has been introduced in 18 states, according to the Movement Advancement Project (MAP).

In 2012, during its regular review update of the DSM, and 39 years after homosexuality was removed as a mental illness, the new DSM-5 dropped Gender Identity Disorder and adopted Gender Dysphoria, shifting the focus from gender non-conformity and/or the desire for gender reassignment *per se* as a disorder to locating the problem with self-reported symptoms of distress. The DSM still pathologizes cross-dressing as "transvestic fetishism" (especially nasty since it stigmatizes cross-dressing as a "fetish"—supposedly a "bad" thing - as if every one of 8 billion human beings doesn't have something special that gets them off).

Said Dr. Jack Drescher, a member of the APA subcommittee that worked on the revision, "There is a whole community of people out there who are not seeking medical attention and live between the two binary categories. We wanted to send the message that the therapist's job isn't to pathologize."

The head of the committee making the change was... Kenneth Zucker.

On December 28, 2014, 17-year-old transgender teen Leelah Alcorn stunned a vast internet audience when she left a suicide note to be automatically posted on her Tumblr account and stepped in front of tractor-trailer.

Explaining that religious therapists retained by her parents had tried to convert her back to being "their perfect little straight Christian boy," she left a hand-written note on her bed ("I've had enough") and pled on Tumblr: "My death needs to be counted in the number of transgender people who commit suicide this year. I want someone to look at that number and say 'that's fucked up' and fix it. Fix society. Please."

A change.org petition for a law to ban transgender conversion therapy received 350,000 signatures, while one at whitehouse.gov received an additional 120,000.

Supportive statements were released by the American Association of Pediatrics, the American Psychological Association, the National Association of Social Workers and the American Counseling Association. Missing was the American Psychiatric Association.

On April 8, 2015 President Obama posted a statement online by the whitehouse.gov petition calling for an end to therapies aimed at "repairing gay, lesbian and transgender youth."

The following November, a local gay man led a successful effort to adopt the section of Interstate 71 where Leelah killed herself.

NGLTF STATEMENT ON GENDER IDENTITY DISORDER AND TRANSGENDER PEOPLE

Washington, D.C., Dec. 11, 1996—The following statement on Gender Identify Disorder and transgender people by the National Gay and Lesbian Task Force (NGLTF) was prepared by Robert Bray, NGLTF communications director. The statement itself is attributable to Kerry Lobel, NGLTF executive director. Prior to the statement is background information and additional resources.

Background

The subject of Gender Identify Disorder (GID) has emerged in the media and within the gay and lesbian movement as transgender visibility and activism continues to grow. GID is listed in the Diagnostic and Statistical Manual of Mental Disorders (DSM), published by the American Psychiatric Association (APA).

While some transgender people use a GID diagnosis to qualify for hormone treatment, surgery and, in limited cases, anti-discrimination protections based on disability, the diagnosis can be used to pathologize transgender people and "gender-variant" youth—i.e., those children who exhibit behavior that may be viewed as "pre-homosexual" or "pre-transsexual." GID is a controversial subject that deserves sensitive treatment. It has broad implications for the civil rights, health and well-being of transgender people.

NGLTF has worked in conjunction with Transexual Menace, International Conference on Transgender Law and Employment (ICTLEP), the National Center for Lesbian Rights (NCLR), International Gay and Lesbian Human Rights Commission, FTM (Female-To-Male) International, Intersex Society of North America, "Hermaphrodites With

Attitude", International Foundation For Gender Education, GenderPAC, BiNet USA, Gay and Lesbian Alliance Against Defamation, and other gay/lesbian/bi/transgender organizations and individuals on the subject of transgenderism, transgender visibility in our society, and GID.

A useful resource on GID and its use against children is the in-depth "Information Sheet" produced by the National Center For Lesbian Rights staff attorney Shannon Minter. A copy of the joint NCLR and International Conference on Transgender Law and Employment Policy (ICTLEP) statement on GID may also be obtained from Shannon Minter at NCLR. The City of San Francisco Human Rights Commission recently passed a proclamation opposing the use of GID against children by the APA. For a copy, contact the Commission. GenderPAC has background information, a Q&A and other facts about GID.

As NCLR and ICTLEP point out, there are now over two dozen jurisdictions with civil rights policies that prohibit discrimination against transgendered people without reference to GID. These include the state of Minnesota and well as its cities, Minneapolis and St. Paul; San Francisco and Santa Cruz, Calif.; Seattle, Wash.; Cambridge, Mass., Evanston, Ill; Louisville, Ky; and Iowa City and Cedar Rapids, Iowa. In addition, the European Court of Justice recently held that employment discrimination against transsexual people violates the fundamental human right to be free of discrimination based on sex. Many transgender activists believe these laws represent the beginning of a new era in transgender liberation—a time in which they can attain equality and health care not through a diagnosis of "mental illness," but through a progressive and comprehensive civil rights agenda.

NGLTF Statement

The following statement is attributable to Kerry Lobel, NGLTF Executive Director.

"NGLTF is sensitive to the differences of opinion within the transgender community on GID and the implications of GID on insurance payments, civil rights and other issues of concern to transgender people. Thus, instead of supporting wholesale GID eradication, we support GID reform. Reform means another diagnosis—possibly medical—that does not pathologize transgender people or gender-variant youth and children. Reform also means increased funding for research on transgenderism and full participation by transgender people in policy decisions that affect their lives.

"We are particularly concerned with the use of GID against children. Gender-variant youth, whether they grow up to be gay, lesbian, bisexual, transgendered or not, should not be stigmatized or mistreated because of a GID diagnosis.

"The struggle for transgender people in 1996 invokes the struggle of gay and lesbian people in the early Seventies when the National Gay Task Force (NGTF) was successful in helping remove homosexuality as a mental disease. We are aware that transsexual people have unique concerns in their lives, including medical treatments such as hormones and surgery, which are different from being gay or lesbian. However, we believe no one—whether gay, lesbian, bisexual, transgender or intersex (hermaphrodite)—should have to accept being pathologized as mentally ill in order to attain wholeness, completeness and civil equality.

"NGLTF strongly supports civil rights protections and affordable health care for transgenders. We loathe discrimination and violence perpetrated against transgenders and stand in solidarity with transgender people in their struggle for visibility, inclusion, equality and justice."

* * *

The National Gay and Lesbian Task Force is a progressive organization that has supported grassroots organizing and pioneered in national advocacy since 1973. Since its inception, NGLTF has been at the forefront of virtually every major initiative for lesbian and gay rights. In all its efforts, NGLTF helps to strengthen the gay, lesbian, bisexual and transgender movement at the state level while connecting these activities to a national vision for change.

Afterword

In the months before starting this book I wrote a column for *The Advocate* called *Transgender Dinosaurs and the Rise of the Genderqueers,* which generated hundreds of comments and literally thousands of online postings—many of them outraged.

In it, I described going to a meeting with a friend and his daughter. Apparently along for the ride was a lovely 13-year-old girl with long blond hair, bright hazel eyes and the budding bosom and hips of the woman she would soon become. I was envious of her bright smile and total absence of my own excruciating self-consciousness when I first dressed in feminine clothing at 28. It must be nice to be born cisgender.

I nodded and then ignored her as I waited for my friend and his transgender daughter. But *this* was his transgender daughter.

Never having passed as female as I'd grown older, I'd finally given up trying. Besides, it seemed somehow counter-revolutionary, as street-cred in the new trans politics is often built around exactly the kind of prominent visibility and defiant non-passing that my doctors at the Cleveland Clinic had assured me were a sign of failure as a transsexual woman.

In fact, my political identity for the past 30 years, as this history hopefully shows, has been tied inextricably to my political visibility, from the first time I pulled on a Menace T-shirt and flew to the Brandon Teena vigil.

Memorial demonstrations, picketing HRC, books on gender theory, public fights with radical feminists and being kicked out of the Michigan Womyn's Music Festival, are thus integral to who I am and how I see myself.

For better or worse, I am a public transsexual.

But what if all that were wiped away? Who would I be? What would I have become? With all the activism and writing which that identity forced on me during the birth of transgender liberation, would I even be writing any of this today?

Androgen blockers, which prevent all the painful, irrevocable pubertal effects that I have spent several years of my life and tens of thousands of dollars trying to reverse—chest hair, beard, Adam's apple—had made this blond 13-year-old into an entirely non-genderqueer woman.

In fact, unless she outs herself, her social identity will likely be completely female to every adult she knows or meets. She doesn't visibly cross gender lines or even rub up against them. She fulfills them fully and completely in a way I could never know.

This is not to say she won't have issues to deal with; she probably will. Or that she will never decide to come out publicly—plenty of young transwomen today bravely choose to do so. Or that having early surgery and hormones makes all your gender troubles disappear. Far from it. But she has experiences I could only dream of, and precious choices I will never have.

With adolescents increasingly taking androgen blockers and the support of a generation of more protective, nurturing parents, one day our public transsexuality will fade out. One day this will become the new standard of care. Pediatricians everywhere will begin recommending it routinely to their transgender patients.

Perhaps, more importantly, any doctor who withholds such treatment will leave themselves open to malpractice. And a parent refusing to provide medical help and forcing their trans-child to go through a disfiguring puberty will be considered child abuse.

It will take time, but the sand is already starting to run out. In 20 or 30 or 50 years, the entire experience I understand as constituting being transgender—along with the political advocacy, support groups, literature, theory and books that have come to define it since transgender burst from its closet in the early 1990s to become part of LGBTQ—all that will likely vanish.

And a century from now, when trans is no big thing and every young person who wants them gets blockers, it will be as if we never existed. These memories, these accomplishments, even this political movement, will all seem to be only historic, something preserved under glass that carries a patina of dust and smells of old people. It will be quaint and about as relevant as silent films or doing the jitterbug.

It reminds me of a prominent writer who was trying to imagine what it would have been like for him to be a gay black man back in the 50s. Then he realized he would have been a "Negro homosexual," a very different thing indeed.

Feeling transgender as we understand it now will not so much become more acceptable, as logically impossible. In other words, I may be a gender dinosaur. And the dinosaurs—who once ruled the world—had no warning that their extinction was around the corner.

Perhaps, in some way, this girl is a sign of our successes, and not of our failure. In any case, if it is becoming obsolescent, it certainly has its upside. For instance, I remember the exact moment I suddenly started to became "normal."

It came from my daughter, DJ, who has perfect social antennae, tuned to the slightest ebb or flow of pop culture tides, relaying and amplifying the Weltanschauung with enormous precision.

When she was six, she was started getting teased and harassed at her school because of me. *"Is that really your mom?"* and *"Why does your dad wear a dress?"* etc. etc. It was from all sorts of kids, black and white, Christian and Jewish, poor and well-off. It's nice to know that transphobia starts so young, and can be so universally embraced.

Our DC school, of course, did nothing to stop this. At one point, DJ quietly asked if she could start addressing me as "Dad" to stop the teasing. I said "No." It's painful seeing your child suffer for something you've done and you're powerless to stop. It was as Francis Bacon said, *"He who has children has given hostage to fortune."*

So when we moved to South Beach, I decided to get the party started early. I wore a dress to drop her off her first day of school. And then waited for the other shoe to drop. It never did. No one said a thing.

It's still a very tolerant, very diverse and very gay community. I'm sure a lot of things were said in private and even more were thought. But the silence we heard was truly deafening.

But then, so much had happened in just the past two years. HBO's *Transparent* was winning awards every year, kids who were transgender were featured in news stories, transgender models were hot commodities on the fashion runways. Lana Wachowski came out in glorious fashion when receiving HRC's Visibility Award. Bruce Jenner had very publicly transitioned to Caitlyn and had a new reality show on TV. And President Obama had appointed the first transgender person to a White House post.

Suddenly trans was everywhere. It was hip, It was almost... normal.

None of this was lost for a moment on DJ. She started taking time on our walks to school to tell me how proud she was of me, how brave I must be and how she would never ever let anyone talk me down again. She started asking me to wear a dress more often. It was quietly thrilling.

Except for this one boy. Each time I dropped her off at school in a dress, I would catch a sour look. I knew something was building. Sure enough, one day when he was seated next to DJ in class, he had his chance and it did:

Boy: "What's your dad's name?"

DJ: "I don't have a dad. I have two moms."

Boy: *[mockingly]* "Then who's the guy in a dress who drops you off at school?"

DJ: "She's transgender, dude—get over it!"

About the Author

Riki Wilchins has been a leading advocate for gender rights and gender justice for 20 years, was one of the founders of modern transgender political activism in the 1990s, and one of its first theorists and chroniclers. In 1995 Riki launched Transexual [sic] Menace, the first national transgender street action group which spread to 41 cities. The following year they launched GenderPAC, the first national political advocacy group devoted to gender identity rights. Riki was an early supporter in the launch of the intersex rights movement as well as the movement for alternative sexualities.

They are the author of four books on gender theory and politics: *Read My Lips: Sexual Subversion & the End of Gender; Queer Theory/Gender Theory; An Instant Primer*; and *Voice from Beyond the Sexual Binary,* (with editors Claire Howell and Joan Nestle). Riki's writing and research on gender norms have been published in periodicals like the *Village Voice, GLQ, Research on Adolescence* and *Social Text* as well as anthologies like *Contemporary Debates in the Sociology of Education, Gender Violence, Feminist Frontiers, Language Awareness, Negotiating Ethical Challenges in Youth Research, Out at Work, Women on Women* and *The Encyclopedia of Identity.* Riki has done trainings on gender norms and nonconformity at the White House, Centers for Disease Control and the Office on Women's Health. *The New York Times* has profiled Riki's work; in 2001 *Time Magazine* selected them as one of "100 Civic Innovators for the 21st Century." Riki is currently working on a book titled *Gender Transformative Practice: A Guide for Funders, Policy-makers, Practitioners, Parents—and the Rest of Us.*

Other Riverdale Avenue Books/Magnus Titles You Might Like

Read My Lips: Sexual Subversion and the End of Gender
By Riki Wilchins

Queer Theory, Gender Theory: And Instant Primer
By Riki Wilchins

Hiding in Plain Sight
By Zane Thimmesch-Gill

Finding Masculinity: Female to Male Transition in Adulthood
Edited by Alexander Walker and Emmett J.P. Lundberg

Outside the XY: Queer, Black and Brown Masculinity
Edited by Brooklyn Boihood

*Queering Sexual Violence:
Radical Voices from Within the Anti-Violence Movement*
Edited by Jennifer Patterson

www.ingramcontent.com/pod-product-compliance
Lightning Source LLC
Chambersburg PA
CBHW070033100426
42740CB00013B/2683